Sean Casteel's
UFOS, ARMAGEDDON AND BIBLICAL REVELATIONS
Signs, Symbols And Wonders—The Whole Truth

Within These Pages You Will Find The Heavenly Light

Conspiracy Journal
PRODUCTIONS

Sean Casteel's
UFOS, ARMAGEDDON AND BIBLICAL REVELATIONS
Signs, Symbols And Wonders—The Whole Truth

Timothy Green Beckley, Sean Casteel, Tim Swartz, Nick Redfern, Dr. Frank Stranges, Prof. G. Cope Schellhorn, Arthur Crockett, Rev. Barry Downing, Diane Tessman and William Kern

Edited by Timothy Green Beckley
This edition Copyright 2020 By Timothy Green Beckley
DBA Inner Light/Global Communications

Published in the United States of America By
Global Communications/Conspiracy Journal
Box 753 · New Brunswick, NJ 08903

Staff Members
Timothy G. Beckley, Publisher
Carol Ann Rodriguez, Assistant to the Publisher
Sean Casteel, General Associate Editor
Tim R. Swartz, Graphics and Editorial Consultant
William Kern, Editorial and Art Consultant

Sign Up On The Web For Our Free Weekly Newsletter
and Mail Order Version of Conspiracy Journal
and Bizarre Bazaar
www.ConspiracyJournal.com

Order Hot Line: 1-732-602-3407
PayPal: MrUFO8@hotmail.com

CONTENTS

1-INTRODUCTION By Timothy Beckley 1

2-Killer Plagues Ancient and Modern By Timothy Beckley and Sean Casteel 4

3-New Testament, Gnostic Scriptures, Second Coming: Are UFOs The Key? 14

4-Finding UFO and Alien Contact in Gnostic Scriptures and Apocrypha 23

5-Mass Landing Myth and Arrival of the Armies of God 32

6-UFOs in the Holy Land By Sean Casteel 41

7-Nick Redfern on the UFO-Demons Controversy 56

8-Dr. Frank Stranges and The Cosmic Countdown By Timothy Beckley 66

9-Religious Odyssey of Reverend Barry Downing By Sean Casteel 84

10-The Wrath of God By Gary Stearman 104

11-UFO Religion-A New Awakening By Tim Swartz 125

12-Son of Man in the Clouds By Prof. G.C. Schellhorn 142

13-Hopi Prophecies by Timothy Beckley 153

14-Saint Malachy Prophecies By Arthur Crockett 165

15-Prophecies of the Presidents By Sean Casteel 181

16-History of Fatima Apparitions By Timothy Beckley 192

17-Madonna's Appeal, Visions in Zeitoun, Egypt By Timothy Beckley 207

18-Lady in White, Visions at Garabandal By Timothy Beckley 216

19-Madonna of Many Faces By William Kern and Diane Tessman 235

20-Conclusion by Sean Casteel 248

Biographies 249

Advertisements 251

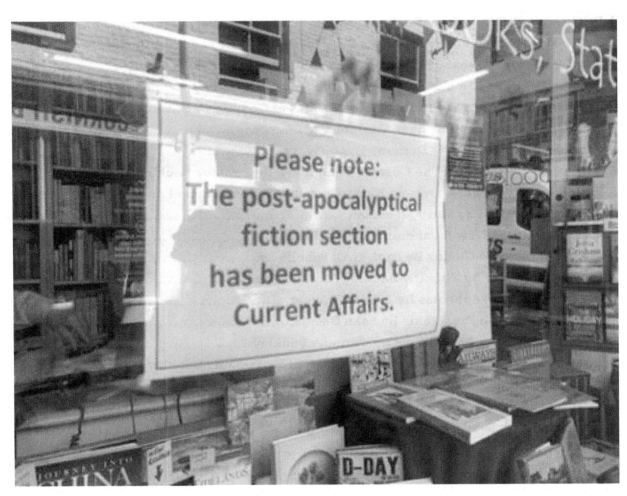

Sign of the Times

UFOS, ARMAGEDDON AND BIBLICAL REVELATIONS

1

JUST A RAMBLING MAN – AN INTRODUCTION...OF SORTS!
By Timothy Green Beckley

Confession time!

I have never been much of a religious person. Too busy recovering from Saturday night to go to church on Sunday.

Besides, the Lord doesn't want to save my ass. I've probably done a lot to offend Him. And He knows that I never have anything left over after buying that last shot of Jack Daniels to put anything into the collection plate. Yes, I am a rambling man, a gambling man...and I'm gambling I'm going to sneak into Heaven one way or the other, even if it's through the back door.

Hey, I've got influence in the afterlife.

Moreover, I have appointed Mr. Sean Casteel as my representative to the Higher Kingdoms. As a Biblical scholar for most of his life, he knows the scriptures much better than I do.

He knows the right questions to ask. And the right "passwords" to get me right with the Lord.

In the meanwhile, I figure I have done my good deed by publishing a number of books that relate to the Bible. In "Flying Saucers And The Holy Bible," we had the opportunity to hear from scholars of the "Good Book" who have diligently and patiently scanned the many pages of the Bible for evidence that the mysterious discs we call flying saucers, UFOs, or UAPs nowadays, have dazzled and influenced the Judeo-Christian religion since before Moses crossed the Red Sea – perhaps having been levitated across, or kept aloft by an invisible army of angels.

Not to be ignored is the work of Reverend Barry Downing. When he first presented his concept that there is a strong tie-in with UFOs and our Lord, he was mocked, even by members of his own congregation. Now he is the "poster boy" for "Biblical UFO Revelations," which just happens to be the title of his book which we published recently.

UFOS, ARMAGEDDON AND BIBLICAL REVELATIONS

Then there was the man who talked to space aliens, the late Reverend Frank E. Stranges. And "strange" indeed he was. Because on one hand he was a servant of Jesus Christ, and on the other hand he met with a spaceman inside the Pentagon. The spaceman had no fingerprints, because where he "comes from," there is no need for them, because there is no crime. His spacesuit could not be destroyed, and he could read minds. His meeting with Val Thor, the "Venusian" who lived inside the planet, sets him apart from other ministers. And like Frank's brother once told me: "My brother would be much more successful at preaching if he just dropped talking about UFOs and spacemen and kept to the Scriptures."

Reverend David Stranges had made a point, and I had to agree with him. Reverend Frank was telling it from the heart. He once told me he almost got tossed out of seminary school because he tried to bring UFOs into the equation.

Indeed, what is the fundamental truth about all things Biblical? And how do we interpret what the Good Book actually says about the Second Coming and the End Times as forecast in the Book of Revelation? I hope our fellow journeymen can offer up a bit of hope for humanity. Some think God is a vengeful God and we get what we deserve. Others believe in the mercy of the Savior. It's a toss-up as far as I am concerned, but that's why I offer you text that lies just beyond my Introduction.

Do UFOs have a place in the Houses of the Holy? I would say maybe ask Jimmy Page of Led Zeppelin, but that would be too cute. And besides, I like the band's cut "Stairway To Heaven" much better. I bring this up, of course, because Zep's Jimmy Page once owned the property near Loch Ness in Scotland where magician Aleister Crowley called up a spaceman-like entity known as Lam. Many think Crowley was cavorting with the Devil, but, hey, Beelzebub plays a role in our investigation. Ask any fundamentalist and he will tell you all aliens are demonic.

I say don't bet on it, but we cover the tale/tail (pardon the pun) of ole Satan, who does have some influence on all things UFOlogical.

The scriptures and all wise men have made it known that we have free will to accept – or NOT to accept – all that is and may be.

Sean Casteel gives us the tools to conduct our search for the true nature of things mysterious and unknown. But, in the end, our heart holds the key. Also, thanks to our fellow devil-may-care (my attempts to be funny get worse all the time) comrades: Reverend Virginia Brasington, Reverend Barry Downing, Gary Stearman, Nick Redfern, Dr. Frank E. Stranges, Tim Swartz, Barry Chamish, Professor G. Cope Schellhorn, William Kern, and the blond Goddess of the Woods, Diane Tessman.

Good luck in your search for the truth, be you a true believer, a heretic, or somewhere on the path in-between.

UFOS, ARMAGEDDON AND BIBLICAL REVELATIONS

mrufo8@hotmail.com

Our YouTube channel - "Mr. UFO's Secret Files," where over 400 interviews await you.

www.ConspiracyJournal.com

www.TeslaSecretLab.com

Photo by Charla Gene

Tim Beckley awaits the Second Coming as he worships an unknown force.

2

KILLER PLAGUES, ANCIENT AND MODERN
By Timothy Green Beckley and Sean Casteel

The sky ran dark as if it were the middle of the night, though it could have been high noon.

The oxygen had seemingly been pulled out of the air, making it difficult – some say impossible – to breathe.

An intense insectoid noise filled the sky, as if a thousand power saws had been turned on all at once. It started as a soft buzzing sound that grew louder and louder until it could easily cause a person's ear drums to burst as well as a loss of one's senses. Some report they blacked out at the sight that suddenly confronted them, so terrorized were they by what they saw blocking the heavens from horizon to horizon.

The locusts had arrived like in a Biblical plague. But the time is NOW as they threaten to decimate two entire continents.

They are the winged terror of bygone ages and of today – and they are not going to simply go away.

TESTIMONIES OF TERROR

One witness described his ordeal this way: "It is a strange sight, beautiful if you can forget the destruction it brings with it. The whole air, to twelve or even eighteen feet above the ground, is filled with the insects, reddish brown in body, with bright, gauzy wings. When the sun's rays catch them – if the sun is still visible – it is like the sea sparkling with light. When you see them against a cloud they are like the dense flakes of a driving snowstorm. You feel as if you had never before realized immensity in number. Vast crowds of men gathered at a festival, countless tree-tops rising along the slope of a forest ridge, the chimneys of London houses from the top of St. Paul's – all are as nothing to the myriads of insects that blot out the sun above and cover the ground beneath and fill the air whichever way one looks. The breeze carries them swiftly past, but they come on in fresh clouds, a host of which there is no end, each of them a harmless creature which you can catch and crush in your band, but appalling in their power of collective devastation."

Another unnamed witness said, "The roads were covered with them, all marching and in regular lines, like armies of soldiers, with their leaders in front; and all the opposition of man to resist their progress was in vain."

Still another testimony: "When they approached our garden, all the farm servants were employed to keep them off; but to no avail. Though our men broke the locusts' ranks for a moment, no sooner had they passed the men then they closed again and marched through the hedges and ditches as before. Our garden finished, they continued their march toward the town, devastating one garden after another. They have also penetrated into most of our rooms. Whatever one is doing one hears their noise from without, like the noise of armed hosts, or the running of many waters. When in an erect position, their appearance at a little distance is like that of a well-armed horseman."

As this chapter is being written, in late spring of 2020, the world is reeling from the effects of COVID-19, a viral disease that has killed hundreds of thousands of people worldwide. It was felt that, in a book about prophecy and the apocalypse, we should include some material on plagues ancient and modern. We begin this chapter with a discussion of the plague of locusts from the Book of Exodus and its resonance with current events in Africa and elsewhere around the world.

THE LOCUSTS OF EXODUS

The Lord sent ten plagues to force Pharaoh's hand and cause him to liberate the Hebrews from their cruel lives as slaves in Egypt. In the tenth chapter of Exodus, God tells Moses: "Go to Pharaoh, for I have hardened his heart and the hearts of his officials so that I may perform these signs of mine among them, that you may tell your children and grandchildren how I dealt harshly with the Egyptians and how I performed my signs among them, and that you may know that I am the Lord."

So Moses and his brother Aaron go to Pharaoh and ask him to humble himself before the God of the Hebrews lest the Lord send upon Egypt a plague of locusts the very next day.

"They will cover the face of the ground," Moses warns, "so that it cannot be seen." Pharaoh refuses Moses' ultimatums, at which point the Lord tells Moses: "Stretch out your hand over Egypt so that locusts swarm over the land and devour everything growing in the fields."

So Moses does as the Lord bids him to do, and the Lord made an east wind blow across the land all that day and all that night. By morning, the wind had brought the locusts.

"They invaded all Egypt and settled down in every area of the country in great numbers." Exodus says. "Never before had there been such a plague of locusts, nor will there ever be again. They covered all the ground until it was black. They devoured everything growing in the fields and the fruit on the trees. Nothing green remained on tree or plant in all the land of Egypt."

Given that the Lord had hardened Pharaoh's heart, it is to be expected that the locusts did not bend the ruler's will to the extent that he would let the Jews go free. It would take even more plagues and the heartbreak of Passover to accomplish that.

LOCUSTS IN OUR OWN TIME

And while Exodus states that there would never be a plague of locusts that devastating ever again, a modern-day plague of locusts began to receive media attention in late winter and early spring 2020. According to a website called "Inside Climate News," in a posting by Bob Berwyn, locust swarms three times the size of New York City were eating their way across two continents. Giant swarms of locusts had spread across East Africa, the Arabian Peninsula and the Middle East, devouring crops that feed millions of people.

"The largest locust swarms in more than 50 years," Berwyn writes, "have left subsistence farmers helpless to protect their fields and will spread misery throughout the region. New swarms are currently forming from Kenya to Iran, according to the United Nations locust watch website.

"The desert locust needs moist soil to breed," he continues. "When rains are especially heavy, populations of the usually solitary insects can explode. In Kenya, one of the biggest swarms detected in 2019 was three times the size of New York City. Swarms a fraction of that size can hold between four billion and eight billion insects. At times, the locusts in East Africa have swarmed so thick that they have prevented planes from taking off and their dead bodies have piled up high enough to stop trains on their tracks."

The website of "The Times of Israel" reported in March of 2020 that "A plague of locusts the likes of which has been unseen for over 30 years is about to hit Africa and the Middle East. Adding to the perfect biblical storm, the current coronavirus pandemic is affecting travel of international experts and in-country gatherings for training to combat the locust threat.

"The desert locust is the most destructive migratory pest in the world. As depicted in the Book of Exodus, when the highly mobile swarms of desert locust form, they are ravenous eaters who consume their own weight per day, targeting food crops and forage. While one locust may not seem like a major eater, the swarms can grow to millions of individuals with the capacity to consume the same amount of food in one day as 35,000 people."

The writer for "The Times of Israel," Amanda Borschel-Dan, warns that the hardest hit countries will include Kenya, Ethiopia, Somalia, Iran, Pakistan and

Sudan, the last of which would likely be affected later in the summer of 2020. Borschel-Dan also writes that, while the plague was set to descend on the Middle East "in time for Passover," it was likely to skip the Holy Land.

DUCKS TO THE RESCUE?

At one point in late winter 2020, it was announced that China might be sending 100,000 ducks to neighboring Pakistan to help tackle swarms of crop-eating locusts. An agricultural expert behind the scheme says a single duck can eat more than 200 locusts a day and can be more effective than pesticides as well as more ecologically friendly. The idea was popular on Chinese social media, where one user wrote, "Go, ducks! I hope you come back alive."

However, it was later decided the idea was impractical because ducks thrive on water and likely couldn't survive in the desert heat of Pakistan. Also, a UN official said that an army of 100,000 ducks could only gobble up 20 million locusts a day. There are not enough ducks, and they could not eat enough desert locusts to have a significant impact.

THE MIRACULOUS SEAGULLS

In another bird-related story, the Miracle of the Gulls is an 1848 event often credited by Latter-Day Saints (Mormons) for saving the Mormon pioneers' second harvest in the Salt Lake Valley. It is claimed that seagulls miraculously saved the 1848 crops by eating thousands of insects that were devouring their fields.

According to an article from Utah newspaper "Deseret News," by staff writer John L. Hart, the story is still vividly recalled over 170 years later.

"During May and June of 1848," Hart begins, "worn-out and malnourished Mormon pioneers discovered that insignificant nuisances had become a deadly enemy: crickets.

"To the starving pioneers," Hart continues, "these thick, black, nearly wingless, inch-and-a-quarter-long insects hopping incessantly forward in indescribably large numbers were an adversary of utmost menace. Chewing the young, green leaves of such crops as corn, beans, wheat, flax and potatoes, the crickets also ate away at the hope of survival of the pioneers. The saving of the remnant of crops from 'the ceaseless gnawing of the ruthless and insatiable invader,' as described by historian B.H. Roberts, came when thousands of seagulls from nearby Great Salt Lake flew in and began feeding on the crickets. This event, known as 'the Miracle of the Gulls,' brought new hope to the struggling pioneers.

"Within time," he writes, "the pioneers accepted what the seagulls did as divine intervention, which ultimately was recognized by the erection of the Sea Gull Monument in Temple Square in 1913, and the establishment of the seagull as the Utah state bird. The story of the seagulls and the crickets has been widely retold from pioneer times to the present."

UFOS, ARMAGEDDON AND BIBLICAL REVELATIONS

THE JEWISH ANGLE TO THE BLACK DEATH

In another Jewish website posting, this time from a site called Hamodia.com, the uncredited writer compares the 2020 coronavirus to the Black Plague of the Middle Ages.

"It's been some 700 years since the bubonic plague ravaged Central Asia, killing millions of people," the site begins. "A decade or two later, in October 1347, a ship from the Crimea docked in Messina, Sicily. Rats in its hold were infested with fleas that harbored the bacterium that causes the sickness. That marked the beginning of the era known as the Black Death. Over the next 50 years, it is estimated that at least 25 million people died, between 25% and 60% of the continent's population."

That Middle Ages disaster is of course recalled because the coronavirus, or COVID-19, is similarly spreading around the world. However, there is a marked difference between the two pandemics.

"The contrast lies in several things," according to Hamodia.com. "For starters, no one at the time of the Black Plague had any idea of what was causing it. At a time of deep ignorance, fueled by Christian lore and superstition, all sorts of theories abounded, none of which did anything to slow the disease."

In the Middle Ages, the plague led people to turn on one another rather than work together to deal with the challenge. Christian leaders abandoned their flocks, parents deserted children, and children their parents. Today, nations and scientists and health workers are working hard to educate people about the current virus, to create a vaccine against it, and to find the most effective therapies for the stricken, if not an actual cure. People might be quarantined, for their or others' benefit, but no one is being deserted.

The Jewish angle to the Black Death, according to Hamodia.com, was the pointing, as usual, of fingers of blame at their Jewish forebears. The plague, it was widely declared, was punishment for Christian society's allowing Jews to live in their midst as Jews. Although Jews, too, perished in the plague, only in much smaller numbers, it was said. The resulting "logic" had it that ending the epidemic lay in converting, exiling or murdering Jews. Despite the declaration of several popes that the Jews were not at fault for the plague, people on the street were sure they knew better.

The general populace also accused the Jews of poisoning the drinking wells of communities in order to harm Christians, a crime to which some Jews "confessed" after suffering horrific torture. Some 2000 Jews were burned to death in Strasbourg's Jewish cemetery and children were torn from their parents' arms to undergo baptism and conversion. The Jewish communities of France, Germany and England were decimated by angry mobs.

"Historians tend to take seriously the contention that Jewish communities were less affected by the plague itself," says the website, "if not from the hatred it unleashed. The ostensible reason that the Black Death may have affected Jews to a lesser degree than Christians lies, the historical consensus has it, in the fact that Jews frequently wash their hands. Upon arising in the morning, before any other ritual, Jews poured water over their hands. And, what's more, they bathed – a luxury back in the Middle Ages – every week in honor of Shabbos.

"We Jews still wash our hands a lot," the site goes on. "But today most of us live in environments where every door knob, subway pole and bus passenger is a vector for the transmission of germs."

The writer advises people, given that COVID-19 is going to get worse before it gets better, to continue the practice of frequent handwashing. This will not only help to protect people from the coronavirus and other infections, but will also serve as a reminder of the self-sacrifice of their European forebears and the moral courage that causes others to reverence God, especially through martyrdom in a time of persecution.

IT HAS HAPPENED BEFORE

In an interview with minister, historian and author Jim Willis, conducted by Timothy Green Beckley and Tim R. Swartz on their KCOR podcast, "Exploring the Bizarre," the subject of whole civilizations being wiped out by disease was discussed.

"The identity of America can be traced back to the Europeans," Willis said, "when they first came over here. They came bearing diseases that the native population simply could not handle. When the Spanish came to Florida, for instance, they brought cholera and they brought measles and they brought mumps. The Indians had no defense. Within just a matter of a decade or two, 95 percent of the population of Florida, the Indians, had died. That's how tough it was.

"The same thing happened in New England," Willis continued. "The Europeans came in, the English especially, and they came across these great open fields. They thought they were natural because they were overgrown and they thought that was the way it was supposed to be. But what actually had happened was, the early fishermen who came over to the Outer Banks, when they would put ashore for supplies in New England, Cape Cod and all the way up to Boston and all the way up north into Maine, they brought diseases with them again. And the New England population of natives, it just decimated them."

Willis also told the story of the first European to travel down the Amazon River, Francisco de Orellane, a cousin of the famous conquistador Francisco Pizarro, in the mid-1500s.

"He reported that along the way there were great villages along the Amazon," Willis said. "Huge villages with great populations. It was about 50 or 60 years before anybody followed up. And by the time they followed up, they didn't find any of these civilizations that he was talking about in the Amazon. They began to think, 'Well, he just made it all up.'"

But now, with the advent of the deforestation taking place in the rain forests, the remains of a huge civilization that existed there and died within 50 years of the first European contact has been discovered, according to Willis.

"It was probably due to diseases," Willis said. "It was just a real tough time. I don't think that's necessarily going to happen to us, but it certainly is enough to make you take these things seriously. It has happened before, and we're getting the idea that we're not quite as in control as we thought we were."

Or, as the rock band Blue Oyster Cult sang in their 1970s hit song, "Godzilla," "History shows again and again how nature points up the folly of men."

The coronavirus has indeed humbled populations throughout the world, and we have learned, as Jim Willis explains, that we are not in control and are still as subject to the whims of nature as we always have been.

[Read Jim Willis' book "Hidden History: Ancient Aliens and the Suppressed Origins of Civilization," from Visible Ink Press.]

Death figure from the Middle Ages appeared as if it were a real individual come to rape the Earth and take millions to their graves.

Monster locusts have been reported – real or urban legend?

China considers readying an army of ducks to take care of a plague of locusts in Pakistan.

Current locust plague in Egypt sparks visions of the Locusts of Exodus. Is that a UFO or a giant saucer-like cloud over the pyramids? www.express.co.uk/

On the podcast "Exploring the Bizarre," minister and historian Jim Willis told about how many Native Americas tribes were wiped off the face of the Earth by the arrival of settlers from Europe and the Old World.

God sent sea gulls to save the Mormons from the locust plague that threatened the pioneers with starvation.

Millions of locusts ravage East Africa.

3

ARE UFOS THE KEY? THE NEW TESTAMENT, GNOSTIC TEACHINGS AND THE SECOND COMING IN LIGHT OF ANOMALOUS PHENOMENA

While their presence may be more subtle than in other scriptures and religious writings, flying saucers do make numerous appearances in the New Testament and are an integral part of the story of Jesus Christ.

In a book released by Global Communications, "Flying Saucers in the Holy Bible," the Reverend Virginia Brasington addresses numerous instances where the New Testament makes overt references to miracles and signs that are consistent with what we in the present understand to be UFO-related phenomena. Throughout her section, which opens the book, Brasington takes as a given that flying saucers are "God's transportation," and this chapter will take that for granted as well.

Publisher/Editor Tim Beckley says he initially met the Reverend Brasington when she came to New York to promote the first edition of her work. "We appeared on the Barry Farber Show with Bishop Allen Greenfield," Beckley reminisces. "She knew her topic remarkably well without being overly preachy. She was a groundbreaker for saying the things she said. The idea that an ordained minister would harbor a belief that Jesus was somehow associated with the UFO phenomena was mind-blowing. And the idea that he had ascended inside a 'cloud' that could have been a UFO was the other side of heresy!"

Among the many passages from the New Testament Brasington uses to make her case is this one:

"When Jesus ascended into heaven," Brasington writes, "the Bible tells us in Acts 1:9 that 'He was taken up; and a cloud received him out of their sight.' A cloud received Him. It was there already. It could have been a dull grey vehicle, or it could have been a vapor around the vehicle. At any rate, the disciples that had gathered, over 500 of them, were told that he would come back in exactly the same way he left."

Verses that speak of him returning "exactly the same way he left" are also included.

Mark 14:62 says, "And Jesus said, 'I am; and ye shall see the Son of Man sitting on the right hand of power, and coming in the clouds of heaven.'" Luke 21:27, "And then shall they see the Son of Man coming in a cloud with power and great glory." Matthew 24:30, "And they shall see the Son of Man sitting on the right hand of power, and coming in the clouds of heaven." Revelation 1:7, "Behold, he cometh with clouds; and every eye shall see him, and they also which pierced him."

Brasington intends for us to read "clouds of heaven" as "flying saucers," which reinforces the reality of the Second Coming. If we know flying saucers are real, does it take any great leap of faith to see the reality of the Second Coming?

"The first letter of Paul to the Thessalonians," Brasington continues, "in the 4th chapter, beginning with the 13th verse, tells about Jesus coming again for the Church. It seems that when He comes, He will be accompanied by a great host from heaven. Read the thrilling words, beginning with verse 16: 'For the Lord himself shall descend from heaven with a shout, with the voice of the archangel, and trump of God; and the dead in Christ shall rise first; then we which are alive and remain shall be caught up together with them in the clouds, to meet the Lord in the air; and so shall we ever be with the Lord.'"

This passage is one of the very few in the New Testament that speak of the Rapture, the miraculous escape of the righteous chosen ones from the chains of an evil Earth staggering under the oppression of Satan. This has in recent decades become a very popular interpretation of this particular scripture and has generated a great deal of speculation and anticipation, as well as the bestselling "Left Behind" series of books that offered a fictional account of the Earth in the post-Rapture era. Belief in the Rapture is a cornerstone of some people's faith, and there have been many who have tried to pinpoint the exact time it will come, in spite of Christ's warning that, "no man knows the day or the hour, not even the angels in heaven."

But beyond the more apocalyptic prophecies, even the Christmas story has a flying saucer element, according to Brasington.

"In the story of the wise men of the East," she writes, "visiting the Baby Jesus and following the star until it came and 'stood over the place where the young child was,' this 'star' has been explained in many different ways – and as far as I am concerned each of them is laughable. The favorite explanation declares the star was the conjunction of Jupiter and Saturn that occurred in 6 B.C. If so, the explanation certainly breaks down if one reads Matthew 2:9, where it says that the star came and 'stood over the place where the young child was.' In the first place, a conjunction of planets couldn't possibly have done this. A conjunction simply means that in their orbiting, at certain times, two or more planets are so positioned that they are seen as one, thus making a very bright appearance.

"In the second place, how could the wise men possibly have followed a star that was presumably in the heavens with the Earth orbiting and, of course, changing the position of the star in relationship to the Earth? Anyway, it would have been so far away it could not have possibly led the wise men even to a large city, much less to the small town of Bethlehem, and much, much less the particular stable, or cave, where Jesus was.

"No, not even the wisest of the wise could have followed such a guiding star. It was bound to have been some special craft or manifestation of God that appeared to the wise men and then guided them to the very spot where Jesus could be found. Evidently this was the first time the 'star' had hovered over a particular dwelling since the wise men had been following it, because we read in Matthew 2:9-11 that, 'When they heard the king (Herod), they departed; and, lo, the star, which they saw in the east, went before them, till it came and stood over where the young child was. When they saw the star, they rejoiced with exceeding great joy. And when they were come into the house, they saw the young child with Mary his mother, and fell down, and worshipped him; and when they had opened their treasures, they presented him with gifts: gold, frankincense and myrrh.'

"Truly, this was an 'unidentified flying object,'" the Reverend Brasington concludes. "It has never been identified unless my ideas are correct! Why did they call it a 'star'? What else would they have called a bright, glowing object that stayed above them in the atmosphere?"

Brasington was licensed as a minister in the State of North Carolina by the Church of the Nazarene. Her book "Flying Saucers in the Bible" was originally published in the 1960s by Gray Barker's Saucerian Press, and later reprinted by Timothy Green Beckley's Global Communications, which is the version portions of this article are based on. One would think it unlikely that a North Carolina minister would end up writing extensively on UFOs in the Bible, but Brasington's back story was a little different than most of her peers in the clergy.

"About 1918, in the late summer," she explains, "my whole family and I were out in the yard after an early supper. We were spending the summer down in the South Mountains, where my father was born and where he had lived as a boy. We did not even have electric lights, and it was necessary to finish our evening chores early. So, we were just sitting around talking when out from behind the mountain back of the house flashed a huge, red, fiery-appearing craft that went across the sky and out of sight behind the horizon. It lighted up the atmosphere in a beautiful pink glow, and was silent as it sped across the sky. When it first appeared, my mother speculated that it was a meteor, but my father thought not because, being so low, had it been a meteor it would have fallen within our eyesight. But this sped straight across the sky and out of sight.

"I was eight or nine years old at the time and remember it vividly. At that time, we didn't know much about airplanes, much less circular, glowing vehicles."

UFOS, ARMAGEDDON AND BIBLICAL REVELATIONS

Brasington goes on to recount other UFO sightings she had had as an adult, including one she shared with another pastor that involved two planes being unable to approach two rainbow-colored, rectangular ships. The local media's subsequent coverage of the sighting could offer no explanation. Her point, she says, is that, as a Bible-believing Christian, the notion of space travel and UFOs is nothing new to her. Seeing them with her own eyes has made her sufficiently familiar with the phenomenon.

Writing many years before stories of abduction by aliens became commonplace, Brasington quoted another apt scripture.

"Paul says in Second Corinthians 12:4 that he 'was caught up into paradise, and heard unspeakable words, which it is not lawful or expedient for man to utter.' Whether it was beyond our comprehension, or whether he just didn't have words to describe it, or whether God told him not to tell us lest we become so homesick for our heavenly home we wouldn't be any earthly good, I don't know. Anyway, he didn't tell what he saw and heard, but he DID say he went there."

Many an abductee has found himself at a loss for words after returning from the experience. Whether because of alien-induced forgetfulness or the traumatic effects of shock and awe, the abductee finds that translating into language what has happened is often impossible, and the accounts given by abductees under regressive hypnosis are often frustratingly incomplete, rife with a groping for words and gaps in the narrative that leave many important questions unanswered. As in the experience of the normally quite articulate Saint Paul, expressing the inexpressible just doesn't come easy.

THE ANDREASSON AFFAIR: ONE OF THE GREAT ABDUCTION ACCOUNTS OF ALL TIME

One of the perks of being a UFO journalist is that publishers are sometimes eager to send me free review copies of their latest releases. Recently, I was very pleasantly surprised to receive an unsolicited – but much appreciated – copy of the recent reissue of Raymond Fowler's classic work on alien abduction, "The Andreasson Affair."

The press material that came with the book made it obvious that it was being marketed for a new audience unfamiliar with "The Andreasson Affair," which was originally published in 1979, over 40 years ago. It seemed as though the publicist had no clue as to what an important and influential work "The Andreasson Affair" really is and how it preceded so much that we take for granted in the present day about abduction research and the methods utilized in that research.

I realize some readers may also be unfamiliar with the events recounted in "The Andreasson Affair," so I will briefly summarize them here. In 1967, New England housewife Betty Andreasson was at home with her children. It was the night of January 25, a typically cold night for the region, and the children had been fed and dressed and were watching "Bozo the Clown" on television. Betty was in the kitchen, finishing up a few remaining chores. Suddenly the lights went out throughout the house and a curious pink glow began to shine in through the kitchen window.

What followed is an alien abduction story that never ceases to both amaze and comfort me. It involves the familiar gray aliens, journeys to and from waiting UFOs, alien medical procedures and frequent episodes of missing time. As with nearly all abduction accounts, most of the narrative information was obtained by the patient and careful use of regressive hypnosis. Another familiar element is that the aliens were obviously interested in Andreasson and other members of her family, abducting not only her but her daughter Becky and her second husband, Bob Luca. Fowler sums this aspect up by saying that alien abduction is almost invariably a "family affair."

But the amazing and comforting part is this: the aliens who spoke to Betty that night spoke of Jesus as "coming soon." They also told Betty not to fear because the Lord is with her. They warned her that she would undergo many trials but that love would guide her and answer her throughout whatever she endured.

The aliens recounted in most abduction literature generally say very little to their abductees. This fact has been compared to, for example, a cat being treated by a veterinarian. What can a veterinarian actually "say" to a cat to explain the various medical processes being carried out in the cat's treatment, let alone their ultimate purpose? But, in Betty's case, the aliens DID speak to her, in terms of her devout Christian faith and with comforting promises that any believer would be glad to hear. Betty has never wavered in her belief that her gray abductors are angelic creatures preparing the way for the Second Coming of Christ.

I first heard of Betty and her angelic encounters when reading Whitley Strieber's "Transformation," his first sequel to his groundbreaking bestseller "Communion." It was 1989, I think, ten years after "The Andreasson Affair" had first been published, and it wasn't easy to get a copy at that point. But I eventually found one through a mail order house and read it eagerly, as well as the sequels that followed. (Those sequels are "The Andreasson Affair, Phase Two," "The Watchers," "The Watchers II," and "The Andreasson Legacy." One can only hope they will all be reissued at some point as well.)

I would later have the privilege of interviewing both Betty and the UFO researcher who told her story so capably, Raymond Fowler, many times. Both Betty and Raymond have been hugely important to my writing career, on the one hand, but, even more crucially, they have helped to shape my beliefs about UFOs and Christianity to a degree I cannot overstate.

UFOS, ARMAGEDDON AND BIBLICAL REVELATIONS

And I am not alone in this opinion. I interviewed Whitley Strieber in 1993 and asked him a question about Betty. He told me that Betty's story was something you grab hold of when you're sinking. She is one of the few people who can take the basic abduction experience and really "make it fly." The rest of us, meaning average abductees, often find ourselves "struggling in the muck," but Betty's story somehow lifts us out of that, Whitley told me. He also said he drew comfort from the drawings Betty had made of her experiences, some of which are included in "The Andreasson Affair" and its many sequels.

Another fascinating – and inspiring – factor in all this is what happened to Raymond Fowler as he was researching and writing about Betty. Raymond came to realize he was himself an abductee who had encountered the same sort of beings that Betty had. Raymond is also deeply Christian and underwent a crisis of faith that ultimately resulted in his bridging the gap between his formerly very conservative religious beliefs and his newfound understanding of some of the moral complexities bound up in the abduction experience. He told me at one point that a few members of his family still considered the aliens to be demonic entities, if viewed in spiritual terms at all, but that he had worked through that sort of limited, black-and-white moralizing to his own satisfaction.

With all that in mind, one should happily snap up a copy of the reissue of "The Andreasson Affair." If you haven't read it, an entirely different understanding of alien abduction – and a whole new world – awaits you.

SUGGESTED READING

FORBIDDEN BOOKS OF HERESY: REVEALING THE SECRETS OF THE GNOSTIC SCRIPTURES, FROM UFOS TO JESUS' LOVE OF MARY, by Sean Casteel

SIGNS AND SYMBOLS OF THE SECOND COMING, EXPANDED AND REVISED EDITION, by Sean Casteel, with additional material by Timothy Green Beckley

PROJECT WORLD EVACUATION: UFOS TO ASSIST IN THE "GREAT EXODUS" OF HUMAN SOULS OFF THIS PLANET, by Tuella and the Ashtar Command

UFOS, PROPHECY AND THE END OF TIME, by Sean Casteel

FLYING SAUCERS IN THE HOLY BIBLE, by Virginia Brasington, Sean Casteel and other contributors

ANGELS OF THE LORD, EXPANDED EDITION, by Timothy Green Beckley, Sean Casteel, Dr. Frank E. Stranges, and William Alexander Oribello

Rev. Virginia Brasington caused a whirlwind of controversy with her approach to Biblical events in light of anomalous phenomena.

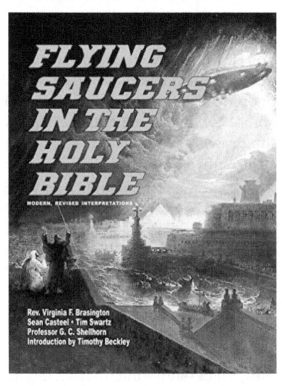

"Flying Saucers In The Holy Bible" is an assault to many on their Christian fundamentalist beliefs.

Could it be that Jesus was actually an extraterrestrial?

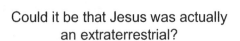

The Star of Bethlehem, which the three wise men followed to the manger where the Christ was born, might have been a UFO and not an astronomical body.

14th Century frescos depicts Jesus on the cross. Notice strange flying machines to his upper left and right.

A close-up of one of the ships that may have taken or followed Jesus into the Heavenly realms.

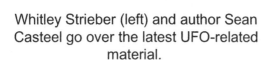

Whitley Strieber (left) and author Sean Casteel go over the latest UFO-related material.

A devout Christian, Betty Andreasson Luca – here undergoing hypnosis – adopts a progressive religious theme into her experiences.

A drawing by Betty Andreasson Luca depicts one of the Elders who seem most masterful and Christ-like.

Figure 53. Betty is greeted by an Elder as she steps out of the blue machine.

4

FINDING UFO AND ALIEN CONTACT
IN THE GNOSTIC SCRIPTURES AND THE APOCRYPHA
By Sean Casteel

Author's Note: For readers unfamiliar with the word "Gnosticism," a little background here. The word means "having knowledge," and originated in the first century AD among early Christian and Jewish sects. The various groups emphasized personal spiritual knowledge, to know God on an individual basis as opposed to the collective experience of the mainstream church. The Gnostics believe that there is a supreme hidden God and an evil lesser force that created the material universe. The physical universe is therefore inherently evil. For centuries, much of what was known of Gnosticism was limited to anti-heretical writings by orthodox Christian figures until the discovery in Egypt of a large cache of Gnostic writings in 1945, which renewed scholarly interest in the previously nearly forgotten faith deemed to be unacceptably heretical.

Also, a word about Enoch may be helpful. Enoch was a Biblical figure from the time before the Great Flood and was an ancestor to Noah. Genesis says that Enoch "walked with God: and he was no more; for God took him." Some Jewish and Christian traditions interpret that as meaning that Enoch entered heaven alive. Three extensive apocryphal books are attributed to Enoch: The Book of Enoch, the Second Book of Enoch and Three Enoch. The books recount how Enoch was taken to heaven and taught all secrets and mysteries, eventually becoming an angel who communicates God's word.

****

While much has been written about the first Book of Enoch, it is perhaps more appropriate here to discuss the lesser-known Enoch Two: The Secrets of Enoch.

Enoch is introduced in scripture as a wise man, much beloved by God, who is given to see the wonders of the heavenly realm, including the "inexpressible singing of the host of the cherubim and of the boundless light." Enoch's story begins when he is 165 years old and begets Methuselah. Enoch then lived another 200 years, for a total of 365. As he lies on his couch asleep, he begins to cry – still in his sleep – completely at a loss to explain his distress.

Two men appear to him, so large there is nothing like them on earth. Their faces, eyes and lips all shine and burn with fire, and they have the telltale wings of angels. They call Enoch by name, and he is roused from his sleep to see that the two "men" are indeed really there. Enoch salutes them and is seized with fear. The angels tell him to have courage. They are sent by God to take him into heaven. Enoch is instructed to tell his sons that he will be gone for a while, and that they are not to look for him until he returns.

The angels bear Enoch on their wings to the first heaven and place him on the clouds. He is shown how angels control the houses of the snow and dew. On to the second heaven, where he is shown rebellious angels being punished as prisoners in a terrible darkness. Enoch pities them, and they ask him to pray to God on their behalf. On to the third heaven. Enoch is shown an idyllic garden with a wondrous fragrant tree. He states that paradise "is between corruptibility and incorruptibility." The garden is guarded over by three hundred angels.

Enoch is told the paradise is prepared for the righteous who suffer greatly yet do good works in the world. Next, Enoch is shown a place of darkness and torture for the punishment of sinners, who practice sodomy and witchcraft and oppress the poor. The fourth heaven is taken up by an astronomical lesson on the goings of the sun and the moon. In the fifth heaven, Enoch sees a race of giant soldiers, called the Grigori, with withered faces and silent mouths. The angels tell him the Grigoris fell with Satan and impregnated the daughters of men to produce the familiar race of giants who "befouled the earth with their deeds." After being questioned by Enoch, the giant soldiers break into song, asking God to pity them. In the sixth heaven, Enoch sees seven bands of angels who guard the sun and moon and stars and regulate events on earth, including world governments and the natural world of rivers and forests, as well as recording all the deeds of mankind. In the seventh heaven, Enoch sees a "very great light and fiery troops of great archangels." These fearsome soldiers serve God with joyful singing.

After showing Enoch the seventh heaven, the two angels leave him alone, which causes Enoch great fear and he cries out for help. Gabriel comes to him. "Gabriel caught me up, as a leaf caught up by the wind." Enoch sees the eighth and ninth heavens, which include the twelve signs of the Zodiac. Finally, in the tenth heaven, Enoch sees the face of God, "like iron made to glow in fire," and emitting sparks. The Lord's face is "ineffable, marvelous, and very awful, and very, very terrible. And who am I to tell of the Lord's unspeakable being and of his very wonderful face?" The Lord instructs the Angel Michael to dress Enoch in "the garments of glory." Enoch is then taught the ways of heaven and earth and writes 366 books of the knowledge that he is given.

God tells Enoch that He was alone before He made creation. Then He made light from the darkness and the visible from the invisible. There follows a wonderful creation story where God speaks in surprising detail and frankness, a much more direct, "first-person" account than is found in Genesis. It begins with the creation of angels as troops with fiery weapons. The Genesis pattern of seven days of creation is also used here in Enoch's version, with man again being created on the sixth day. But there are fascinating differences, namely the "seven consistencies" from which man was made.

First, his flesh was made from the earth. Second, his blood from the dew. Third, his eyes from the sun. Fourth, his bones from stone. Fifth, his intelligence from the swiftness of the angels and the clouds. Sixth, his veins and his hair from the grass of the earth. And seventh, his soul from the breath of God and from the wind.

As in Genesis, God then rests on the seventh day. But God also talks of an eighth day, a day without time or the measurement of time. "A time of not counting, endless, with neither years nor months nor weeks nor days nor hours."

Enoch is then told to return to earth for thirty days to tell his household what he has seen and to write down his journey for the sake of future generations. Enoch is returned to the couch on which he slept at the book's beginning, where his son Methuselah has been keeping watch for him and is amazed to see his return. Enoch, with weeping, tells of how being in the Lord's presence is "endless pain." Enoch also tells his son he now knows everything, being shown the utter and complete truth of mortal and universal existence by God.

Again, details of the workings of astronomy and the natural world are recited, which are then followed by exhortations to be righteous and to give no unclean gifts to God. Enoch tells his sons that the fate of man's soul is fixed even before he is born. God bids us to be meek, to endure attacks and insults, and not to offend widows and orphans. Enoch instructs his sons to pass along his books to others and then begins to speak of how it is important to treat the poor well. The moral injunctions Enoch speaks of are all familiar from the Old Testament, but there is an urgency and intensity to Enoch's version that stems mostly from the strangeness of his journey and the fact that he will be taken again by the angels, this time for good.

The word of Enoch's impending departure into heaven becomes widely known, and two thousand men arrive to kiss him goodbye and ask his blessing. Enoch again prophesies a world where time is not measured, a paradise that cannot be corrupted, and says those gathered to see him off must walk before the Lord in "terror and trembling."

The Lord sends darkness on the earth. Enoch is taken up, and the light returns. Enoch's sons erect an altar at the place where Enoch has been taken up and make sacrifices there. The people and the elders gather together for a great feast with his sons and they make merry for three days, praising God, who had favored them with the sign of Enoch's heavenly departure, the story of which is to be handed down from generation to generation and from age to age.

SOME FINAL THOUGHTS ON ENOCH

The events described in Enoch Two are very similar to what we read in modern day UFO abduction accounts. We see the standard scenario in which the abductee finds himself partially awake but in a dreamlike state. He is then taken up from his bed and transported into another world very different from the normal waking world, accompanied by men or angels or the now familiar gray aliens.

When Enoch says that being in the Lord's presence is "endless pain," one is reminded of the stress factor in the alien abduction experience. In an early interview I did with "Communion" author Whitley Strieber, who was among the first to popularize the abduction experience, he quite flatly told me, "You cannot imagine how awful it is." Some abductees, such as New England housewife Betty Andreasson Luca, believe the alien abductors are angels sent to announce the Second Coming of Christ. But Luca also recalled some genuinely frightening moments onboard the UFOs. Strieber, meanwhile, acknowledged that alien abduction can be a beautiful experience, but rarely in the sense of "sweetness and light."

Perhaps all of that is a testimony to the authenticity of what Enoch, Strieber and Luca and many others have undergone. Alien abduction can be seen to be linked to Enoch Two as part of a tradition stretching back thousands of years. The spiritual mysteries of one age are continued in the next, and maybe we can draw comfort from believing that the Eighth Day that God speaks of in Enoch Two, a day when no time is measured, may be just around the corner on the Cosmic Calendar.

[The following are excerpts from the newly published "Forbidden Books of Heresy: Revealing the Secrets of the Gnostic Scriptures – From UFOs to Jesus' Love of Mary," by Sean Casteel. The two sections provide an overview of alien contact as expressed in ancient times, using scriptures from the Gnostic book "The Acts of John" and the apocryphal "The Second Book of Enoch."]

THE CHANGING FACE OF JESUS

There is no one face or personality for the Jesus described in the Gnostic scriptures, but instead a series of incarnations and embodiments that each serve a different purpose and lead the believer from one point of revelation to another, the various "masks" of the deity.

This idea is expressed quite eloquently by the late, great scholar of comparative mythology, Joseph Campbell. Campbell is best known to the general public for his 1987 PBS television series, "The Power of Myth," in which he was interviewed by journalist Bill Moyers. In part three of his landmark series of books, "The Masks of God," entitled "Occidental Mythology," Campbell relates an interesting story of Jesus in disguise from the Gnostic book called the Acts of John.

"The Messiah has just come from his desert fast of forty days," Campbell writes, setting the scene, "and his victory there over Satan. John and James are in their boat, fishing. Christ appears on the shore. And John is supposed to be telling, now, of the occasion."

The scripture commences.

"For when he had chosen Peter and Andrew, who were brothers, he came to me and James, my brother, saying, 'I have need of you, come unto me.' And my brother, hearing that, said to me, 'John, what does that child want who is on the shore there and called to us?' And I said, 'What child?' And he said again, 'The one beckoning to us.' And I answered, 'Because of the long watch we have kept at sea, you are not seeing right, my brother James. But do you not see the man who is standing there, comely, fair, and of cheerful countenance?' But he answered, 'Him, brother, I do not see. But let us go and we shall see what he wants.'

"And so, when we had brought our boat to land, we saw him also, helping us to settle it; and when we had left, thinking to follow him, he appeared to me to be rather bald, but with a beard thick and flowing, but to James he seemed a youth whose beard had newly come. We were therefore, both of us, perplexed as to what we had seen should mean. And as we followed him, continuing, we both were, little by little, even more perplexed as we considered the matter. For in my case, there appeared this still more wonderful thing: I would try to watch him secretly, and I never at any time saw his eyes blinking, but only open. And often he would appear to me to be a little man, uncomely, but then again as one reaching up to heaven. Moreover, there was in him another marvel: when we sat to eat he would clasp me to his breast, and sometimes the breast felt to me to be smooth and tender, but sometimes hard like stone.

"Another glory, also, would I tell to you, my brethren: namely, that sometimes when I would take hold of him, I would meet with a material and solid body, but again, at other times, when I touched him, the substance was immaterial and as if it existed not at all. And if at any time he were invited by some Pharisee and accepted the invitation, we accompanied him; and there was set before each of us a loaf by those who entertained; and with us, he too received one. But his own he would bless and apportion among us. And of that little, every one was filled, and our own loaves were saved whole, so that those who had invited him were amazed. And often, when I walked with him, I desired to see the print of his foot, whether it appeared on the earth; for I saw him, as it were, sustaining himself above the earth; and I never saw it."

An important point to make here: the description of Jesus as "rather bald" and "a little man, uncomely," who never blinked and left no footprints but rather seemed to float above the earth as he walked, contains many elements of our present-day descriptions of the gray aliens of abduction literature. One is reminded that the gray aliens are universally described as bald and small in stature. Whether or not they are "uncomely," meaning "unattractive," is a matter of personal taste. The oval gray heads with unblinking black eyes are nowadays a ubiquitous cultural icon, and the gray aliens' ability to float just above the ground as they "walk" is a very familiar feature of abduction accounts. Abductees are often conveyed to and from the waiting ships in this same manner.

The Apostle John concludes by saying, "And these things I tell you, my brethren, for the encouragement of your faith in him; for we must, at present, keep silence concerning his mighty and wonderful works, in as much as they are unspeakable, and, it may be, cannot at all be uttered or be heard."

Campbell explains that this ancient view of a chameleon-like Jesus holds that Christ's body, as seen by men, was "a mere appearance, the reality being celestial or divine, and its appearance, furthermore, a function of the mentality of the seer, not of the reality of the seen; a mere mask that might change but not be removed."

The face and body of Jesus could be anything, anywhere, anyone, according to Campbell. It is understandable that the orthodox hierarchy would reject such a view of Jesus. A carefully choreographed game of "Now you see him, now you don't" is a hard and elusive thing to grasp even in this supposedly more enlightened age, and a Jesus with a perpetually changing face doesn't exactly fit one's notion of "that old-time religion," does it? But it is an enthralling mystery, nevertheless, and one worthy of continued contemplation by those seeking a truth not often told in the mainstream churches of our time.

THE BOOKS OF ENOCH

The apocryphal Books of Enoch are a marvelous addendum to the Bible as we more commonly know it. We share in Enoch's wondrous adventure as he travels to both heaven and hell, bearing witness to the innumerable mysteries and testifying always for the sake of the righteous as they battle, suffer and endure the wicked. The fall of the evil angels called The Watchers, who take earthly wives and breed a horrifying race of giants; the birth of Noah as a strange and supernatural child of the great unknown who utterly terrifies his father; the creation story told by God, which begins with God as a solitary figure creating the visible from the invisible, all combine to fascinate and enthrall the reader who takes up the Books of Enoch and joins the prophet on his fearsome ride through the cosmos. Space and time melt away, and the promise of an eventual paradise where there is no time becomes the goal of Enoch's journey, and our own as well.

To author Sean Casteel all men mighty and small – and alien – are equal in the eyes of the Lord.

An angel is said to have shown Enoch the way to Heaven.

Ezekiel knew his way around the high kingdoms – in a technologically advanced craft much like today's UFO.

Was Enoch taken to Heaven with the angels? Was the "Kingdom of God" perhaps a giant Mothership as depicted in "Close Encounters of the Third Kind"?

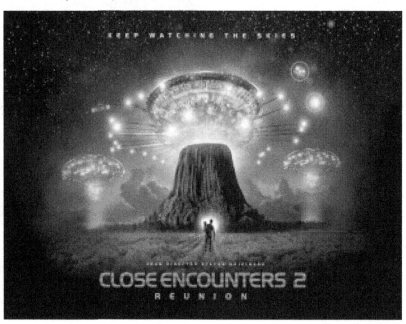

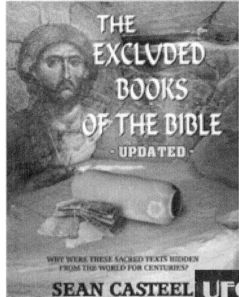

THE EXCLUDED BOOKS OF THE BIBLE
- UPDATED -

WHY WERE THESE SACRED TEXTS HIDDEN FROM THE WORLD FOR CENTURIES?

SEAN CASTEEL

The Heretic's UFO Guidebook:
Revealing the Secrets of the Gnostic Scriptures
From Aliens to Jesus' Love of Mary

Sean Casteel

UFOs, PROPHECY AND THE END OF TIME

SEAN CASTEEL

Some noteworthy books by
Sean Casteel

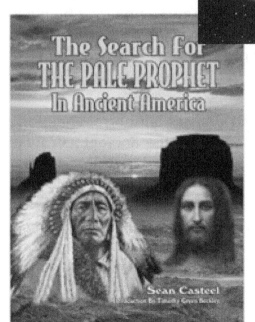

The Search For THE PALE PROPHET In Ancient America

Sean Casteel

SIGNS AND SYMBOLS OF THE SECOND COMING

Contains:
o Book
o Audio CD
o Report or Update

WILL HE ARRIVE ON A CLOUD OF GLORY? INSIDE OF A UFO? SURROUNDED BY ANGELS? OR AS A HOLOGRAM SEEN ALL OVER THE WORLD?

SEAN CASTEEL

5

MYTH OR REALITY? A MASS UFO LANDING AND
THE ARRIVAL OF THE ARMIES OF GOD

There exists a prevailing belief among a great many within the UFO community that there will someday come a "mass landing," a revelation to the entire world of the flying saucer reality we have only seen the briefest hints of so far. We somehow believe we are "owed" a climactic revelation as to the true nature of the flying saucer phenomenon, that we will one day have paid our dues and will receive a payoff in the form of some kind of ultimate truth.

One of the most common ways this idea is expressed is with the phrase "a landing on the White House lawn," which presumes the U.S. president would be the first person the alien presence would want to communicate with. This is sort of an extension of the old 1950s cliché in which the aliens land and say, "Take me to your leader." Perhaps the White House landing myth implies that they have eliminated the middleman/informant and gone straight to what Americans in their national pride would like to assume is the leader of the free world.

Another myth this basic concept incorporates is that of a morally indifferent alien force that wants to talk politics at the White House and eventually be interviewed on CNN. Any number of similar scenarios can be imagined while the waiting for some kind of open disclosure of the alien presence by the UFO occupants themselves continues. We wait, without being able to define what we're waiting for.

But what if we're waiting for the wrong kind of mass landing? What if the UFO occupants are not morally indifferent at all? What if the ancient astronaut interpreters of the phenomenon are right and the aliens are the gods that created us and at least tried to teach mankind a set of moral codes, a system of ethics that reflected their own "alien" morals and ethics? Perhaps the Old Testament word would be "righteousness," and the prophets crying out down through the ages for truth and justice were not merely raving in some kind of sacrosanct psychosis but were, as they claimed, pressed into service as a "mouthpiece" or advocate for God?

There has always been a thin line between madness and genuine religious experience. The story of Abraham and his near-sacrifice of his son Isaac is a frequently used example of this problem. Abraham claims to hear a "voice," which he assumes to be God, telling him to "sacrifice" his son. If Abraham were to walk into a courtroom today and tell a judge his "voices" told him to murder his own child, one would hope he would receive immediate hospitalization. It is typical of the schizophrenic to use what psychiatry would call "religious delusions" to justify any number of violent or otherwise antisocial behaviors.

Complete with "miracle beam," a spaceship can be seen hovering above in this rare religious mural.

Yet from childhood we are taught that Abraham was not psychotic and was having a genuine conversation with the true God. We are also taught that God chose at the final instant to take mercy on both Abraham and Isaac, providing a sacrificial animal, seemingly out of nowhere, to substitute for a frightened and confused Isaac. God's real point had been to test Abraham's faith, in a manner appropriate to the historical context of the ancient world.

As UFO believers, we too would like some kind of assurance that we are on the right side of that same thin line. While the morals of this country and the world around us may be said to have deteriorated to a depressing, even dangerous degree, there still exists a kind of social contract, law and order, and an agreed upon effort to maintain a level of ethical behavior we can live with comfortably enough to survive.

UFOS AND THE SECOND COMING

We think we know what is right and who among us could somehow trust an invading alien army to tell us different? Would these faceless, unknowable flying saucer occupants necessarily have a moral agenda at all? And should they have such an agenda, would they automatically want to impose that on us or even deign to teach it to us?

What to fear and who to trust about that fear? These kind of unanswerable questions inevitably grow wearisome to even the hardiest of UFO speculators. But this book on UFOs and the Second Coming is an attempt to answer some of those questions by blending the prophecies of the Bible with what little is known of the UFO phenomenon. Admittedly, in the marketplace of truth as it exists today, we already have two strikes against us. We are taking up two sharp sticks of something society has seen numerous examples of in the context of insanity – Biblical prophecy and UFOs – and giving ourselves a painful poke in the eye. Many a maniac with an axe to grind has wrapped himself in one or both of these subjects, usually to nauseating effect.

But nevertheless, we persist in this line of inquiry, of careful painstaking research. I have interviewed a group of experts on the subjects of Biblical prophecy and UFOs. Some have made the leap of faith and believe they are two inseparable parts of an overall whole, while other interviewees quoted here tend to carefully avoid expressing a belief in some future violent apocalypse.

For instance, what does the Second Coming mean to ordained minister Dr. Barry Downing? Downing's impressive academic background in both science and religion, combined with a longtime study of the UFO phenomenon, makes his opinion as "expert" as they come.

Biblical prophecy scholar Gary Stearman discusses how the long awaited Rapture will be timed to events in Israel and explains how UFO waves in that embattled stretch of Earth have always been an expression of God's unfolding plan in the modern world. One must learn to live with the idea that the Day of the Lord will arrive as a "thief in the night," catching the entire world off-guard and entering our reality unannounced.

There are also chapters offering the aforementioned less apocalyptic view of the Second Coming. In interviews with religious and UFO scholar Dr. Brenda Denzler and prophecy researcher G.C. Schellhorn, Christ's return is portrayed as a quieter transformation of humankind's collective consciousness, a kind of moral rebirth taking place on levels too subtle to be readily apparent to the unenlightened observer. What if Christ and the other prophets can achieve their merciful ends without a "blood and guts" confrontation with the wickedness of the world?

THE TEAM OF BRAD AND SHERRY HANSEN-STEIGER

The legendary husband and wife team of Brad and Sherry Steiger are interviewed for separate chapters about their beliefs on the Second Coming. Brad recalls his youthful days in Bible class and explains how his views are now less extreme, less black and white, regarding what we mean when we discuss things like the fearful aspects of the Book of Revelation.

Meanwhile, Sherry also feels her childhood religious beliefs and even time spent in a Lutheran seminary as a young woman did not prepare her for the truths she would later discover. What should be emphasized, she believes, is the commonality between all world faiths and the peaceful, good intentions of the prophets who introduced them to us. Yet she concedes she is troubled by portions of Book of Revelation and believes the Mark of the Beast could easily become a reality. Read her chapter in "Signs and Symbols of the Second Coming" to find out why.

Did the late Dr. Frank Stranges correctly identify the Antichrist? He is among the many who have tried to "name names" in that regard, but in this exclusive interview he explains his reasoning for doing so in some detail, while at the same time decrying the "fear mongers" who use the Second Coming to terrify rather than to inspire. Will the UFOs eventually spread the wisdom and grace of Christianity to the entire universe after carrying out the Second Coming on Earth?

UFOS, ARMAGEDDON AND BIBLICAL REVELATIONS

Finally, I touch on the possible use of holograms to stage a false Second Coming and offer a checklist of signs to watch for in the countdown to the Day of the Lord, as provided by Gray Stearman.

Returning to the subject that began this chapter, it is my belief that we should not be waiting for a morally indifferent landing on the White House lawn. Should the mass landing come, it will more likely be from the skies over Armageddon, when the UFOs arrive en masse to combat the armies gathered by the Antichrist. Jesus Christ is often thought of as the teacher who cautioned us to turn the other cheek but he also said he came not to bring peace but the sword. In Revelation, Chapter 19, he is called the Word of God, he from whose mouth issues a sharp sword with which he smites the nations. He is accompanied by the "armies of heaven" who follow behind him on white horses. Would you not agree that all that stands in marked contrast to "moral indifference"?

In a book published by Tim Beckley's Inner Light Publications, called "Project World Evacuation," the late contactee, Tuella, lays out in exquisite detail another take on what the Second Coming will include: the promise that some UFOs will assist in the "great exodus" of human souls off this planet. Tuella channeled Ashtar, her name for the alien Space Brother who "spoke" to her and other fellow believers. "You will be hosted by us, fed and housed comfortably in a great mother ship," Ashtar told her. Another Space Brother entity, called Andromeda Rex, even volunteered information about the food: "It will be as nearly normal to your accustomed foods as we can arrange it. It will include some drinks and foods that are new to you, but we are attempting a cuisine that will be favorable to all, with personal choices where needed."

It is comforting to know that the Chosen Ones will be well-fed in outer space, but the most joyous aspect of the great adventure will be "in the mingling of beings from all worlds," when the evacuated earthlings will be introduced to their galaxy and universe.

The exact time of the great evacuation is not known of course, but is contingent on events on Earth. For example, one message given in "Project World Evacuation" declares that, "We will not allow the entire planet to be destroyed. If atomic warfare does become activated, that will be the point of immediate mass evacuation by us of the prepared citizens of the Earth."

Tuella knows her audience. She is not preaching to the masses but rather to a specialized group prepared to understand her.

"Just as many are called but few are chosen," Tuella writes, "likewise, many who read this book will neither understand nor receive the information. But those special souls for whom it is intended will rejoice in its guidance and accept its timely and imperative revelation.

"This information is not entertainment," she continues. "It is comparable to 'sealed orders' given to dedicated volunteers on a strategic mission. It is dispersed to them, compiled for them and will be cherished by them. It is neither defended nor justified. It is data recorded as given and passed on to those for whom it is intended."

There is a vaguely militaristic overtone to some of that passage; the phrases like "sealed orders" and "strategic mission" seem to imply that the Ashtar Command speaking through Tuella is extremely well organized and is definitely playing for keeps. But when you're talking about the rescue and salvation of yourself and your loved ones, who would have it otherwise?

It is unfortunate that Tuella passed away before she could be interviewed for this book because her input would have been fascinating. Her Space Brother contacts have given her a beautiful blueprint for an alien Rapture complete with information on the living arrangements onboard the ships afterward. As a race, we stand on the cusp of Doom and Salvation, and the mysterious, ubiquitous UFOs will be a crucial element of both.

SUGGESTED READING

SIGNS AND SYMBOLS OF THE SECOND COMING, EXPANDED AND RE-VISED EDITION, by Sean Casteel, with additional material by Timothy Green Beckley

PROJECT WORLD EVACUATION: UFOS TO ASSIST IN THE "GREAT EXO-DUS" OF HUMAN SOULS OFF THIS PLANET, by Tuella and the Ashtar Command

UFOS, PROPHECY AND THE END OF TIME, by Sean Casteel

FLYING SAUCERS IN THE HOLY BIBLE, by Virginia Brasington, Sean Casteel and other contributors

THE HERETIC'S UFO GUIDEBOOK, by Sean Casteel

UFO believers have long been hoping for a UFO landing on the White House lawn.

Inspirational artist Carol Ann Rodriguez foresees the way a mass UFO landing might look.

An Ashtar Command book – "Project World Evacuation" — channeled by Tuella — devotes almost 200 pages to describing how a possible "lift off" might remove the "worthy" from Earth to a new home in space. Heaven?

The late research team of Brad and Rev. Sherry Hansen-Steiger mixed metaphysics and spiritual beliefs. Brad's father was a minister – a closely guarded secret?

Gary Stearman has mixed feelings about UFOs and the arrival of their occupants. He describes their shapes and sizes with L.A. Marzulli on Stearman's television program "Prophecy Watchers,"

Dr Frank E. Stranges told of meeting a man from another world, who he identified as Val Thor.

Here he is seated with "Mysterioso" talk show host Greg Bishop. Photo by Adam Gorightly.

The "Venusian" known as Val Thor as photographed by Augie Roberts at a spacecraft convention. He met with the late Dr F.E. Stranges inside the Pentagon

Rev. Barry Downing holds a book he recently wrote on UFOs and Biblical revelations.

UFOS, ARMAGEDDON AND BIBLICAL REVELATIONS

6

UFOS IN THE PRESENT DAY HOLY LAND
By Sean Casteel

While most of this book is focused on UFOs and their frequent appearances in the pages of the Bible, there is a wealth of interesting sightings and abduction cases from present day Israel that are also worthy of mention here.

Perhaps the best-known Israeli UFO researcher is journalist and author Barry Chamish. In this chapter we will look at some of the more exciting case histories Chamish has collected over the years, and then move on to look at the prophetic aspects of the sightings witnessed in Israel since the late Nineteenth Century.

THE UFOs FIND BARRY CHAMISH

It is quite common for someone with little or no interest to stumble onto the UFO phenomenon through no conscious intent of their own. Such is the case with Barry Chamish, who was serving in the Israeli Air Force in the early 1980s when he and a comrade-in-arms, Adam Reuter, sighted strange objects flying over their post in the desert. The strange sightings continued for more than three months, and, over time, were seen by nearly everyone at the airbase.

The objects bore no resemblance to what they had been trained to identify as part of their military education, and when Chamish reported the UFOs to his superior officers, he was told to ask no further questions and to tell no one else what he and his friend had witnessed. As word spread through the other airmen at the installation, Chamish was singled out for the usual ridicule that typically accompanies a person's decision to honestly report what they have seen.

"As the summer wore on," Chamish writes, "Adam and I were the sole advocates of the UFO theory, and I especially was subjected to mockery. The most common theory among the unit was that a new weapons system was being tested, but over time, that explanation did not suit even the most hardened critics.

"One morning at assembly," Chamish continued, "the unit asked our officers to request an explanation from the Air Force. A few days after the request was submitted, a colonel from the Meteorological Division came down and addressed us. His message was plain and simple, 'We don't know what you are seeing but we request that you do not talk about your sightings and do not tell outsiders since that only spreads rumors.' So the arguments over the lights continued, and as the strongest advocate of the extraterrestrial visitation hypothesis, I was ribbed ruthlessly."

At that point, Chamish adds a dramatic statement to the mix.

"This would not happen today. Back in 1980, very few Israelis had seen UFOs."

The implication being, of course, that UFO sightings in Israel became so commonplace that there are few doubters left there anymore.

CONFIRMATION OF THE UNKNOWN

In spite of all the ridicule he endured, Chamish was intrigued enough to begin some investigating of his own. He quizzed some of the pilots at his airbase about whether they had ever encountered UFOs themselves.

"I was serving at a large Air Force Base, and pilots would occasionally lecture us on tactics for aiming and shooting our missiles. Once the lecture ended, I approached the pilots and asked them if they had ever chased UFOs.

"Because I was a fellow soldier, the pilots let down their guard. Two admitted that they had chased ships of unexplainable origin. One was glowing blue and the pilot chased it over Haifa until it tired of the pursuit and sped over the Mediterranean at a speed the pilot's state-of-the-art Phantom could never hope to achieve. The other chase was over Jerusalem. The object was red in color, twice as large as a Phantom and disappeared before his eyes."

Chamish was later told that he had had a rare privilege in getting a pilot to talk to him at all. A reporter for the official magazine of the Israeli Air Force, identified only as "Julie," was doing a story about the UFO wave and was interviewing some of the same people as Chamish was for his own research.

"She told me outright," Chamish said, "that there is a special unit within the Air Force investigating UFO incidents but as far as anyone was concerned, it was nonexistent. The Air Force would not help one of its own journalists get near the unit or its files. And pilots were ordered not to answer her questions."

Chamish told the story of a former Air Force radar operator who spoke to him.

"He told me the operators often get strange blips on their screens, such as objects flying at impossible speeds which shouldn't be there or objects making gravity-defying turns. These are reported and planes scrambled to chase them.

"'I was personally responsible for two reports that led to chases. I saw the pictures the pilots took. They were of cigar-shaped craft. The Air Force feels these craft are intruders and a security risk so it will not publicize such incidents, partly to avoid panic and in part because there is no answer to them if they turn hostile."

"Because the Air Force had effectively covered up UFO encounters," Chamish continued, "and because there were so few sightings, until the late 1980s almost all Israelis viewed UFOs as pure science fiction. Then, in 1988, two UFO incidents were well filmed and documentary evidence was presented to the public."

THE MODERN ISRAELI UFO FLAP BEGINS

Chamish recounts the amazing story of the initial salvoes in the modem Israeli UFO wave.

"On the 26th of February, 1988, Rosetta Kalphon was having a gathering at her apartment in Haifa on Israel's northern Mediterranean coast. Included among her fifteen guests was a professional photographer from Ashdod who had brought his video camera with him. As the evening drew to a close, all sixteen people stood on Rosetta's balcony and watched a spectacular UFO, while for seventeen minutes it was filmed professionally. Shortly after, journalists were invited to Rosetta's apartment to view the film."

Chamish was not present with those first journalists, but he did see a frame of the film reproduced in a local newspaper.

"The UFO is somewhat umbrella-shaped," he said, "and on the side shown in the shot were eight smallish orange lights and, in the middle of them, an orange light twice their size."

Later, on June 26 of that same year, the Israeli papers carried an account by one Yossi Ayalon.

"'Two nights before,' Chamish writes, "at 1:30 AM, he stood on his balcony in Herzlia, ten miles north of Tel Aviv, and saw a point of light appear on the horizon out of nowhere. 'I called my wife,' Ayalon reported to the newspaper, 'but the light had disappeared by then. Suddenly it reappeared as big and bright as the sun at dawn. I knew I was seeing something strange something I'd never witnessed before, so I ran inside for my video camera and started filming.'"

Chamish takes up the story again.

"Yossi did not call the police," he said, "but rather sent the film to Israeli Television for public scrutiny. He, however, refused to appear on television, explaining, 'I never believed in UFO stories and I don't want to become a joke. But I just can't ignore what I filmed and what I saw.'

"Nor could many viewers. Yossi's UFO is clearly round and like many of the Israeli UFOs, emits a bright orange light. The roundness is broken by a dark colored square from the rim in the middle, taking up about twenty percent of the ship's size.

"Thus, in 1988, two UFOs were videotaped in Israel, and this evidence is important to me," Chamish solemnly states. "Only by gathering the strongest physical evidence in the present could the more difficult Biblical thesis be made possible."

In other words, if we choose to believe that UFOs interacted on numerous occasions with the personages of the Bible, it is essential to prove the reality of UFOs in the present day to make that belief in ancient encounters truly concrete.

MODERN ISRAELI ABDUCTEES

After the initial trickle of sightings reported above, a virtual flood of UFO reports began in Israel, many of which were documented by videotapes that fully supported the claims of witnesses. And just as it takes place throughout the world, the strange phenomenon quickly jumped from simple UFO sightings reports to the ever-increasingly complex abduction accounts.

In one of his numerous articles, Chamish relates the history of three Israeli abductees, the first of whom is Ada, a medical electronics technician from Kfar Saba.

Ada's testimony begins: "In the afternoon after work during the summer of 1993, I went to my bedroom to sleep. I saw within a three-dimensional being less than a meter from me. He was tall and wearing a 'spacesuit' of silver and green.

"The being emitted white beams from his waist area. I felt the energy of the beams first in my feet, then throughout my whole body. The feeling was wonderful. A feeling of fullness, well-being, joy and purity, then the being left. It took small steps and it was gone. For weeks I walked around with this feeling of fullness. My views on life and death have changed since then. When I am not afraid, I can let loose and call up visions of all kinds of beings. I feel their presence everywhere, in my home, my car and other places.

"That year, despite my overall feelings of warmth, I was often very tired and slept too much. In this period, they helped me in many ways, even finding a complete solution to my problems with my husband. I couldn't complain about this first learning period."

The aliens at some point leave behind a calling card on Ada's body, a series of 20 blue spots, what she called "tiny blood dots."

"The spots went away in two days," she continues, "and then the aliens returned in the middle of the night. They literally smothered me with a feeling of love, and I felt a wave of heat. That night, a sinus abscess that I had suffered for ten years disappeared.

"I was told that there are two types of aliens, good and bad. The good wish to promote harmony, but the bad have the upper hand right now. They are responsible for the UFO landings and the mass abductions and have no concept of the pain they cause."

UFOS, ARMAGEDDON AND BIBLICAL REVELATIONS

The next story Chamish offers is that of a woman named Chani Salomon. "On May 2, 1997, during the afternoon rest time, I felt a presence in the bedroom. I tried getting out of the bed, but failed. I saw an elliptical image 60 centimeters high of a brightly lit and glowing object. It approached me and I felt it was operating on me. It was a most uncomfortable feeling. My eyes were wide open and I saw what was happening to me, but I was helpless to react. A most worrying situation. I felt I was being drilled into from place to place. The center of the operation was in the heart. I felt a pain there that is indescribable. I was that unfamiliar with it.

"I tried to scream to alert my family, but no sound came out. I tried to say Shma Yisrael [which Chamish explains is a holy Jewish prayer, traditionally recited before death] but don't recall how many times. I went to the beach a few days later and saw all the people glowing and translucent. Then I felt an odd sensation in my forehead, between my eyes. The rest of the week, the area behind my ears hurt, though there was no sign of injury or wound. Two weeks after the first incident, I had a dream connected to UFOs, something which never happened before. In it, I'm with a group of people and we're all startled by the appearance of UFOs in the sky. A voice asks for volunteers to go up in the craft. A white beam lights up my knees, though I don't recall volunteering. The dream awakened me to the fact that there are others in the cosmos trying to reach us and help us. We just have to be sensitive to the infinite pool of energy and exploit it for our own health and care."

The third case Chamish gives details of was first published in a Tel Aviv newspaper on May 30, 1997. Chamish said he was initially reluctant to include it because the experiencer was not named in the article, but decided to go ahead with it because of the newspaper's reputation for integrity. "The witness describes herself as a rationalist and a skeptic, then tells her frightening story," Chamish says by way of introduction.

"Things began almost innocently," the anonymous woman said. "I would have the sensation at night of being between sleep and a dream state, something that was difficult to control. Every morning I'd wake up confused, with deep pains centered around my right ear. Then I'd go to sleep at night and have the feeling I was choking, like I was breathing in smoke.

"Strange beings would appear in the dreams. Sometimes they'd be tall and long haired, with a stunted nose and giant nostrils, and sometimes like bald, skinny children with a mask-like face and huge eyes. After the dreams, I felt pain in the legs and the armpits, which included sores that disappeared later. I would feel that time was lost and I was very tired. For six or seven days, we experienced electrical blackouts whose cause was not known.

"On May 14, 1997, at night, I awoke from my sleep. But I felt tied down to the bed. I felt like I was choking, and my throat burned like I had drunk something caustic. The house stank of a crippling odor. I went into panic. I felt a smothering, heavy feeling in the atmosphere. The smell even emanated from my son's room.

"I could sit up in bed, and did so. Half an hour later I heard a sound in my ears which began like a cricket chirping and ended like a jackhammer. The sound emanated from somewhere above me. When the sound dissipated, I went downstairs and saw a shocking image: the windows and blinds were covered with a fluorescent blue light whose source seemed to be in the room, flowing outside. In the morning, I saw two of my photos scratched and torn like rats bit it, a sculpture had its throat damaged, and a doll's face was ripped off.

"Outside were two twenty-centimeter black circles that stunk of last night's smell. Around the twenty-centimeter circles were a number of eight-centimeter circles that formed the shape of a scorpion's tail. I'm not a paranoiac, but I have a feeling I've been violated inside. I think they've formed a bond with me and will be back. Especially the little ones with the big eyes."

It should be obvious to the reader that the abduction experiences the three women reported are very similar to stories told in the United States and throughout the world. The aliens come by night, typically terrify the abductee, and often leave little medical anomalies behind them in their wake. The feeling of being loved by the aliens, or of forming a "bond" with them as reported in the third case above, are also quite commonly reported by abductees worldwide.

THE "DEMONS"

Among the many strange case histories collected by Chamish are some extremely eerie instances of Arab Israelis encountering what they believe are demons. Chamish cites some cases reported in the respectable daily newspapers Yediol Ahronot and Maariv.

"Dr. Harav Ibn Bari, a physician at Hasharon Hospital in Petach Tikveh, was returning from Beersheva by car with his cousin Dudi Muhmad at the wheel. He relates, "After passing the bridge to Tel Aviv at 3:30 AM, I saw a strange figure on the opposite side of the road. We did a U-turn and stopped the car. The figure came out of the shadows and into the light. He was small, and his body color light.

"He lifted his right leg and approached us at terrific speed. He had huge, bulging, round black eyes. They contrasted with the white color around them. It was as if he was reading my thoughts and I couldn't take my eyes off his for six seconds. He lifted his right hand and Muhmad pressed on the gas and took off."

A few days later, Chamish writes, another similarly frightening episode occurred. "Khaj Muhmad Jamal Kavah, 45, a Tel Aviv cab driver who lives in the Arab village of Al-Arian, met his cousin Ataf Kavah at 6 PM at Mei-Ami Junction to drive to a dinner party.

UFOS, ARMAGEDDON AND BIBLICAL REVELATIONS

"I saw him and signaled that he wait a moment while I relieved myself first. I heard him say, 'Okay.' When I was finished I approached the car and saw that Ataf was wearing a shiny suit. I thought to myself, in his whole life, Ataf never wore material like that. I bent down to open the door and saw that Ataf wasn't sitting in the driver's seat. I stared over but the driver paid no attention to me. Then I saw the weird creature. He had long hair reaching to his shoulders; his nose was enormous like an eggplant, colored purplish black. I almost had a heart attack. But I regained my senses and began walking backwards towards the highway.

"My plan was to make a break for the cars if he followed me. But I couldn't run because I felt something holding me in place for fifteen minutes. Then Ataf opened the door and came out looking totally confused. I shouted at him, 'You're not Ataf! What do you want from me?'" Ataf recalls sitting in the car and wondering why it was taking Muhmad so long to get in. He got out of the car and asked him what he was waiting for. He remembers Muhmad yelling, "You're not Ataf! Who are you? Where's the shiny suit you were wearing?"

Chamish goes on to say that Muhmad took and passed a polygraph test arranged for him by one of the newspapers. Muhmad"s home "became a pilgrimage center as dozens of people a day came to hear his story. Included among them are Muslim religious leaders who have concluded that Muhmad met a demon and irritated him by relieving himself in his territory. They say the demons are rising because so many Arabs are straying from their religion."

STILL MORE STRANGE ENCOUNTERS

A few more days passed and still another incident occurred. This time the victim was named Eli Hawald, a 33-year-old resident of a village near Haifa called Kfar Hawald.

"The tiny village has no electricity," Chamish begins, "and when Eli Hawald went outside at 11:00 PM, all was too clear for him. 'Out of nowhere, I saw a gigantic green light,' Hawald said, 'the color of a traffic light, fall out of the sky. I ran into the house, locked the door, and watched from the window. When the craft was about ten meters above the ground, the light was dimmed and three figures were "shot" to the ground from it. I began to shake.

""They had humanlike bodies," Hawalt continued, 'but because they were 20 meters from my house, I couldn't distinguish their faces, just their color, which was completely black. They acted oddly. They would fan out, quickly return to one formation, and fan out again. I remember two things distinctly. They reformed after a siren was sounded that resembled puppies crying. And their speed was fantastic, tens of meters in two seconds. At this point, I alerted my wife and children and we escaped through the back door.'"

And the spate of demon encounters continued. Again, Chamish's source was the respected newspaper Yediot Ahronot.

"A Jenin resident picked up a hitchhiker on the Jenin-Dotan road. A few moments after he sat in the front seat, the driver looked at him and saw his face had become that of a dog with one eye. The driver stopped his car, got out and fainted after he saw the hitchhiker disappear. That incident has become the talk of Jenin. Some of the religious leaders believe that the passenger was a demon who lives in the area. Others believe he is a devil known as The Blind Liar who has returned to presage the arrival of the messiah. The driver is still in shock and is being treated at the Jenin Hospital."

The use of the guise of a dog in that last story is very interesting. Traditionally, dogs are regarded as "unclean" animals by Jews and Moslems both, and the idea that an "unclean" spirit or demon would make some kind of use of that tradition symbolically is not much of a stretch.

Chamish concludes by saying, "I make no claims to understanding why there has been a wave of demon-like entities witnessed among Israeli Arabs in the past year. But I can verify that the wave has been characterized by the high quality of the testimony associated with it. If one can generalize, Israeli Jewish encounters since 1993 have mostly been with giant entities and UFO activity has always accompanied the incidents, while Arabs of the region are mostly encountering grotesque monsters, with less direct UFO activity involved. Both the giants and the monsters are capable of disappearing into thin air." (See the book: Invisibility and Levitation by Commander X for additional accounts of UFOs and invisibility.)

CHAMISH ABANDONS UFO RESEARCH

Unfortunately, Chamish eventually felt it prudent to leave his UFO research behind. That decision resulted from what he took to be direct harassment from the Israeli government and media, both of whom began to use his history of interest in the UFO phenomenon as a weapon to wage war against a controversial book Chamish had published about the cover-up involved in the assassination of Israeli Prime Minister Yitzhak Rabin.

"Yitzhak Rabin was not murdered by the patsy imprisoned for the crime," Chamish declared, "but rather by his own bodyguard in a coup from within his own political circles. I collected my findings into a book called Who Murdered Yitzhak Rabin, which was published in five languages. For exposing the truth about Rabin, I have gained a large number of enemies, no small number from within the Israeli ruling establishment. Their main proof that my Rabin research is wrong is because I wrote about UFOs, therefore, I must be a nut. My UFO work was badly affecting my credibility. So I chose to distance myself from it."

Chamish's decision leaves us all a little disappointed as well, but perhaps one day the situation will change and Ufology will become a respected science in its own right, If so, Chamish's diligent research into UFOs in Israel will be an important link in the chain of truth.

GARY STEARMAN AND THE CHARIOTS OF WONDER

Gary Stearman is a well-known author and formerly co-host, with his partner, the late Dr. J.R. Church, of a television program called "Prophecy in the News." Stearman now hosts his own program, "Prophecy Watchers," broadcast on satellite, cable and the Internet. .

In an interview with Stearman conducted specifically for this book, the theological and prophetic aspects of the modern UFO phenomenon and its interaction with the modern state of Israel are given a thorough examination.

"The fact about UFOs," Stearman began, "is that they seem to correspond in many ways to what human beings have associated for centuries with spiritual events. There seems to be a spiritual quality within the UFO world and, specifically, it can be seen as part of perhaps a spiritual struggle.

"And with that in mind," he continued, "it's very useful to compare UFOs, the history of UFOs in the modern era, with the occurrences of UFOs in various parts of the world. First of all, the Bible speaks of fiery chariots. The chariot in Hebrew is called the merkavah. It has been suggested, in fact, several modern Israelis have suggested, that UFOs in the Hebrew be called merkavah mophtim. And mophtim means 'wonder.' So what you have in the Hebrew would be 'chariots of wonder,' or vehicles of wonder.

"And the vehicles of wonder have been seen in the Middle East literally for centuries. But in the modern era, particularly late 1947 through 1948 in Israel, they were seen not only in the United States and Europe, but also throughout the Middle East. They were reported as disc-shaped, sometimes cigar-shaped. Sometimes they were suspected of being Russian secret weapons. At other times, invasions from another planet. But they were nevertheless seen at the time."

THE TIMING OF THE UFO FLAPS

Stearman explained the pattern of how UFO sightings flaps were timed around crucial events in Israel. "UFOs made their first dramatic appearance, really dramatic appearance, in 1947 and 1948. That would be the Jewish year 5708, or 47-48 in the Christian calendar. Of course, that was the year of the rebirth of Israel. And these were years when great battles were being fought by human beings in Israel, but the idea is that perhaps someone else was taking notice of this on a higher plane.

"Just about ten years later, in early October of 1956, during the great Sinai Campaign of Israel against Egypt, there were great numbers of sightings of UFOs. It was quite commonly reported in the newspapers of the Middle East, particularly the Israeli newspapers.

"And then again, in the Jewish year 5727, which of course was timed with late spring of 1967, the Six Day War erupted. When the Six Day War came to pass, there was a great UFO flap throughout the world. Then, during September and October of 1973, when the Yom Kippur War against Israel took place, sightings were again very common.

"So when you lay this out," Stearman said, "you have the years 1948, the date of Israel's statehood, and 1956, the Sinai Campaign, as well as 1961, when another massive anti-Israeli movement was begun, of Arabs against the Israelis, 1967, the Six Day War, and 1973, the Yom Kippur War. All of those were the dates of historic UFO flaps. So that's sort of the beginning thesis that leads us to other ideas."

ANOTHER RELEVANT SIGHTINGS WAVE

Stearman made another connection between a major UFO sightings wave and the modern state of Israel, with the surprising year being 1897.

"The beginning of the state of Israel," Stearman explained, "was in the year 1897. That was the great year of the first Zionist Congress in Basel, Switzerland. And in 1897, the world experienced, and I'm talking about the entire world – and it's heavily reported in all the UFO literature – the world experienced a flap of UFO sightings. But they were not called UFOs. They were called airships.

"I believe that the 1897 flap was timed with the rebirth of Israel. From 1897 to 1947 of course is precisely 50 years, and the two great UFO flaps happened in those years."

Stearman related a familiar anecdote from the 1897 flap. "There was the famous case of Alexander Hamilton of Leroy, Kansas. April 21, 1897. An unidentified airship was sailing low over his farm and it lowered a rope and trapped one of his cattle. A two-year-old heifer, bawling and jumping, was lassoed and hauled up into this airship. And it flew away. Well, there is an affidavit published in a number of the UFO publications from Alexander Hamilton. It was signed by the local sheriff, the town banker, and the registrar of deeds, attesting that this really happened. And there are, just as you know, dozens if not hundreds of reports from 1897. 1 link those to the first Zionist Congress, which essentially was the meeting that established the Zionist Movement and the state of Israel."

FROM ROSWELL TO THE PRESENT

"To me," Stearman said, "the biggest year in the history of Ufology is 1947, the year of the Roswell Incident, timed perfectly with the foundation of modern Israel. Of course, everyone's read about Roswell.

"I believe that the Roswell event actually had an effect on the shaping of the government of the United States, in that it established an Above Top Secret mentality in the old Army Air Corps, which later became the Air Force. And a brand new bureaucracy was established to keep secret the fact that we had been contacted by alien beings, and that they had crashed. The most famous crash was at Roswell, New Mexico, but there are other reported crashes around that same time.

"And to bring this up to the present date," he continued, "right at the moment there is an incredible acceleration in UFO sightings, just in the last little while. Not just in Israel or the Mideast, but over the entire planet. I think it coincides with Arial Sharon's declaration that the Temple Mount belongs to the Jewish people. He made that statement in September of the year 2001.

"And from that time to this, there have been just huge numbers of strange flying triangle sightings – low altitude flying triangles that move along very slowly are being seen all over the world now. I see that as a current wave of UFO activity, but again timed with extremely critical events in the Middle East. We're at a point where we may be at total war with Iraq, and of course Israel could become involved in that. If that happens, I would say that UFO reports will increase in an alarming manner."

BUT WHAT DOES IT ALL MEAN?

After Stearman had explained the timing of major UFO sightings waves with events in Israel, the question then became, "What does it all mean? What are the UFO occupants trying to say about their relationship to Israel?"

"Well," Stearman replied, "this takes us back to the fact that these are merkavaim, plural, and that's what the Bible calls them. The Bible speaks of the fiery chariots being like heavenly ambassadors, or sometimes they're called heavenly messengers, or angels. You can call them beings from another dimension. They're commonly called aliens. But the prophets of ancient Israel said that these were the watchmen watching over Israel. And they were acting on behalf of the people of Israel, according to the will of God. Now, that's what the Bible specifically says."

So did Stearman feel that the UFOs are making a show of force, letting the world know that they intend to protect Israel?

"Yeah, I do," he answered. "Or perhaps there is a battle, an ultra-dimensional battle, shall we say, a battle behind the scenes, taking place between those who favor one side or the other. You can state it any way you want to, but there's an earthly battle going on and there appears to be an ultra-dimensional battle going on, too."

Did Stearman mean something like the War In Heaven spoken of in the Bible's Book of Revelation? "The War In Heaven, yeah," he said. "And it seems that every time Israel is threatened, the War In Heaven also seems to accelerate so that it becomes visible in this dimension as UFO and strange creature reports."

THE SERVANT'S EYES ARE OPENED

Stearman made reference to a story in the Bible, from Second Kings, Chapter Six, beginning in verse Fifteen.

"And when the servant of the man of God was risen early and gone forth," Stearman read aloud, "Behold, an host – that's an army – encompassed the city, both with horses and chariots. And his servant said unto him – of course 'he' being Elisha the servant – said unto him, 'Alas, my master, how shall we do?' In other words, we are in deep trouble. And he answered, 'Fear not, for they that be with us are more than they that be with them.' And Elijah prayed and said, 'Lord, I pray thee, open his eyes that he may see.' And the Lord opened the eyes of the young man who saw and behold the mount was full of horses and chariots of fire round about Elisha."

Stearman then illuminated the text a bit more. "Now what was going on here in Second Kings, Chapter Six, is that there was a great battle being fought in which Israel was threatened, deeply threatened. And the prophet Elijah went out on behalf of Israel. The king of Syria had invaded Israel, and Elijah went down to deliver God's message to the leaders of Israel. And he had a servant with him. And the servant was deathly afraid that they were going to be killed, and Elijah prayed and the servant's eyes were opened and he was able to see that they were surrounded, the Israelites were surrounded by these chariots of fire, these merkavim. We could call them today the 'chariots of wonder.'

"And I believe this is an Old Testament reference to what we would call UFOs today, fighting on behalf of Israel."

SAME AS IT EVER WAS

"The same phenomenon exists today," Stearman concluded. "And so every time that Israel is threatened, the battle becomes pitched and becomes more visible to human eyes. And I believe that, Biblically speaking, you can make a strong defense for this because in the Old Testament, one of the titles of the Lord is 'Lord of Hosts,' or 'Jehovah of Hosts,' as he is called. And that title essentially is a military title. It's like being the General of the Heavenly Army.

"Of course, one of the major Bible themes is that the Lord fights on behalf of his people. In fact, one of the meanings of the name Israel is 'for whom God fights.' And so it can be very well said that the hosts of heaven are fighting on behalf of Israel and that each time Israel is in peril, what we call UFOs, but what really are probably better termed merkeva mophlim, these vehicles of wonder, these fiery chariots, roll into action on behalf of Israel."

A controversial figure, the late Barry Chamish collected hundreds of reports from Israel of unexplained aerial objects and their occupants.

Barry's "Return of the Giants" did exceedingly well in a country not overly familiar with UFOs or their occupants.

No, he's not about ready to fend off the aliens. It's Barry Chamish in the Israeli Air Force.

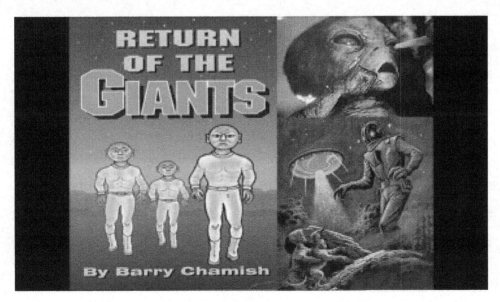

On January 30, 1965, or during the night of March 7, 1965, at 2:00 a.m., he claimed he was walking along Selva Beach, or along the Manresa Beach (the date and the place change with the various versions) and heard a whistling sound similar to that of a jet plane. Looking up, he saw to his "great amazement" a craft, 15 meters in diameter, land before him. He described it as a totally "classic" flying saucer. He wanted to run away, but a voice came from the craft, called his name, and told him no harm would be done to him.

The hundreds who saw the UFO over the Kaputz say it was utterly creepy.

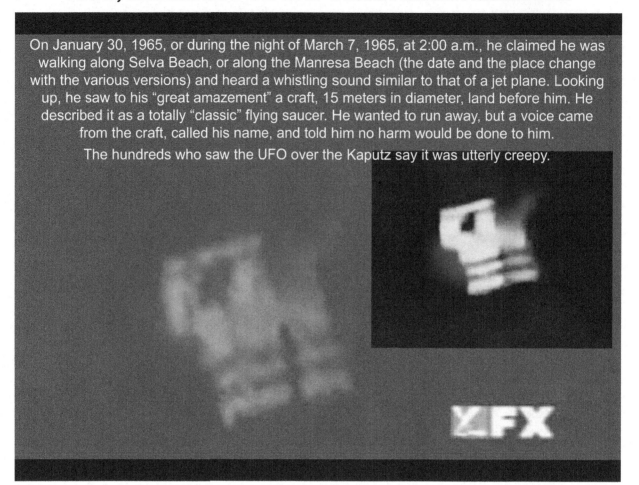

Fast-moving lights over Israel.

Flying saucers have frequently landed in Israel
UFOs over the Dead Sea. What could they be?

Original – privately published – edition of Cecil Michael's "Round Trip to Hell In A Flying Saucer."
A more recent, greatly expanded edition has been published by Tim Beckley and can be found
on Amazon.

7

NICK REDFERN ON THE UFO-DEMON CONTROVERSY
A Q AND A CONDUCTED BY TIMOTHY GREEN BECKLEY

In September 2010, Anomalist Books published Nick Redfern's book, "Final Events And the Secret Government Group on UFOs and the Afterlife," which looks at the history of a hidden think-tank within the US Government that believes that, rather than having alien origins, UFOs are really a tool of the Devil. We sat down with Nick and spoke with him about his "Final Events" book and the beliefs of those in the government who hold to the "aliens are demons" theory.

One does not have to be associated with the UFO mystery for any length of time before it becomes obvious there is a rather big divide between the "scientific community" among UFO researchers and those who are taking a more fundamentalist approach, guided by their interpretation of Biblical scriptures. Their minds are made up! If it's not in the Bible, it either doesn't exist or it is under the control of Satan. Not very scientific. Not very logical. But that's the way the Good Book goes for some people.

In "Round Trip To Hell In A Flying Saucer" I pointed out that this UFO/demonic aspect was the dirty little secret of UFOlogy – something that only a few insiders dare discuss amongst themselves. For example, Lord Hill-Norton, the late five-star Admiral and the former head of the British Ministry of Defence, believed strongly in the existence of UFOs. But he did not see them in a positive light, professing instead in his privately printed UFO Concern Report: "UFOs are essentially a religious matter rather than a military threat and furthermore there is certainly a degree of psychic involvement in almost every case. Quite often, however, such experiences are definitely antithetical to orthodox Christian beliefs."

Journalist and author of "The Mothman Prophecies" (made into a film starring Richard Gere) John A. Keel was adamant when he stated: "The UFOs do not seem to exist as tangible manufactured objects. They do not conform to the accepted natural laws of our environment. The UFO manifestations seem to be, by and large, merely minor variations of the age-old demonological phenomena."

I like Nick. In addition to having a good reputation among most in the field, he has always acted as a friend, been a guest on our podcast, "Exploring the Bizarre," and has the proper – middle of the road – attitude when it comes to all things weird and unexplained.

BECKLEY: When did you get wind that there was actually a think tank or secret group in the government who took seriously the idea that demons and UFOs go hand-in-hand?

REDFERN: The lead came from a man named Ray Boeche. Ray is an Anglican priest and he is a former State-Director of the Mutual UFO Network (MUFON), for the state of Nebraska. In late 1991, Ray was contacted by two physicists working on a secret Department of Defense project to contact – and to try and exploit the mental powers of – what they called "Non-Human Entities," but that are more commonly known as the Grays. Ray met the guys for a clandestine discussion in Lincoln, Nebraska, in November 1991, and that's how the story started. It was as if there were people in the official world that wanted to see if the mind-power of the Grays could be utilized as a form of mind-weaponry by the Pentagon. In other words, it was something along the lines of a next-generation Remote-Viewing type program. But the idea was that instead of training the mind to psychically spy on the enemy, it would be to psychically assassinate them using powers of the mind, gleaned from the Grays. But, the DoD physicists told Ray Boeche that the further they got into the project the more they came to believe that the Grays were highly deceptive, and they also came to believe the Grays were actually – and quite literally – deceptive demons from Hell, who were here to deceive us about their true agenda – which was to bring people over to the dark-side and prepare things for Armageddon, but to do it under the guise of a faked alien appearance.

The DoD physicists wanted Ray's opinion on all this, because he had a background as a priest and as a MUFON State-Director. And it was when I began to investigate Ray's story in 2007, after extensively interviewing him about it, I got on the trail of the think-tank group behind all this – that calls themselves The Collins Elite – and managed to get some interviews with them, and copies of their files too. And, when I had enough data, that's when I decided to write my book on the subject: "Final Events: And the Secret Government Group on UFOs and the Afterlife."

BECKLEY: What evidence did they offer you that there is a relationship or a link that would prove their theory?

REDFERN: The Collins Elite did not offer any evidence at all. Like all worldwide religions, Christianity is faith-based, which essentially equates with the idea of belief without demonstrable evidence of literal existence. So, they had a lot of belief-driven ideas, theories and conclusions. But all of them were lacking in terms of having actual evidence to support the notion that the UFO presence on Earth was a Satanic deception, but it is what they believed. So that people will not be in any doubt at all as to where I stand on all this, my personal view is that the conclusions/beliefs of the Collins Elite are wrong. I think the whole idea that this is all Satanic and that only Christianity has it right is far too simplistic.

How do they know other religions are wrong? The answer is simple: they don't know, they just believe all other religions are wrong. How do they – or we – know that any religion is correct? I would agree with the Collins Elite on a couple of things, however: I actually gave up on the E.T. hypothesis a long time ago, and I suspect we're actually dealing with extra-dimensional entities, and they may not have our best interests at heart. I do believe that they might be malevolent and deceitful, and that we're not seeing the full picture. But that doesn't automatically mean they are something that stepped straight out of a Hell that no one can prove exists. I don't personally believe in the whole Heaven and Hell concept. I think it's far too simplistic, and is a scenario created to control people via fear and guilt. But, the fact that there are several groups within the Department of Defense and the Pentagon that do believe this, is what makes it a fascinating story, and why I decided to write my "Final Events" book.

BECKLEY: Did they offer you up any specific cases?

REDFERN: Yes. They claimed that the whole modern era of Ufology was the work of Aleister Crowley and Jack Parsons. From January to March 1918, Crowley received a series of visions via his "Scarlet Woman," one Roddie Minor; this is the infamous Amalantrah Working. Throughout his life, Crowley had a number of these Scarlet Women, all of whom essentially acted as channels or vessels for the transfer of messages perceived to be of angelic and/or demonic origin. But Crowley was interested in more than mere messages; it was his deep desire to invite, or to invoke, the entities behind the messages into our world and to engage them on a one-to-one basis. Crowley was certainly no fool and he was fully aware of the potentially hazardous and disastrous implications that might very well result from his planned door-opening activities. This did not, however, in any way dissuade him from enthusiastically pressing ahead.

And, it seems, he succeeded beyond his wildest dreams – or nightmares, maybe. It was during the Amalantrah Working, which included the ingestion of hashish and mescaline to achieve an altered state of consciousness, that Crowley made contact with an inter-dimensional entity known as Lam, a large-headed figure that could have quite easily passed for a close relative of the enigmatic being that stares eerily forth from the cover of "Communion," Whitley Strieber's alien abduction book published in 1987. The Collins Elite also focused, as I mentioned, on the brilliant, maverick rocket-scientist Jack Parsons, who died under controversial circumstances in 1952. Parsons, a devotee of Crowley, undertook in 1946 the infamous Babalon Working. Like Crowley, Parsons was fascinated by the notion of opening dimensional gateways, and this is precisely what the Collins Elite believe happened – that Crowley and Parsons opened the doors to this demonic deception in a fashion that allowed for (in the Collins Elite's view, at least) these entities to confront us – in a build-up to the final battle between good and evil – but under the guise of aliens.

As for other cases, the Collins Elite also came to believe that the whole Contactee/Space Brother movement was demonic. For example, the fact the 1950s Contactee George Hunt Williamson made some of his contacts via Ouija-boards was seen as evidence by the group that he was being deceived, because the Collins Elite concluded Ouija-boards are tools that demons can exploit. On this same issue, when they began to research George Adamski, they found that his co-author on his first book, "Flying Saucers Have Landed" – an Irishman named Desmond Leslie – had a very interesting background. Desmond Leslie's father, Sir Shane Leslie, was a big student of the occult, and had a deep fascination with the teachings of the aforementioned Aleister Crowley. So, the Collins Elite was putting together strands like this to support their theories and beliefs.

BECKLEY: Were all the members of this group Christian fundamentalists, or did the group include atheists and agnostics as well?

REDFERN: They were all, or came to be, Christians, and some of them were indeed full-blown Fundamentalists. So, in other words, their investigation that concluded UFOs are demonic was hardly what we could call an unbiased investigation and conclusion.

BECKLEY: Are any of its members famous?

REDFERN: As far as I can tell, all the members were regular people in the military, government, intelligence world, and Department of Defense. However, it does appear to be the case, from the story I uncovered, that they deeply influenced the mindset of none other than President Ronald Reagan, who was highly interested in UFOs and who also had a very disturbing interest in "End Times" scenarios, both of which, of course, are central aspects of the beliefs of the Collins Elite.

BECKLEY: What exactly is their concept of a demon? Are we talking Satan's henchmen here?

REDFERN: Yes, that was their conclusion – that these things are the literal manifestation of Satan's hordes. However, they believe that such demonic entities lack physical form. In other words, their natural appearance is not of the typical horror movie image of horns, glowing eyes and a fork-tail etc. Rather, they believe these entities are essentially non-physical, and along the lines of pure energy. But that they can create deceptive imagery with which to deceive us that looks physical, but really isn't. In other words, they believe the whole UFO phenomenon is illusion-based, and they believe abduction stories are actually nothing more than solely illusions projected into the minds of the abductee to further instill this alien imagery. The Collins Elite do not believe that any abduction experience has ever taken place outside of the confines of the human brain – partly due to these entities not having physical form as we understand it.

BECKLEY: What is the weirdest idea they laid down to you?

REDFERN: That these demons farm human souls, as a form of energy, as sustenance, an answer I'll get into deeper with the John Lear question below.

BECKLEY: Are they shape shifters? Do they abduct humans? Experiment on them? Cut them into little pieces?

REDFERN: No, the Collins Elite do not believe that these entities have any physical interaction with us – at least not in the way that we understand the term. They believe the whole alien abduction scenario is a scam – a series of brain-induced hallucinations provoked by these entities as a means to reinforce the idea that they are aliens here to experiment on us, etc. In other words, for the Collins Elite, abductions are a way for these creatures to deceive us further. So, there's no actual physical interaction with us at all, the group believes. But they can provoke hallucinatory imagery in the mind: aliens, goblins, Bigfoot etc, to make us believe we're seeing something physically and externally, the Collins Elite concludes.

BECKLEY: The always controversial John Lear has said that aliens are sucking human souls? Did anything like this ever come up with the group you are in touch with?

REDFERN: Yes, this was one of the central themes of the beliefs of the Collins Elite. They came to the conclusion that the Earth is a farm, and that we are the cattle. They came to accept – based on interviews with a number of people who had Near Death Experiences, theologians, experts on Demonology etc. – that these entities essentially harvest and feed upon a poorly-defined "soul-energy" upon our deaths. In essence, the Collins Elite thinks that because these demonic creatures are basically energy-based, that our energy feeds and fuels them. The group interviewed a number of NDE witnesses who claimed to have seen vast, never-ending "soul-factories" while in a near-death state, and who also claimed these Gray-like entities process us, slaughter-house/farm-like one by one, and extract energy – rather like the idea of a demonic vampire.

BECKLEY: Any tie in with human sacrifices or animal mutilations?

REDFERN: Ray Boeche was told about human sacrifices connected to the project, but the information given was literally just that, and not expanded upon. I do have information on animal mutilations, however. I didn't put this in my "Final Events" book, so this is a bit of a scoop for you! One of the things that a former member of the Collins Elite told me was that there were several groups in government that believed in the demonic angle. But, whereas the Collins Elite were supposedly trying to keep these entities at bay, groups like those that approached Ray Boeche were trying to enter into Faustian-style pacts with them. And one of the things that I was told was that there was a group buried very deeply in the U.S. Army that was involved in the cattle mutilations, but that had nothing to do with aliens, but that did offer an explanation for the whole "Black Helicopter" angle. Supposedly, this Army group doing the mutes were actually killing the cattle and taking blood and organs as sacrificial items, that would then be used in ancient rites and archaic rituals to both appease and summon up these "Non-Human Entities" as they described them, in an effort to try and engage them and use their mental powers.

BECKLEY: So were they at any point looking to tell the public of their findings?

REDFERN: Yes, they were. This was a very controversial area, because they were unsure for a while how to do this. Whether their belief-system has any merit to it or not, they did recognize that telling the public the truth as they saw it, would be a fraught task, and one that could lead to the collapse of society, when the realization sunk in that we are essentially living on a farm that is designed one day to allow for the reaping and "digestion" of our souls. They came to the conclusion that subtly, bit by bit, government and the intelligence world should be infiltrated to a greater degree by Christian extremists and then combine that with trying to almost create like a fascist-Christian government that would rule the nation with a rod of iron, instill this belief system about UFOs in the population, and tell them that a strong denial of these beings can actually hold them at bay. That's what the Collins Elite believes – that if we deny their existence or deny their power, it actually has a way to lessen their ability to interact with us. But the Collins Elite concluded that for the entire population to hold such deep beliefs would require the nation being placed in literal lock-down status, and near-totalitarian indoctrination of old-time religion. And, if we look at the world today, we do see more and more people (some of them quite insane people, too) trying to make the government and the military more and more dominated by religion. So, maybe they really are beginning this process.

BECKLEY: Do they believe an actual day of tribulation is at hand?

REDFERN: Yes, they do. They believe these entities know they are doomed when the final battle between good and evil, God and Satan, comes to pass, and they believe these demons – as Judgment Day draws near — will create a worldwide, faked, UFO sighting wave all across the planet, and that we will be deceived into thinking these are friendly aliens come to help, when in reality – the Collins Elite believes – these will really be the demons, seducing as many millions as they can with their ET-driven lies, as a means to take as many of our souls with them when the final battle arrives. At least, that's the Collins Elite's conclusion on it. Personally, I'm always very wary of prophecies, future-predictions etc.

BECKLEY: What did they figure would be the reaction of religious leaders and of the average guy in the street? Isn't this likely to blow the minds of everyone? I know it would blow mine, probably yours as well.

REDFERN: The sheer fear of learning that we are basically cattle whose whole existence is geared so that these demonic entities can feed on our souls after death – in the form of ominous, never-ending soul factories – was deemed as being too terrifying to tell people, at least right now. Which is why the Collins Elite concluded the best way to do this would be by spending the next 10 or 15 years basically, secretly building up a kind of Christian dictatorship that would have an iron-grip on the population and then when we're under their vise-like control, even if there was mass panic the government would invoke the worst parts of the Patriot Act and lock-down the country with martial law, curfews etc., and have constant indoctrination in schools, on TV etc., until people came to accept it, and came to believe that they could hold these creatures at bay with deep, fundamentalist belief. But the problem, as the Collins Elite sees it, is how to get the population into that mindset – and that's where this whole religious "New World Order" plan comes into play.

BECKLEY: So is Satan real? Has he or is he paying us a visit in a flying saucer?

REDFERN: My personal view is that, no, Satan and his minions are not paying us visits in flying saucers, or under a deceptive guise of aliens. Ironically, for someone who has written a book about how a group in the government really does believe this is going on, I'm personally not a religious person at all. I have never been to church, aside from weddings and funerals. And, I find it hard to understand how anyone can say with confidence that this religion, or that religion, or any religion is definitely wrong and that someone else's religion is definitely right. I'm not saying there's definitely no afterlife. But, when we have countless religions all across the world that have varying beliefs – sometimes wildly varying beliefs – then I don't see how anyone can say for certain their view is right, without hard evidence. And as for the Collins Elite, their conclusions lack hard evidence and are based solely on belief and faith, which is never a good thing. If any religion could provide me with proof – not deeply held beliefs or deep faith, but actual proof – they're right, maybe my personal views might change. But, no religion in the history of the planet has ever proved anything, and the Collins Elite can't prove that demons from Hell are visiting in flying saucers. They can only offer their beliefs that this is going on, and that's not enough.

BECKLEY: Wouldn't you say this sounds pretty outlandish? Certainly Stanton Friedman isn't likely to add your theory to his lecture program. Do any serious UFOlogists accept this theory?

REDFERN: It certainly is outlandish! I think that what the story I relate in "Final Events" tells us is that the government often secretly funds think-tank groups with unusual ideas and theories. And the reason the government does this is to try and determine if there is any intelligence/espionage or national security issue that has a bearing on the work of the group, and if any sort of advantage can be gained in these intelligence and national security areas by looking into things along the lines of the Collins Elite. Yes, there are a number of Ufologists who do believe the demonic theory for UFOs is correct. There's the aforementioned Ray Boeche, who was a State-Director with MUFON, and who did a lot of work in the 1980s into the famous Rendlesham Forest, England, UFO landing case in 1980. Michael Heiser, author of the book, "The Facade," is a strong believer in the demonic angle. As are authors/researchers Guy and Nicole Malone, and Joe Jordan, who works at NASA's Kennedy Space Center, and who is heavily involved in researching alien abduction cases in relation to the demonic angle.

SUGGESTED READING

FINAL EVENTS

ROUND TRIP TO HELL IN A FLYING SAUCER

UFOS - WICKED THIS WAY COMES

WITHOUT CONSENT — THE SUM OF OUR DARKEST FEARS

Occultist Aleister Crowley conjured up his own negative spirits, including "Lam," who looks remarkably like a Gray described in current UFO abduction accounts.

THE WAY

Lam is the Tibetan word for Way or Path, and Lama is He who Goeth, the specific title of the Gods of Egypt, the Traveler of the Path, in Buddhistic phraseology. Its numerical value is 71, the number of this book.

Pastor Nick hangs out with our
homies Allan Benz
and Charla Gene.

Dr. Ray Boeche met with two
members of the Department
of Defense who revealed to
him the existence of the
Collins Elite.

The Collins Elite:
Theocratic Surveillance State vs Demonic Entities

FINAL EVENTS

AND THE SECRET GOVERNMENT GROUP ON DEMONIC UFOS AND THE AFTERLIFE

NICK REDFERN

Bryan Fischer says that UFOs are just a "ruse from Satan" to distract us from the coming End Times. Fistastic.com

Are demons hanging out inside the Pentagon? Hey, is Val Thor a secret member of this group? Doubt it!

Evil lurks behind the face of the aliens – or at least some Christian fundamentalists would have you believe.

Is the Collins Elite the shadow "UFO government" of the Pentagon — or a simple coffee clutch of workers operating on their own time?

< In his controversial book, "Final Events and the Secret Government Group on UFOs and the Afterlife," Nick Redfern "blows the whistle" on the Satanic/UFO connection.

8

THE COSMIC COUNTDOWN HAS BEGUN
By Timothy Green Beckley,
Based On Interviews With Tuella And Dr. Frank Stranges

There is sufficient reason to believe that we have passed the Eleventh Hour on the countdown, and that the hands of the cosmic clock are pushing Midnight. Throughout our research, we are told to look for certain "signs," which will alert us to the fact that time is running short. As previously stated, not even the space people know the exact hour, since the future is subject to change. This seems to confirm Matthew 24.29-36 for those who are interested in tying this in with a Biblical reference: "But of the day and hour knoweth no man, no, not even the angels (space beings?) of heaven."

I find it rather fascinating that much of what has been revealed to us via extraterrestrial sources seems to be quite similar to religious texts, Christian as well as other sects. There seems to be almost a universal understanding that something very traumatic is going to happen during the period in which we now find ourselves.

Remember Ashtar's prediction to the effect that there would be a strange haze in the atmosphere which would turn the moon and sun a weird color, making it difficult to tell the difference between day and night? Well, there are several references in the Bible to just such an event. Take, for example, Isaiah 13.9-10: "For the stars of heaven and the constellations thereof shall not give their light; the sun shall be darkened, and the moon shall not cause her light to shine." Or take Amos 8.9: "And it shall come to pass in that day, sayeth the Lord, that I will cause the sun to go down at noon, and I will darken the Earth in the clear day." Nor should we forget Joel 3. 15 which says: "The sun and the moon shall be darkened, and the stars shall withdraw their shining."

To an extent, we might have already been given a sample of what could happen on a much larger, more intense scale. On several occasions in recent years, pollution caused by waste being released into the atmosphere has cut visibility down to less than a foot in several large cities. One day soon we could very easily have the three days of darkness spoken of so often in prophecy, and we will know with a strong conviction in our heart that the End Times are upon us.

MYSTERY MESSAGES

Another sure-fire sign that we are approaching the close of an age, and that extraterrestrial intervention (to whatever degree is allowed) is at hand, is said to be the taking over of our broadcasting facilities by the UFOnauts. According to the messages channeled for the past several decades, our space friends will interfere with our normal radio and television reception, and will issue a communication directly to the people of earth. Supposedly, they will "cut in" over our regularly scheduled programs and will issue forth a proclamation that will be seen and heard in every country around the world.

Thelma Terrell – who took the name "Tuella" for channeling purposes – had recently received one such channeled message which deals with this precise subject: "Our technology is readied to super-impose our frequencies over your television and radio broadcasting systems if necessary, to reach the masses in the quickest possible manner. We can also extend our frequencies into your telephone lines for a brief message. We have systems similar to your public address systems, available from the smaller scout ships which operate with a volume and power unheard of in your technology.

"We have many ways of reaching quantities of persons simultaneously. We project into your thinking at this very date, that fear of us and our presence or our appearance, or lack of understanding of our motivation, will combine to produce such a negative field around your physical form that we would be unable to assist you."

The channel then goes on to say, once again, that time is short. "We cannot promise you another decade. We cannot even promise you all of this one. Your destiny is in your hands."

Pretty explicit words, wouldn't you agree?

As an experiment to prove to us that such a massive take over of our communications systems can be accomplished, the UFOnauts have already beamed several important messages over our television stations. The following is a complete transcript of the "Voice from Outer Space" as broadcast on TV, in the Hennington area of Southern England at 5:05 P.M. on Saturday, November 26, 1977.

"This is the voice of Glon, representative of the 'Asteron Galactic Command,' speaking to you. For many years you have seen us as lights in the sky. We speak to you now in peace and wisdom as we have done to your brothers and sisters all over this, your planet.

"We come to warn you of the destiny of your race in your world so that you may communicate to your fellow beings the course you must take to avoid disaster which threatens your world and the beings of other worlds around you.

"This is the order that you may share in the great awakening as the planet passes into the New Age of Aquarius. The New Age can be a time of great evolution for your race, but only if your rulers are made aware of the evil forces that can overshadow their judgement. Be still now, and listen, for your chance may not come again for many years.

"Your scientists, governments and generals have not heeded our warnings. They have continued to experiment with the evil forces of what you call nuclear energy. Atomic bombs can destroy the Earth and the beings of your sister worlds in a moment. The wastes from atomic power systems will poison your planet for many thousands of years to come. We who have followed the path of evolution for far longer than you, have long since realized this, that atomic energy is always directed against life. It has no peaceful application. Its use and research into its use must be ceased at once, or you will all risk destruction. All weapons of evil must be removed.

"The time of conflict is now passed and the races of which you are a part may proceed to the highest planes of evolution, if you show yourselves worthy to do this. You have but a short time to learn to live together in peace and good will. Small groups all over the planet are learning this and exist to pass on the light of a new dawning, the New Age to you all. You are free to accept or reject their teachings, but only those who learn to live in peace will pass to the higher realms of spiritual evolution.

"Hear then the voice of Glon – the voice of the 'Asteron Galactic Command' – speaking to you. Be aware also that there are many false prophets and guides at present operating on your world. They will suck your energy from you, the energy you call money, and will put it to evil ends, giving you worthless dross in return. Your inner divine self will protect you from this. You must learn to be sensitive to the voice within that can tell you what is truth and what is confusion, chaos and untruth. Learn to listen to the voice of truth which is within you and you will lead yourself onto the path of evolution.

"This is our message to you, our dear friends. We have watched you growing for many years, just as you have watched our lights in the skies. You know now that we are here and that there are more beings on and around your Earth than your scientists care to admit. We are deeply concerned about you and your path towards the light and we will do all we can to help you. Have no fears, seek only to know yourself and live in harmony with the ways of your planet Earth.

"We are the 'Asteron Galactic Command'; thank you for your attention. We are now leaving the planes of your existence. May you be blessed with the supreme love and truth of the cosmos."

Wouldn't you agree that this is a most inspiring communication? The authorities attempted to attack the validity of the message, stating that a vandal had taken over a deserted transmitter in a wooded area of the city and had somehow managed to broadcast the message, overriding the normal TV signal. What the spokesman for the television station neglected to mention is that there was actually more than one message, and they lasted for a considerable period of time, not the 15 or 20 seconds they tried to make everyone believe.

I have received a number of letters from readers who claim to be picking up strange "alien communications" on their ham radios. Many of these messages deal with End Time prophecies and many of the things talked about in this book. It's hard to believe that hoaxers got hold of some very expensive equipment and transmitted just for the "fun" of it. More likely, these messages fit right into the puzzle we are trying so desperately to solve.

"VALUABLES" TO BRING ALONG

Naturally, if the world blows up, turns to ashes, or flips on its axis, all the tea – or money – in China won't be of any use to survivors. Yet, if your house is burning down, or you are on a ship and it is sinking, you usually don't leave behind all your valuables. It's human nature to take that which is dearest to you, or that for which you have worked the hardest. If our cities collapse and we have to take to the road, as has been predicted, what should we make certain to take with us?

Chicago psychic Warren Freiberg has a few thoughtful suggestions on this matter. "Forget about taking money with you. Paper money and even coins won't be worth anything," he points out. "Food will be scarce and people won't want to part with what they have in exchange for worthless currency. Remember, a dollar bill isn't worth anything in itself; it's only valuable because the U.S. Government stands behind it. In all likelihood the government as we know it will be dissolved or at least totally ineffective to the point where nobody will be willing to listen to our former leaders as they will come to see the folly of their ways. If possible, start saving things like silver and gold pieces, and also gems. Such items are always of value, but best of all they are relatively small and easy to carry on your person. My suggestion would be to turn your savings into diamonds or small gold coins. Eventually, the banks will shut down and all your life savings will go down the drain, so do something about it before it's too late."

Robert Short's space contacts have informed him during several channeling sessions that the bartering system may return in the Last Days. "If you recognize that all have their methods, and thus if they return to their original teaching, which teaches abstinence from those paths which lead only to wrongdoing, and that which has replaced the people's ability to trade among themselves in humility and honesty, which is called a 'barter system.' They (the banking system and governments) have replaced this with that force which is MONETARY and thus have sold men's minds, bodies and souls into slavery upon your planet. If this ceased among the nations, then will peace come, not rapidly, but it will begin to replace the wrongdoing which had begun centuries before in your time when those of the human race who had placed value upon metals and gems, and other methods of exchange – in lieu of that which was the original verbal agreement and handshake between neighbors who were able to trade in true value among themselves. . ." This message was received on February 2, 1979, and in recent conversations, the head of the Solar Space Foundation has revealed that a return to the barter system may become a way of life before the end of our age.

When the time comes to be taken aboard a spaceship for a quick trip out of this manmade hell, several of the space entities who have spoken through our channels agree that it's alright to bring your personal necessities. "There are many personal items you might desire, which we could not provide, and if these few small things will make you content and happy while you wait, then they should be included. Your own ingenuity will be exercised here, keeping the contents few but vital," remarks Capt. Avalon of the Interplanetary Council.

So remember, keep a small overnight bag packed under your bed and ready to go. I can't say for certain, but they might not have your favorite brand of toothpaste in the outer reaches of the solar system.

SIGNS AND WONDERS

There is only one man I know of who is knowledgeable when it comes to UFOs and believes their mission is an honorable one, and is also a practicing evangelist who has placed his faith in God. Most religious leaders will tell you that flying saucers are the devil's messengers and that when they promise to save us they are only lying. (The late) Dr. Frank Stranges made a serious study of the UFO mystery, Frank Stranges is quite different in this regard. Not only is he a man of the cloth, but this evangelist claims to have actually met and conversed with a being from another planet. Several years back, Stranges was introduced to a spaceman who said his name was Val Thor, and that he had been living on Earth for several years attempting to establish contact with the heads of government. Stranges claims that he spoke to Val Thor in the Pentagon, where the human-looking alien had been staying after proving his superiority and the fact that he came from an advanced civilization. In addition to his church work, Dr. Stranges is the only preacher I know to actually run a UFO group, the National Investigations Committee on Unidentified Flying Objects,

Though much of Frank Stranges' teaching is based upon Biblical scripture, he is also familiar with the plan that the UFO intelligence has in store for us, and is thus able to incorporate his thinking on the matter of the End Times. According to Dr. Stranges, a third world war is not that far off. He believes the next global conflict will involve Israel, the Arab states, the countries of Western Europe, the USSR, and the United States. This is how he sees the order of events transpiring in the

UFOS, ARMAGEDDON AND BIBLICAL REVELATIONS

Last Days:

1. MILLIONS WILL VANISH FROM THE FACE OF THE EARTH.

2. CHILDREN WILL BE REPORTED MISSING (remember the prediction that the Space Brothers will take our youngsters first), LOVED ONES GONE, GRAVES OPENED.

3. DISTRESS OF NATIONS, SUCH AS HAS NEVER BEFORE TRANSPIRED ON THIS PLANET. '

4. TRANSPORTATION WILL BE A MAJOR PROBLEM.

5. FROM THIS POINT ON, A SERIES OF PRESIDENTIAL ORDERS WILL BE ISSUED TO THE AUTHORITIES ON THIS PLANET, PLACING EVERY LIVING PERSON IN THE U.S. UNDER COMPLETE DICTATORSHIP!

6. ONCE THE "CHOSEN" HAVE BEEN REMOVED, THE PRESIDENT WILL:

A. Take over all communication media.

B. Take over all petroleum, gas, fuel, electric power, etc.

C. Take over all food resources, farms, etc.

D. Take over all modes of transportation, highways, and airports.

E. Mobilize all civilians into work forces under government supervision.

F. Take over all health, welfare and education.

G. Postmaster authorized to conduct nationwide registration of ALL persons.

H. Take over all airplanes, aircraft, including private planes.

I. Take over all housing, financing - to relocate people, build with public funds in certain designated areas.

While touring California years ago I had the pleasure to be invited by Dr. Stranges to speak at his Saturday night lecture program in Van Nuys. After the evening's official schedule had been concluded, Frank and I wandered down the hall to the seclusion of his private office for a more personal chit chat. Here we discussed some of his personal transformational views which incorporate the following earthly changes he sees as being on our door step. As we get nearer to the midnight hour, Frank paints a frightening apocalyptic vision that he believes will unfold all around us in the Earth, in the Heavens and in the stars. He sees his vision as being backed up by both orthodox Biblical teachings as well as being verified through the channelings and thinking of many contemporary New Age teachers. Here is his breakdown on what events are likely to occur in nature.

THE SUN

Jesus said: Immediately after the tribulation of those days shall the sun be darkened, (Matt. 24:29). The Apostle John was shown an apocalyptic vision of the world during the last days of the Great Tribulation, and he wrote that because of the sun men were scorched with great heat. . .(Rev. 1619).

71

UFOS, ARMAGEDDON AND BIBLICAL REVELATIONS

The Prophet Isaiah wrote of this time, the light of the sun shall be sevenfold, as the light of seven days. (Isaiah 30:26). For many years astronomers concluded that our sun could maintain its present heat energy output for at least 8 million more years, because its hydrogen supply was only about half exhausted. However, more recently, some astronomers have reappraised this theory, and now believe that once a star (our sun is a medium size star) has expended half its hydrogen, it is in danger of experiencing a nova.

Larger stars, supernovas, blow up, and the smaller stars, like our own sun, nova, get brighter and hotter for a period of from 7 to 14 days and then become darker. There are about 14 novae a year in the observable universe. Some astronomers now believe that the increased sun-spot activity is a sign that our own sun may be about to nova. The increased solar storm activity predicted could be the trigger that would set off the atomic collapse of the sun. A nova of our sun would most assuredly: (1) cause the sun to become unusually bright (as Isaiah prophesied) (2) become seven times hotter as Joel prophesied, and (3) then become dark as Joel and Jesus prophesied.

MOON

Isaiah prophesied. . .the light of the moon shall be as the light of the sun.(Isaiah 30:26) Joel said of this time, The sun shall be turned into darkness and the moon into blood (Joel 2:31) Jesus said, The sun shall be darkened, and the moon shall not give her light. (Matt 24:29)

Inasmuch as the moon has no light of its own, and reflects only that light which it receives from the sun, the prophetic word is in perfect harmony with science. It naturally follows that when the sun becomes 7 times brighter, as Isaiah prophesied, reflected light upon the Earth will make the night as hot and bright as the average day. Then, when the sun becomes dark, as Jesus said it must, the moon will naturally give off no light. However, Joel indicates that at this time the moon will be turned into blood, or become red in appearance. The prophecy of Joel about the moon could well take place as the scientists believe there will be strange lighting effects in the heavens in our time.

EARTH

The environmental changes on Earth preceding the return of Jesus Christ, will be varied and severe.

Storms: The Scriptures indicate that terrible storms and floods will occur at the beginning. We have always been of the opinion that the battle of Ezekiel 38 occurs at the first of the Tribulation Period. We read in verse 22 of great hailstones and an overflowing rain. It is also prophesied in Revelation 16:21 that upon men will fall a great hail out of heaven, every stone about the weight of a talent. A talent is equal to about 10 pounds. A sudden shift in the winds with increased velocity conjointly with great disturbances in the upper atmosphere is predicted by scientists.

Drought: After the sudden shift in wind directions and temperature, resulting in violent storms, the wind will stabilize and a drought will prevail over the Earth. Joel prophesied of the time of great distress, the seed is rotten under their clods . . . How do the beasts groan? The herds of cattle are perplexed, because they have no pasture. The beasts of the field cry also unto thee, for the rivers of water are dried up. (Joel 1:15-20)

We read in Revelation that no rain will fall upon the Earth for 1,260 days (about three and a half years), and could be a factor responsible for the world's changing weather patterns. It is significant, in the light of the Bible prophecy, that the scientists predict great disrupting weather patterns around the globe.

In Time: Jesus said of the time factor during the Great Tribulation, And, except those days should be shortened, there should no flesh be saved. The duration of the Tribulation Period is already established by God. It will be seven years - no more and no less. The second half of the Tribulation Period, also called the Time of Jacob's Trouble, will be three and a half years (42 months - Rev. 13:5). Calendar-wise, the Great Tribulation cannot be shortened. Therefore, it seems obvious that Jesus was referring to the shortening of the hours of the days (literally, the days themselves will be shortened by several hours.) The evident truth of Jesus' prophecy is verified in Rev. 8:12, and the day shone not for a third part of it, and the night likewise.

Earth's Orbit: The Scriptures indicate that before the flood, rain did not fall upon the ground. The earth was watered by a mist. A layer of water vapor in the upper atmosphere served as an air conditioner, and there was an even temperature from pole to pole. Then this vapor was removed at the flood, the earth tilted on its axis 23 degrees, and a great amount of this water was frozen at the ice caps. The resulting change in environment decreased the life span of man from several hundred years to three score and ten. We read in the 34th chapter of Isaiah, that at the time. . . the Lord of hosts shall reign in Mount Zion and Jerusalem, and before his ancients gloriously (verse 23), that the Earth shall reel to and fro like a drunkard (verse 20).

There is an excellent probability the Earth will be righted on its axis and pre-flood conditions restored. During the Millennium, we are informed by the Scriptures that all deterrents to a fruitful Earth will be removed, and people shall live to be several hundred years old (Isaiah 65:19-25).

Famine: Jesus prophesied of the last days, and there shall be famines (Matt 24:7). World health and food experts have predicted that one billion people could starve to death. Already, 28 nations around the equatorial belt have experienced drought and famine. This assuredly, will have an effect on agriculture, and make feeding the exploding population of the Earth more difficult. If drastic weather changes take place as predicted, then the expected one billion victims of famine within the next ten years may be a conservative estimate.

Earthquakes: Jesus said also of signs related to His Second Coming, and there shall be. earthquakes in diverse places. Jesus meant that at the time of the end of this age, earthquakes would occur in increasing numbers in many places. It is remarkable that scientists have warned there will be many earthquakes, large and small. These are almost the exact words that Jesus chose to describe one of the judgments that would be visited upon the earth at the time of His return. As much is said about earthquakes in the end of the age as any other heavenly or earthly phenomena during the Great Tribulation. Revelation 6:12 There was a great earthquake; and the sun became black and the moon became as blood. (Revelation 11:13), And the same hour there was a great earthquake, and the tenth part of the city Jerusalem) fell, and in the earthquake were slain of men seven thousand. (Revelation 16:18.20), .and there was a great earthquake such as was not since men were upon the Earth so mighty an earthquake, and so great, and every island fled away, and the mountains were not found.

SIGNS IN THE EARTH

Scientists say that there will be drastic weather changes; fierce changing winds: rapidly accelerating solar activity connected with an outward gravitational pull that may cause the Earth to become exceedingly hot for several days; the ice caps may melt and earthquakes occur all over the Earth. If the predictions of the scientists measure up to even 26 percent of expectations, then soon there may be a time of desolation and tribulation. Jesus said of His coming again, as recorded in Luke 21:25-28, that there would be fearsome signs in the heavens and upon the earth, distress of nations. Since 1945 the world has witnessed on several occasions the rising of pillars of smoke and fire into the atmosphere from the explosion of nuclear devices. Joel said this would be one of the signs of the last days.

As we have already brought out, earthquakes will be only a part of the drastic environmental changes on Earth that scientists believe will take place. However, earthquakes are perhaps the most important, from a Biblical standpoint, because earthquakes have always signified dispensation changes in God's dealings with mankind. There must have been great earthquakes at the flood, because we read in Genesis 7:11 that the fountains of the great deep were broken up.

There must have been another great earthquake at the time that God divided the nations at the time of the Tower of Babel. God divided the nations by race, languages, and cultures; and He divided them by mountains, rivers, seas, deserts and oceans. Science has now verified that the continents were all one huge land mass but something happened and they broke up and floated apart. For example, the east coast of South America fits like a puzzle piece against the west coast of Africa. And if you will consult an earthquake map of the fault lines around the world, they generally follow the coasts of the continents, indicating that a great earthquake most likely caused the continents and islands to separate.

DAYS OF DARKNESS

This channeled message has been circulated among various groups and individuals and purports to be directly from The Christ. It was received through Anna, the prophetess who considers herself a messenger of God. We fully realize it is of a controversial nature and present it because so many have expressed interest in material regarding specifically "THE DAYS OF DARKNESS" so many have predicted. Interestingly, it is quite similar to other such channeled messages being received worldwide.

**

This is thy Lord, Jesus Christ. I have spoken of three phases of Cleansing. The first is the three days of Darkness; the second is the Seven-Year Famine; and the third is the Battle of Armageddon, at which time the Children of God will not be on Earth, but will have been evacuated.

There have been cleansings in which there were three days of darkness in the time of Noah; and in the time of the flight of the Children of Israel out of Egypt; and in the time of Enoch; and in the time of Abraham. When Abraham was, the Earth had existed twenty-six hundred years, but there was no written history. The history of the Earth is written in God's Book of Life, where those who can go to the Akashic Records can read it. Atlantis was at the time of Enoch. Lemuria was at the time of the flight of the Children of Israel out of Egypt.

When ye see this writing, the time will be short before the beginning of the first cleansing. When the three days of darkness begin, it is well to think only thoughts of love and kindness to all that cross your mind. This will alleviate the pressure of unforgiven feelings.

Those who are not able to cope with the hearing of these events are not yet right in their love relationship with God. When a person knows God is in charge of all things at all times, they can cope with anything God plans for them or the Earth. They may be somewhat frightened, but will receive comfort and guidance by looking to God.

When the first Cleansing begins, it will be on a clear day in the middle of the day. The sun will fade away and darkness will begin to come over the land. There will be several hours before total darkness will be on all sides. There will be time for all enlightened to bring home their family; put water and feed outside for their animals and birds; and obtain supplies of food which does not need to be prepared and clean drinking water where it can be reached in the dark. Have warm clothing and bedding to remain wrapped in for the duration of the darkness, which will last three days. By the third night stars will be seen in the heavens. The fourth day the sun will shine again. During these three days of utter darkness, it is necessary that those in the houses do not look outside. It is necessary that they cover their windows with heavy covers which keep out the cold and keep the warmth inside.

The light that can be used for a short period of time has to be a battery-operated light. No fires or open flame light is to be used in the first three days. This will use up oxygen, which is already low in the atmosphere of the earth. Those who have respiratory problems will have a difficult time surviving. It is well if the door not be opened to anyone or for any reason. After the first three days, candles may still not be used for two more days; then ye can use any light or heat ye wish. Electricity should be re-established in a matter of time after the sun shines again.

You can use whatever light or heat ye wish after the first three days, but are required to stay inside your home another eleven days without opening the doors or looking out the windows. This is to know only that which is in thy house. The memory of the outside would not be easily removed. The commodes should flush the entire time. The freezers will be off during the time the electricity is off. Food could be spoiled; test before eating. Not all those who are outside of God's care will leave the body. Some will live through it through sheer perseverance on their part – the will to live. This terrible thing must happen because the people have hardened their hearts. At the close of each age a cleansing is necessary. We are in the transitional period between the Piscean Age and the incoming Aquarian Age.

Those who will keep their animals inside to protect them will suffer the consequence of disobedience. God is not mocked. There is reason for what He asks of the people of the Earth who have gone far astray from His laws. The animals are cared for by my beings, who are on Earth for this reason. None will die. This cleansing is not for the animals or for little children. The little children who are left on Earth without their parents are in God's care. The angels will care for and comfort the little ones. There will very quickly be found loving homes for them to be raised in. The parents with little ones need not worry how they will be cared for. God's plan is complete.

After the three days of darkness are past, stay inside another eleven days. This is to re-establish the atmosphere on the Earth and to give the Space Brothers sufficient time to take care of the debris the destruction has caused, and to remove the bodies of those who are no longer living. When the people come out of their houses on the fourteenth day, they will see no sign of the terrible things that happened. These will have been through a cleansing in their terrible experience, and will now accept God into their lives.

When the sun shines on the fourth day, those who are yet alive need to thank God. It is not better to be dead than alive when God is carrying out a cleansing plan on the Earth. When they are yet alive, they have yet an opportunity to establish a closer walk with God which will assure them a safer place in God's kingdom. By safer, I mean an area where God's laws are yet obeyed. After the three days of darkness and before the Battle of Armageddon, is a time when the people will wish to learn how to obey that which God has said they can do as the Lord Jesus Christ is able to do. When the aftermath of this terrible destruction is past, the world will then be in a famine for seven years. During these seven years, the church and the school will be established with the help of angelic guidance.

In the time given for this activity, these lessons will be learned sufficiently that those who come back to Earth will bring back the knowledge and the talents which they took with them. After that will follow the Battle of Armageddon. Those who are in God's care are not on Earth during this time. They will have been taken up with me into a beautiful and peaceful area where they will stay until the aftermath of the last battle on Earth is cleared awdday.

Then chosen ones will be returned to Earth the same way they were taken. This will be done by our Space Brothers and their spaceships. One phase will go directly into the next. The Children of God will not be brought back until the debris of all the cleansing is cleared away and the Earth is fresh and clean. The Children of God will have been in a state of heaven, and will have forgotten happenings on the Earth.They will be taken with their bodies and brought back with their bodies. Nothing at all will be left on earth. Some things of this civilization will be found hundreds of years from now, or even thousands, and will be called "Artifacts of the Lost Civilization of Earth."

When the Children of God are returned again to Earth, they will be beamed back asleep and will awaken on Earth in an area close to where they were when they were taken up. They will not remember it but many will feel comfortable with their atmosphere, as if they had been there before. They will arrive in comfortable weather and will have nothing with them except some tools which the Space Brothers will leave with each adult. With these tools they will slowly begin to carve out a pattern for life. They will begin to plant seeds which will be left for them. They will carve dishes out of wood. They will build fires to keep warm and to cook food. They will find vegetables and fruit growing and seeds and nuts, and things which grew in the area when they were taken away. It will be much like the Garden of Eden.

The Children will have Angels and Space Brothers with them on Earth to help them build homes; establish the various systems such as government, financial, educational, and the system in which people are made well when something affects them adversely. This will not be a medical system in which doctors use chemical and other harmful procedures for which they can charge an exorbitant price from the already impoverished patient or the patient's family. This healing system is called "The Well-Making by Mental Power." Each person will learn how to apply his own mental powers to all phases of his life. When a person is too ill to accomplish this, there will be practitioners who will help the patient heal himself by directing the patient's thoughts.

My thoughts will be picked up by all when I am giving them guidance or comfort. This they will have learned in the interim between the time they were taken and the time they are brought back. When the Children of God come back they are no longer called by the name they had when they were taken. They will have forgotten. In time they will think of something to call each other. They cannot read or write now. The schools must teach this very soon. The Angels will teach the teachers and build places to learn in. There will be animals of other kinds; some were on Earth before. There will be no vicious animals. All animals will love each other as people do.

The only supplies people will have will be those they can find around them. They will soon learn to make clothes to cover them up and keep them warm on cold nights. They will come back with the clothes they had on when they were taken. The weather will not be cold for some time – that is, until the people have learned to make clothes and bedding for themselves to protect them against the elements. Their God would not bring bad things upon them without giving them a way to protect themselves.

The Angels will have similar flesh bodies as they did at the time the Sons of God were upon the Earth and found the daughters of man very fair, and loved them and had children with them. There will be children born of these attractions, who will be normal children. The fathers will disappear, one after another, when their work is done. The mothers of the children will know their husband was a Son of God and would be leaving again. They will raise the children with love and loving memories of their fathers. The children will be the same in all ways as are children on Earth. To get to this beautiful Garden of Eden with God and the Angels, one must now give his or her heart to God to be forgiven and guided by God into a life of service to God.

Those returning will be much wiser and purer in mind and body. They are then given a piece of ground and tools to make their living and to learn to survive with the help of the Angels which God is sending with them to guide, guard, protect, comfort, and supply their needs. The tools and other equipment are not of the Earth kind.

This is the age when God is ruling in the hearts and lives of those on Earth. They will live closely with their Angels. The Angels will be protectors and companions to them. The people will have learned to communicate with God and with the Angels assigned to them by their Lord, Jesus Christ. The Angels are an ever-present help in all things.

Those who return to Earth will have no recall of their families or homes. The healing work will have been done in them while they are where they awaited return to Earth. People of all ages will return. Those who have family with them will stay with their kinfolk, though they will not know they are kin. This will keep family love and ties between them. Those who are without family will be grouped in a way that they can soon become family. Their Angels will be a great help in this area. The Angels will express much love to them and create a feeling of togetherness by a bond.

Space Brothers are highly evolved Beings of great light who operate space vehicles to do the work which God requires in all areas of the Universe. They are involved with this very important work on Earth. They live in their vehicles when they are not based doing clean-up work. They wear uniforms which resemble those of an army. The uniforms are not clothing; they are of a substance which is formed over the wearers. The Space Brothers do not have names except when they are assigned to a person or a group who can communicate with them. The name is relinquished when their work with that person or group is finished. The name is given to them by God and usually denotes a status. The spaceships also have names at that time.

The time is now when those who have the light of understanding need to heed this message and prepare the best they can. Where there is not enough money because of the economy to buy that which they need, and their heart is with God, they can count on their Angels providing that which they need. They will find they need less than they think. Their Angels have many ways to bring necessary things to them. In the wilderness the Children of Israel were given quail when the Children were tired of spiritual food and were complaining loudly to God. Spiritual food is fruits and vegetables, nuts, seeds, honey, and grains. There was plenty of that for them.

Before they left Egypt they were eating meat, and they thought they needed meat to have strength to travel. They did not need meat, but God gave it to them because they thought they needed it.

Meat-eating is against God's laws for man. In the coming age, God will re-establish this battered law. There will be no eating of the flesh of any of His animal kingdom; neither will their skins be used for clothing for man. This was never the intent of God's animal kingdom. God has permitted it to be until this time because men learned to depend on animal flesh when Noah and his family came off the ark and found no food. Then God said, "Take an animal and kill it and stay alive." Since that time, man has enjoyed eating the flesh of God's animals, but the time is now when God will reclaim His animals as He is reclaiming His souls. God is staging a final campaign to give the souls who have free will the choice to come.

If the animals had a choice, they would choose not to be slaughtered and eaten by man. They also have intelligence and feelings, and emotions, as man does. With this message which is given by me, thy Lord, Jesus Christ, THE PEOPLE

UFOS, ARMAGEDDON AND BIBLICAL REVELATIONS

HAVE BEEN WARNED. Those who have given their hearts and lives to God are in God's care and are surrounded by His Angels. Only those who are yet outside of God's care have a great worry.

SUGGESTED READING

COSMIC MESSAGES FROM THE ASHTAR COMMAND

A NEW BOOK OF REVELATIONS

COSMIC TELEPATHY

STRANGER AT THE PENTAGON

ON EARTH ASSIGNMENT

PROJECT WORLD EVACUATION

TRANSMISSIONS FROM THE SPACE BROTHERS

Are the hands on the cosmic clock pushing Midnight, thus spelling out disaster?

Some UFO beings – such as this one drawn by the late Canadian artist, Gene Duplantier – are said to be angelic in both appearance and attitude, and could be here to help save humanity from its own self-inflicted demise.

Alien television broadcast interruption.

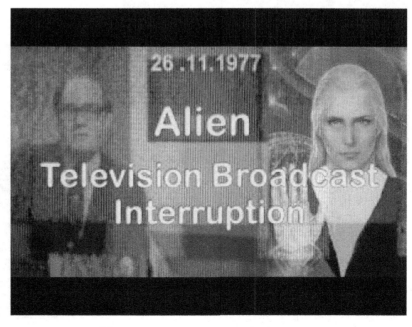

Tuella at the lectern speaking on behalf of the Ashtar Command.

The final book from Tuella, the primary channel for the Ashtar Command.

The late Rev. Robert Short was among those who originally channeled under Giant Rock, in a massive room cut out under the boulder in the Mojave Desert.

UFOS, ARMAGEDDON AND BIBLICAL REVELATIONS

Supposed "spaceman" Valiant Thor in the Sixties and more recently. A comparison shot.

As we look all around us, we could definitely be living in the End Times.

9

OTHER DIMENSIONS, PHYSICS, THE BIBLE
AND THE PARTING OF THE RED SEA
Slow Train Coming: The Continuing Religious Odyssey
of Reverend Barry Downing
By Sean Casteel

Science and religion could end up complementing each other. New – more "radical" – trends in physics point to the existence of parallel universes and other dimensions which could assist in explaining many Biblical mysteries and miracles, at least according to one Protestant minister who has spent more than a half century pondering the reality of UFOs and extraterrestrials and their possible connection to the seemingly bizarre and unexplainable tales of the Old and New Testaments.

Reverend Barry Downing, who resides in upstate New York, was among the first to see that it wasn't a given that the "good book" was in conflict with the lore of the flying saucer and the possibility that our universe might be constructed of a bit more than just physical matter. He posited that heaven could be a real place – if not in our timeline then perhaps in a parallel existence just beyond our reach. Could that other dimension possibly be accessible through the guidance of Godly ultra-terrestrial beings and their vehicles? What we think of as spaceships could, in some cases, be divine.

*** Reverend Barry Downing has been preaching the gospel of "UFO angels" for more than 50 years now, since the publication of his 1968 book, "The Bible and Flying Saucers." Downing has recently released a new book called "Biblical UFO Revelations" that incorporates hard won wisdom and perspectives gleaned in the intervening years as he steadfastly continues to make his case for his particular take on Christianity and the aliens.

*** Downing is not just an ordained minister and a religious expert, he is also well-versed in physics, having earned his bachelor's degree in the field. So he is uniquely qualified to analyze Biblical miracles like the parting of the Red Sea

UFOS, ARMAGEDDON AND BIBLICAL REVELATIONS

from the Exodus both scientifically and as a man of faith. Read more about the "environmental impact" that the pillar of cloud and fire exerted for the sake of the fleeing Israelites.

*** How does one approach the extreme levels of fear experienced by witnesses to angels in the Bible? Is the fear a UFO witness experiences an example of that same kind of fear? Are we actually wise to approach the two phenomena in abject terror and trembling? At what point does a heavenly love enter the picture and cast out all fear?

****

I was on the air this past summer with Timothy Green Beckley and Tim Swartz, the hosts of the KCOR podcast "Exploring the Bizarre," with their special guest, the Presbyterian minister Dr. Barry Downing. In a commercial break, during which we all chatted but the audience could not hear us, Downing informed us that he had sufficient new material for a physical/print book.

Thinking quickly on his feet, Tim Beckley wasted no time in offering to publish Downing's more recent writings through Beckley's company Global Communications/Inner Light. And so the process began for "Biblical UFO Revelations," a book that is a long overdue reprise from an important pioneer in the ancient aliens school of UFO interpretation.

Downing made his initial entry into the UFO community in 1968 with his groundbreaking tome "The Bible and Flying Saucers." The book explored the possibility of extraterrestrial influence in the development of the Old and New Testaments, with particular emphasis on the notion that one can equate the "angels" of the Bible with the "aliens" of our modern era. Which, at the time, was fairly new and unfamiliar territory for the relatively young field of UFO research.

Before writing that first book, Downing had already earned a Ph.D. from the University of Edinburg in Scotland. His dissertation, called "Eschatological Implications of the Understanding of Time and Space in the Thought of Isaac Newton," combined the religious, the philosophical and the scientific into the kind of whole that would serve Downing well in his years spent researching and writing about UFOs.

When Downing returned from Scotland in May of 1966, he set up shop in his in-laws' basement and wrote his book while he awaited his first church assignment as a newly ordained minister. He finished the writing one week before taking a job at the Northminster Presbyterian Church in Endwell, New York, in February 1967, and the book came out the following year.

"I was hopeful that conservative Christians would be more positive than liberal Christians," Downing told me by email. "It turned out to be the case that neither liberals nor conservatives liked my book. So in a sense I was treated 'fairly' by both sides."

UFOS, ARMAGEDDON AND BIBLICAL REVELATIONS

THE 'ENVIRONMENTAL IMPACT' OF A UFO

The parting of the Red Sea is particularly interesting to Downing, and he gives it 20 pages of examination in "The Bible and Flying Saucers" and devotes a chapter to it in the new book, "Biblical UFO Revelations."

"My argument is that the Exodus UFO, the pillar of cloud and fire," he explained, "which appeared cloud-like during the day and glowed in the dark, used its propulsion system to split the waters of the Red Sea and save Israel from the Egyptians. The reason the parting of the Red Sea is so important is that it tells us in detail the environmental impact of the UFO presence. Modern researchers go to landing spots with Geiger counters and all kinds of equipment in order to study the environmental impact of a flying saucer landing. Exodus 14:19-30 is a very detailed environmental impact statement."

Downing says he differs from the standard biblical interpretation that a "strong wind" was used to part the sea, because a wind strong enough to do that would also have blown Moses and the Israelites into the sky. The biblical text says the ground was dry when the Israelites crossed over, but since the escape was taking place at night, it could not have been dried by the sun. Downing suggests that some kind of microwave effect may have been involved.

"I believe the best explanation for the parting of the Red Sea," he said, "is that the pillar of cloud and fire was some type of spaceship, and those in charge of the spaceship planned the parting of the sea well in advance, to save Israel from the Egyptians and to keep Israel from going back to Egypt, once the Jews discovered that the whole Exodus process was not a walk in the park."

THE NEW PHYSICS: WHAT THE YEARS HAVE TAUGHT DOWNING

Downing has kept up with the worlds of UFOlogy and physics. His bachelor's degree is in physics, which he earned while on scholarship at Hartwick College in Oneonta, New York.

"When I published 'The Bible and Flying Saucers' in 1968," Downing writes in "Biblical UFO Revelations," "I had one major concern about connecting UFOs to biblical angels. The biblical view of angels was they were eternal beings, they had eternal life. My understanding of the scientific worldview at that time was that we live in a 'running down universe,' meaning that at some time in the future the universe will run out of energy and die. If this were true, then no one living in this universe could be eternal.

"I began to explore the possibility,' he continues, "that there might be more than one universe, that there might be a way to escape from the space-time continuum of our universe into a world that did not decay, did not run down. I thought Einstein's Theory of Relativity offered us the freedom to explore some possibilities within the framework of the as yet unfinished science of advanced physics. With that in mind, I began to look at the New Testament ideas of the angelic world, looking for 'some way out' of our universe, and looked for the possibility that UFOs did not come from our universe, but rather from another dimension."

These ideas are a large part of chapter five of the first book. Downing's optimistic search for a dimension that is truly eternal was met by the typical scorn his work receives from mainstream Christianity.

"The Christianity Today review of my book," Downing writes, "was predictably negative about Chapter Five. 'Space does not permit a complete account of the scientific distortions contained in the book. In the preface, Downing states that he is not an authority on Einstein or on heaven. This does not deter him, however, from devoting a chapter to the question, "Where Is Heaven?" He admits that his discussion reads very much like science fiction and is not necessarily true, but it may, he says, "help to set our minds free from the somewhat depressing agnosticism we now find ourselves in when we even begin to entertain the idea that we might live eternally – as part of God's plan." He then proceeds, with complete abandon, to do violence to both Einstein and heaven with over 20 pages of pure speculation.'"

[The review, which was published in the June 21, 1968, issue of Christianity Today, was written by Albert L. Hedrich and entitled "Flying Saucers in the Bible?"]

In that same section of "Biblical UFO Revelations," Downing summarizes the liberal and conservative objections to his work.

"Liberals do not want me to take stories like the parting of the Red Sea literally," Downing writes, "they want it to be poetry, mythology. They want to keep science out of the Bible. Religion is not about reality. It is about something that we make up in our heads, much like music and poetry. Religion may have a beauty about it, it may represent human psychological longings, but it has nothing to do with the physical world.

"The issue with conservatives is quite different," he goes on. "It has been around 50 years since the publication of my book and I still can't understand the conservative attack on my work. The conservative Christian mentality seems to be this: the church is a fort, the fort protects the basic treasure we have, which is the gospel, and the task of Christians is to attack all enemies who are trying to destroy the fort. They might be atheists (or other non-Christian religions, New Age mysticism, etc.) or they might be false prophets, or, as Gary Bates says of me, 'former believers who have fallen away.' Within this assumption, everyone has to be tested to see if he or she is a true believer or an enemy."

Downing says it is obvious that the point of view of people like Hedrich is that Downing is the enemy, having done violence to both Einstein and heaven. Downing's speculation amounts to bombs being dropped on the Christian fort.

"Does Hedrich know where heaven is?" Downing asks. "If he does, he does not tell us in his review. Apparently he thinks it is sinful even to wonder about it.

UFOS, ARMAGEDDON AND BIBLICAL REVELATIONS

Since when is being full of wonder a sin? Since when is it a sin to believe that 'with God all things are possible?'" (Matthew 19:26)

The church is not a fort built to defend the gospel, according to Downing. God himself is our fort. We are not called to live in a fort, we are called to live in the wilderness with God, on a journey where we are moving toward the kingdom of God.

"If you hole up in a fort, you will not arrive at the kingdom of heaven," Downing cautions. "The incarnation of Christ means this journey through the wilderness is so important to God that God became human in Jesus, and lived, and died, on the journey with us. On this trip, we look for signs of buried treasure." (Matthew 13:44)

THE UFO PHENOMENON AS 'BURIED TREASURE'

For around 50 years now, Downing has been pointing at UFOs and saying, "This may be buried treasure hidden for us to find."

The UFOs are not buried in dirt, of course.

"They're buried by the greed and lust for power of the military-industrial complex," he writes, "which decided years ago that UFO truth needed to be kept from us. Our modern Pharaohs are no different from the Pharaoh who challenged the God of Moses. I suspect that many world leaders did not want us to even think about the possibility that the angels of God are not only watching us, but are, on occasion, shutting down our nuclear missile sites.

"And I suspect that for many conservative Christians, defending fortress America and fortress Gospel are so similar, that seeing UFOs as demons, rather than angels, enemies of both America's military power, and enemies of the Gospel, was a very natural way to interpret the UFO mystery. This is my best understanding of why I am not only the enemy of liberal Protestants, but also conservative Protestants. By and large, it is Roman Catholics who have not demonized me."

THE ROLE FEAR PLAYS IN THE UFO DRAMA

When I interviewed Downing by email for an introduction to "Biblical UFO Revelations," I asked him about how fear often plays a major role in the UFO drama, especially in terms of the alien abduction experience.

"We are inclined to think fear is a bad thing," he replied, "and in a sense it is. If God in His essence is love, then 'There is no fear in love, but perfect love casts out fear.' (1 John 4:18) At the same time, we are called, according to Paul, 'to work out your own salvation with fear and trembling.' (Philippians 2:12) The biblical view is, the closer we come to knowing God's love, the less we will fear. Nevertheless, inclined as we are to sin, to pride, to jealousy, we need to live our lives in fear and trembling, aware that we are never more than a bad thought away from offending God and hurting the divine love bond.

UFOS, ARMAGEDDON AND BIBLICAL REVELATIONS

"Fear is very much a dimension of our modern UFO story," he continued. "One reason for governments of the world keeping UFO information secret is that release of the information would lead to panic, the stock market would crash, the world economy would be destroyed."

Downing also offered an interesting analogy.

"If a stranger walks into my house and points a gun at me, fear will be my response, and it is a very appropriate response. I may die if I do not fear the intruder; I may die even if I do fear the intruder. But fear in this situation gives me a survival edge, a better chance of not being killed. I will treat the stranger with the gun with respect. The basic idea of God is that He is the one with the gun. He has the power to take our life, or save it, even to raise us from the dead. So fear of God as a sign of respect is an appropriate response."

When the angels appeared to the shepherds in the fields, Downing said, fear was the understandable response of the shepherds. "The angel said to the shepherds, 'Be not afraid, for behold, I bring you news of great joy.' (Luke 2:10) Fear of angels when they appear is a frequent response reported in the Bible. An angel of God descended from the sky and rolled back the tomb where Jesus was buried. 'And for fear of him, the guards trembled and became like dead men.' (Matthew 28:4)

"Whenever we meet a strange power greater than ourselves, fear is a natural response. It is a frequent response for by those who have a UFO encounter, or have an abduction experience, or have a bedroom visitation from an alien. Fear of aliens is no more proof they are evil than fear of angels proves THEY are evil."

Downing also commented on the abduction experiences of Betty Andreasson Luca and Whitley Strieber, calling their stories "mini forms of disclosure."

"They are not disclosure at a political level," Downing said, "that is, landing on the White House lawn and saying 'Take me to your leader.' But modern UFO abductions are a limited form of disclosure, examples of what I call 'targeted intervention.' The Second Coming of Christ, according to Christian hope, would be a form of an angelic army invasion. At the same time, the biblical story of the angel at the tomb of Jesus, or the conversion of the Apostle Paul on the road to Damascus, represent forms of 'targeted intervention.'

"The story of the Jewish Exodus from Egypt seems to be something like a major invasion," he continued, "but the 'pillar of cloud and fire' keeps its distance from both Pharaoh and the Jewish people. And the Jewish story has spiritual and moral power in human culture to this day – proof that targeted intervention can have consequences for human culture for thousands of years.

"The work of the pillar of cloud and fire during the Exodus should make us aware that, even if modern UFOs are working for our good, they represent a power of judgment over us such that 'fear and trembling' may be a very wise response to the UFO presence."

More from Dr. Barry Downing: The Soul Takers

Will humanity someday force God's hand, by way of rampant corruption and environmental decline, even nuclear terrorism? Does God intend to use the Second Coming only as a last resort?

Was Christ deceived about the timing of his own Second Coming? Should we continue to wait for a savior who may never come? Or is there some middle ground between the various extremes?

Does the nature of faith require that we remain in the dark about some aspects of God? Would the landing of Jesus on the White House lawn somehow make faith less necessary?

Ordained minister Dr. Barry Downing is a very well-known name in the field of religiously oriented Ufology. His 1968 book, "The Bible and Flying Saucers," is considered a classic with about 300,000 copies in print.

Downing's credentials as a Presbyterian minister are also very impressive. After earning a degree in physics, he went on to receive a divinity degree from Princeton Theological Seminary, and later earned his Ph.D. from the University of Edinburgh in Scotland, specializing in the relationship between science and religion.

After returning from Scotland, Downing said he began to contemplate the spatial nature of the universe and where theology was at the time.

"And where theology was then," Downing said, "was to doubt that the whole idea of heaven even held water anymore. Once we started thinking in spatial terms and sending up rockets, the whole idea of God being up in the sky kind of died. In fact, the 'Death of God' movement in the 1960s happened just a year before I was ordained. So this kind of stuff was going through my mind."

In the early 1950s, while Downing was still in high school, his father gave him some books by UFO pioneer Donald Keyhoe to read. Meanwhile, Downing had also read the Bible through completely once and then half again by the time he graduated from high school.

"So I had a background in physics and UFOs and the Bible," he said, "and it came together about the time I was finishing my Ph.D. dissertation. I'd been doing the concepts of space and time and the whole issue of eschatology, which includes the Second Coming of Christ as a theological issue. The whole question of angelology is obviously involved if you're going to deal with the Second Coming, and so those were areas of interest.

"Liberals in theology," Downing continued, "tended to see these as mythology, whereas conservatives took them literally. Conservatives still take them literally, and don't like the idea that they might be space beings. So my position is not well received by either conservative or liberal Christians. I take things like the parting of the Red Sea too literally for liberals, and I've got technology involved in the parting of the Red Sea, which is a no-no from a conservative point of view. So conservatives see me as heretical and liberals see me as silly."

THE TWO FORMS OF THE SECOND COMING

Having established some personal background on Downing, the interview moved on to address more directly the Second Coming.

"I think there pretty much has to be two forms of the Second Coming," he said. "One form is, what happens when we die? I assume that our bodies decay. We see this, or we have them burned up if we're cremated. In any case, the body ends. What happens to the person? I think that some Near-Death-Experiences give us a clue that there's part of us, another spiritual dimension to us that seems to coexist with our body and is not destroyed by death and goes on to some other form of life.

"One of the possibilities," Downing continued, "is that one of the tasks of UFOs, or the angels, is to collect the souls of people when they die and take them off to another world where they begin the next life that they have. This is not the Second Coming as we usually think of it. But when Jesus says in John 14, 'I go to prepare a place for you. And if I go and prepare a place, I will come again and take you to be where I am.' For this to be true, I think it has to be true when someone dies. That's probably how it works.

"Likewise, Jesus says to one of the thieves on the cross, 'Today you will be with me in paradise.' So I assume there's a kind of 'coming for us' when we die, and it's kind of like a return of Christ to take us, or at least the return of the angels to take us. But it's not the end of history. Obviously my death or your death is not the end of history."

Downing began to describe the kind of Second Coming that is the end of history.

"From my point of view," Downing said, "God is reluctant to bring down the curtain of history, because the scientific evidence suggests that the universe is about 15 billion years old. Our sun is five billion years old. It took millions of years to get the Earth and human civilization to the point it is now. And life on Earth as we see it now has been planned by God, and therefore is serving God's purpose. To bring it to an end, only to have to start over again, either on another planet or on Earth, sometime after a new Ice Age or something, is just, to put it bluntly, a big hassle.

"So if I were God," he said, "having created Earth as it now is, and the human condition as it now is, I wouldn't be anxious to bring it to an end."

UFOS, ARMAGEDDON AND BIBLICAL REVELATIONS

FORCING GOD'S HAND

"It may be," Downing explained, "we humans will force God's hand in some sense by blowing the Earth up or blowing ourselves up, so that human history no longer serves God's purpose. If that were true, then I would say that the Second Coming might occur at that point. Certainly if you look at the types of disasters that you read about in the Book of Revelation, they may be hints about the kinds of things that humans could do to cause an ecological breakdown of the Earth."

Downing also cautioned against setting a particular time for the Second Coming to occur, citing verses where Jesus says, "It is not for you to know the times and the seasons the Father has fixed by his own authority," and "Not even the Son knows when the return will happen."

"The angels don't know," Downing said, "and the Son doesn't know. So one of the main warnings I would give is to be extremely careful about setting dates, as some religious Christian leaders have done in the past, predicting when Christ was going to come. There is an evangelist who came to my county and predicted that Jesus was going to return on July 4, 1976, to help America celebrate its 200th Anniversary. This kind of stuff just brings discredit on Christianity because before you know it, you're past the date. Obviously, the guy either was a fraud or a liar or didn't care about making a joke of the Second Coming. That's what I would consider that to be.

"You have to be careful not to go setting dates, but at the same time to believe that God is in charge and if God wants the Second Coming to happen tomorrow, that's fine with me. Certainly if God wants to do it, God should have the right to do it."

A TROUBLESOME TEXT

The question was asked regarding Jesus' promise that some of those standing there with him would not taste death before the Coming of the Kingdom of Heaven.

"This is a text that has bothered a lot of Biblical scholars," Downing said, "and I don't know what to make of it. One of the possibilities is to look at it in terms of character. There are parts of the scriptures that refer to the Second Death. I suppose that the Second Death happens when you go in for a Day of Judgment and God says, 'Okay, you're worthless, and you're going to a place where worthless people go.' That would be the Second Death. Or, 'You have failed to live a life that is satisfying to me.' And so you're pretty much consigned to nothingness. You could look at it from a moral point of view rather than an End of Time point of view. If you look at it from a moral point of view, it means I wouldn't taste what death is like until I stand before God and God says, 'You're going to hell.' That would be a taste of death.

"And if I had a nice, successful life going," Downing continued, "all the world's goods, and thought I was quite a good person, and then faced God's judgment, and heard God's judgment on me basically say that I'd deceived myself about how good I was, or how worthwhile I was, that would a tasting of death. And I would not have tasted death until I saw the Judgment of Christ coming. So I think that's a possible way to interpret that passage, rather than having it be a prediction that Jesus would return before, say, the Apostle Paul died or Peter died or the other people of then- generation."

The alternative to that rather unsettling interpretation is also a little bothersome.

"Obviously," Downing said, "if you think that Jesus meant that he was going to return then, then you have to conclude that Jesus himself was deceived about God's plan or his place in God's plan. And by the way, this particular text contributed to Albert Schweitzer's book, written in 1907 or 1908, entitled 'The Quest for the Historical Jesus.' This was a huge issue, and people were concluding with Schweitzer that Jesus was deceived. Either Jesus was deceived or his disciples were deceived about his Second Coming. Since it hadn't happened by this time, 1900 years later, it was probably not going to happen, and we ought to give up believing in this silly teaching."

The liberal side of the church followed in Schweitzer's direction, and stopped even hoping that the Second Coming would occur.

"And that particular text was the key text," Downing said, "that led them to say either the church was deceived and the church wrote that into the text and not Jesus, or Jesus himself was deceived when he said it, and therefore he didn't know what was going on or he had deluded himself or whatever."

CAN WE TRUST IN GOD?

All of which leads to the question, can we trust in God?

Downing talked about a Biblical passage in which the prophets lie to a foreign king.

"They're inspired by God to lie to the king," he said. "And then another prophet comes along and basically says that God has asked him to lie. The whole issue of how do you know if you can trust God gets right upfront here on this.

"An issue for me that's big," Downing continued, "is the whole concept of faith and why faith is big to God. If you look at the Book of Hebrews, Chapter 11, it's a huge, long chapter just dealing with the fact that the people of God were a people of faith. Abraham went out not knowing where he was going. He had to just trust God. He didn't really see the future clearly. And all the people of the Bible who were heroes trusted God without really seeing the end of the story clearly. The chapter ends by saying that they finished their lives without obtaining the prize, because apart from us, they would not be complete. So again it gives you the idea that until all of human history is finished, the whole nature of the purpose of the church and the purpose of the people of God won't be clear."

THE ROLE OF DOUBTING THOMAS

"Another thing I want you to think about," Downing went on, "is the way in which Jesus appeared to Doubting Thomas. He appeared to the ten disciples first, and they saw him and they believed and then they reported to Thomas that they'd seen the risen Christ. And Thomas said he wouldn't believe unless he saw and touched with his own hands. Then of course it happened and he believed. And Jesus said, 'Blessed are those who believe who have not seen.'"

Which creates still further complications, according to Downing.

"Notice that when the Second Coming happens," he said, "and Jesus returns with the angels and lands on the White House lawn, or perhaps in the European Union or the Middle East, or however he does it, there's no more doubt now about who Jesus is and what the power of God may be. Just like with Doubting Thomas, once he saw Jesus' hands and touched him, he didn't have grounds for doubting anymore.

"The other issue was that now it didn't require faith for him to believe in that Christ. 'Blessed are those who believe who have not seen.' Somehow, you see, it's big to God that we believe in this story or what I call, 'to believe in God's game,' without proof. And the problem with the Second Coming of Christ is that the game is over when Christ lands or when the angels return. And therefore faith is not necessary anymore. The faith game is up.

"So when I said it's taken God a long time to set up life on Earth as we have it now and to set up what I call the 'faith game' that we have going—I don't think God's in a hurry to destroy the game. Now it may be that humanity will force God's hand in some way, by the weapons we've made or the ecological breakdown that we're bringing about. Who knows? But in any case, I just think that God's purpose is to see the extent to which humans can trust God without proof.

"And that's what faith is," Downing said. "Faith is trusting without proof. It doesn't mean that you don't have any evidence, but it means you don't have proof."

THE PLAUSIBLE THROUGH UFOs

Downing made reference to one of many articles he was written for The Mutual UFO Network UFO Journal, entitled "Is UFO Midnight A Possibility?" which appeared in the May 2000 issue.

"What I argued was," Downing said, "that I think that one of the roles of UFOs would be to move us to the point where the Biblical faith is more scientifically plausible. You've got a huge split in American culture now between fundamentalists who believe the Bible just because God inspired the Bible, and therefore it must be true. Then you have university types who don't see the Bible as different from any other book and pretty much don't believe that God is any part of the universe. They believe the universe was in some sense 'self-created' by ways we don't yet understand and therefore there's no divine force behind anything that we see. Our kids may be brought up in a Christian home and then are shot into this agnostic university system.

"You end up," Downing continued, "with the political split like we've got between Republicans and Democrats now. We've got this kind of schizophrenia, you know. We've got either this kind of fundamentalism that insists on believing with its eyes closed, or you get the atheism of the far left. That's pretty much the dominant force in what we see in American culture.

"So the question is, how do you get faith back in play? Not based on the Bible alone, but based on modern evidence that says, 'Hey, the angels may still be here.' To me, that's where the UFOs come into the scene. Fundamentalist Christians, of course, tend to see UFOs as demonic. The assumption of fundamentalists is that if UFOs were really the angels of God, they'd show themselves openly. Yet, obviously, the angels of God do not show themselves openly to us. Otherwise, we'd all see them. There's some part of God that holds God's self back, that doesn't reveal God directly to us. That's what makes the 'faith game' both necessary and possible."

But Downing said that conservative Christians have a hard time understanding that basic condition of God's efforts to communicate with humanity.

"At the same time," Downing explained, "if God stays too hidden, we won't believe. Nobody wants to believe in a God that doesn't exist. So God has to walk this thin line of revelation whereby God shows enough that belief is possible, but at the same time hides enough so that belief is not required. It's a choice you can make. And the argument I made in the MUFON Journal article is that I think God is more likely to use the UFO force to get faith back in business in what you'd call the intellectual side of our culture now, which is very atheistic."

And where does Downing place himself in all that?

"I walk a line," he said, "that's somewhere between where Christian fundamentalists are, who would be the ones most likely to be upfront about believing in the Second Coming, and the liberal elements, who figure that the Second Coming of Jesus is like a Santa Claus story that we'd be better off without."

WHY DOES THE HOPE PERSIST?

In a world torn apart by opposing extremes of blind faith and atheistic materialist thinking, the hope of an almost immediate Second Coming of Christ still persists among some people. But why?

"This gets excitement up," Downing said. "If I knew Jesus was going to be returning tomorrow, or even next week, it would change my view of how I go at things. I probably wouldn't worry about putting the garbage out on Thursday, as I normally do. You change your value system if you think history is coming to an end within two or three days. It sets you free from a lot of anxieties about the future.

"So I think that why the hope for the Second Coming stays with us is that we want history to make sense, we want there to be a big plan somewhere up in the sky that somebody made, so that life isn't like Shakespeare says, 'Full of sound and fury and signifying nothing.' The hope of the Second Coming is positive in the sense that it says that somebody is minding the store here, and even though we can't see the person in charge, eventually it will all come out and we'll know what the truth is and what the purpose of our own lives is and what the purpose of human history is. The idea of the Second Coming gives meaning to our struggle. That's why the hope of the Second Coming stays alive.

"Also, anyone would hope that a Day of Judgment is coming when God will undo all the unfair things that may have happened to us or people we care about. So we want justice. The hope of the Second Coming is actually connected to our hope that there is a God who judges fairly and fairness will be established once and for all. I think those things are involved in keeping the hope of the Second Coming alive."

THE TERRORS THAT MAY COME FIRST

The Book of Revelation describes a host of terrors on the Earth that are prophesied to occur before the Second Coming. When asked about that aspect of things, Downing replied, "I don't have a firm opinion on this. It looked like we were well setup for a nuclear disaster, and that therefore we will definitely have the fire next time. Yet that seems to have receded, at least in terms of the press.

"Obviously," he continued, "if terrorists learn how to make nuclear weapons in their basement, why then we may have nuclear terror on our hands, even coming from we know not where. So those kinds of things may still be 'plagues' that are going to be in our near future. I think the population explosion is going to put the resources of the Earth very much on trial, in terms of the ability to sustain human life without plagues. All you have to do is have a pretty major weather interruption, and suddenly your six to eight billion population of the Earth would not be able to sustain life very well.

"Our American economy now is so oil-dependent. You read about it in the paper and everyone says, 'Yeah, I have to pay $2 for gas now. It's terrible.' But the whole American economy has been built around oil. You get in your car, you can drive to McDonald's, you can drive to the store. Half of America I bet doesn't live within walking distance of a grocery market. So we're automobile-dependent, and if they turned off that spigot, what would happen in American life? How would Americans treat each other? What would happen in terms of violence in this country? There are a lot of things that can happen just in the way in which human culture is maintained right now, what we would call our scientific and technological culture, that could blow things up pretty fast. Now whether or not these things would then lead to the Second Coming of Christ, I don't know."

Why does God feel it necessary to subject us to those kinds of potential horrors?

"I don't like it," Downing answered, "but the fundamental story is that you have to be crucified with Christ before you can be raised with him. It's sort of like until you experience the bad news, you can't appreciate the good news. I wish there were a better way to say it, and I wish it were not true, but that's how it seems to be."

A "STAR WARS" SECOND COMING?

The question was posed to Downing as to whether there is an End Times relationship between UFOs and the Second Coming? Will Jesus be arriving in a UFO? Is the antichrist equipped with his own army of UFOs? Like a sort of "Star Wars" fulfillment of the Second Coming?

"These are tricky things," Downing acknowledged, "and I think it's important to deal with them as best you can in the book. Let's start with the issue of if UFOs carry the angels of God. And I say 'if' because I don't have proof that it's true, but that's a big question that I think our culture needs to be asking. I think that religious people would have been asking it if the government had not lied about it. The religious people have trusted the government too much on this, you know?

"Religious people should have remembered Pharaoh. Pharaoh's not a guy to trust. They should have remembered Pilate and Caesar and these guys. They're not God-friendly people. They may lie to you under some circumstances, so you should stay alert. It just appalls me that religious people have been happy to take the word of the government on this.

"In any case," he continued, "if it should be true that UFOs carry the angels of God as we understand them Biblically, then that would certainly seem to be the way in which the Second Coming would happen. If Jesus was taken up into the sky at his Ascension in a UFO, which is what seems to be said in the Book of Acts, Chapter One, then the other thing that's said in that same chapter is this: 'This Jesus, who was taken up from you into heaven will come in the same way as you saw him go into heaven.' That's Acts, Chapter One, verse eleven.

"So it seems to me that what's referred to here is some type of a bright object that carried Jesus off into the sky. Actually, it's referred to as a cloud. The cloud then refers to the whole 'pillar of cloud by day and pillar of fire by night' tradition of the Exodus, the major UFO of the Exodus. It also refers to the bright cloud that hovered over Jesus at the Transfiguration in Matthew Chapter Seventeen, and brought both Moses and Elijah to Jesus at that point. So these clouds provide the heavenly transportation system. If that heavenly transportation system in the Bible is the same as the UFOs that we have now, then that's how Jesus will return with his angels."

In other words, as he departed in a UFO, so will Jesus come back again in a UFO. One begins to see the pattern of how UFOs make miracles plausible, as Downing was explaining earlier.

THE POSSIBLE ROLE OF THE ANTICHRIST

There is, as always, the proverbial fly in the ointment, however: the antichrist. Again, Downing said he is unsure about what to think.

"I don't know whether the antichrist is a supernatural power," he said, "that flies around in the skies in a 'Star Wars' fashion and is in a battle with the angels of God. I can't rule it out. I don't like the idea, but it might be true. My own inclination is to think that the antichrist is actually the biological forces of greed and dominance and similar things that we all have in us. Almost animal forces. My theology of sin comes more from studies of etiology and socio-biology, rather than UFOs. Most Christian fundamentalists tend to see the devil and his angels as flying up in the sky, but the main times when UFOs in the Bible are reported, they're all connected to God. They're not connected to the devil."

Downing then moved on to his personal understanding of demonology.

"The demons, he said, "seem to inhabit human bodies when they have a chance, and I don't know of any times when they're actually seen 'live.' Jesus was tempted by the devil in the wilderness, but the devil is never described there. The whole issue of seeing the devil in a bodily form is very, very 'iffy,' compared with angels, who are in such bodily form that when angels come to visit Abraham in the Book of Genesis, he feeds them. I'm skeptical about the bodily forms of demons and the devil and therefore of the antichrist."

A more mystical, symbolic understanding of the antichrist suits Downing better.

"I'm more inclined to think it's our struggle for dominance," he reasoned, "which is an instinct we share with the animals. If you study the way in which baboon males fight for their territory, and have their own females—the relationship between sexual reproduction and dominance of males over other males in order to have access to females—this kind of thing, in my opinion, is what has carried over to the human race. So when we battle for territory, we don't use horns to fight our enemies, the way animals do. We use nuclear weapons, which is a lot more dangerous.

"But that's where we are," he said. "If the desire is in us to dominate others, instead of giving our lives for each other, as Christ gave his life for us, then the desire to lord it over others, in fact to crucify others, to put ourselves on top, that to me would be the antichrist. The spirit of the antichrist is the spirit of the world. The war in Iraq has been about who can be top dog in Iraq. That's the antichrist. That's the spirit of the world."

LIFE AFTER THE SECOND COMING

While Downing resisted too much apocalyptic, End Times speculation throughout the course of the interview, he did offer a little in the way of imagining what life might be like after the Second Coming.

"There will be no death," he said. "There will be cooperation. You won't therefore have to worry about working to survive. Instead, you can work to the glory of God. I would think that life after the Second Coming would be life with joy and no fear. If I'm right about UFOs basically being the transportation system for the angels, I would also think that we've got travel throughout the universe available.

"Is the angelic world a high-tech world? No Christians have ever thought about this. We've always assumed that if the Red Sea parted, it was done by a supernatural power. We've never supposed that it might have been done by some kind of high-tech power. For conservative Christians, this is not what they want to hear because I don't say it's a supernatural act. But then why do we suppose that the angels don't have some kind of advanced technology?

"A lot of our jokes have to do with what kind of car are you going to have when you get to heaven? We don't have any trouble imagining that we can project our own technology into a heavenly world. But why not suppose that the heavenly world has a technology that is way advanced over ours and gives you transportation throughout the universe or into other universes, if there are such? This is highly speculative, but at the same time I think it's the kind of speculation that the Christian Church needs to do. And I think it will emerge if the government starts revealing that UFOs are real and that they apparently are piloted by beings that are in some ways superior to us and have a purpose that includes watching over us in some way."

Downing discussed the concluding chapters of the Book of Revelation in this same high-tech vein.

"It does say that there's no darkness there," he said. "It sounds like you've got a world which operates by something that's an eternal sun. The question then is, can we comprehend this other world even if we're taken into it in some kind of journey? Can we really understand what we're seeing? Could John understand his Revelation vision really? And can we interpret it properly? This is the tricky thing, you know.

"I mean, it's one thing to read a travel brochure on, say, going to Venice," Downing said. "And it's quite a different thing to actually go there. The Book of

UFOS, ARMAGEDDON AND BIBLICAL REVELATIONS

Revelation is kind of a travel brochure on the future. I'm not sure how much of it we can really figure out until we get there."

SUGGESTED READING:

BIBLICAL UFO REVELATIONS, by Dr. Barry Downing

UFOS, PROPHECY AND THE END OF TIME, by Sean Casteel

SIGNS AND SYMBOLS OF THE SECOND COMING, by Sean Casteel

THE EXCLUDED BOOKS OF THE BIBLE, by Sean Casteel

UFOs: ARE THEY YOUR PASSPORT TO HEAVEN? by Diane Tessman and Timothy Beckley

SUGGESTED VIEWING:

MR. UFO'S SECRET FILES

Over 400 videos on our Free YouTube channel

The initial edition of Reverend Barry Downing's book was way ahead of its time, for which he received condemnation.

The now-retired minister began the wave of UFO books devoted to delving into Biblical scriptures.

Reverend Downing believes the three wise men were following a UFO and not a star or a planet, as most astronomers believe.

UFOS, ARMAGEDDON AND BIBLICAL REVELATIONS

Biblical Armageddon, the Day of the Lord, as foreseen by the Church of God.

It is not unusual for UFOs of one type or another to show up in art from centuries past.

102

Reverend Downing believes the angels of the Bible might be what would be considered aliens in present times.

Is it possible we will see Jesus coming out of a UFO during the Second Coming?

Could the Biblical tale of Sodom and Gomorrah be related to a radioactive UFO crash? Those who watched the UFO and its angelic occupants might have turned into a figurative "pillar of salt" due to the atomic fallout.

10

CHURCH PASTOR GARY STEARMAN ON THE WRATH OF GOD AND A COMING PARADISE

Since 1983, Gary Stearman has been the pastor of the Bible Church in Oklahoma City—Grace Fellowship, where he and his congregation are "devoted to deep investigation and application of God's truth as expressed in Scripture." Beginning in 1987, Stearman was a researcher and writer for the late Dr. J.R. Church's television ministry "Prophecy In The News." As the name implies, the ministry was focused on Biblical prophecy as it is fulfilled by current news events. In the years after Dr. Church's death, Stearman established his own television ministry, called "Prophecy Watchers," as well as publishing a magazine on the ministry's research with the same title.

Stearman said that he came to the Bible by a nonstandard route. When he grew bored with his studies at university in engineering, he switched his major to psychology, which he pursued about halfway through a master's degree. However, it was his minors in linguistics, creative writing and literature that would later come to serve him best. He took a job as a writer and supervisor of commercial publications at Beech Aircraft Company.

"But essentially my university work was creative writing, history, and English, specifically Shakespearian studies," Stearman said. "I even took Greek. I feel in retrospect that the Lord was kind of leading me toward Bible study. It was not until after I graduated and had been in the corporate world for several years that I received Christ at the age of thirty-two. I was taken completely by surprise, having never been raised in a Biblical environment. I was utterly overwhelmed by the Bible. From the first minute that I received Christ, I began to study.

"I was in comparative Shakespearian studies," he continued, "which involved studying the history of language, linguistic comparisons. I discovered that all of that work transferred itself into Bible study. And the more I studied, the more I discovered that scripture is indeed divinely inspired, divinely ordained, and controlled in every aspect by God."

UFOS, ARMAGEDDON AND BIBLICAL REVELATIONS

Stearman said that he has collected a large library of two or three thousand volumes on the Bible and has spent the last fifty years totally immersed in the subject. In 1983, he founded the aforementioned church in Oklahoma City, called "Grace Fellowship." He was working as a freelance scriptural writer when he met J.R. Church, the founder of "Prophecy In The News," at a lecture Church was giving in 1987. The two men talked at length about Biblical prophecy, with Stearman offering some discoveries of his own.

"It became very obvious to both of us," Stearman recalled, "that I could be of help to him as a researcher. So anyway, that's kind of a strange bio. I started out in commercial business and the Lord took me into pastoral work and Christian writing."

ISRAEL'S MODERN REBIRTH

One of the fundamental bricks that modern understanding of Biblical prophecy is built of has to do with the rebirth of Israel as a nation in the 20th Century. Without a State of Israel to provide a staging ground for the predicted events to center around, there might not be any real credibility owed to the many prophets of the Bible.

Stearman said that, beginning in the early 1830s, several scholars began to look forward to the establishment of a new Israel, and the Zionist movement that sprang up soon afterward set the wheels in motion for just such an event.

"A number of men," Stearman said, "taught that Israel would soon be established as a nation, and when it was, it would be a fulfillment of prophecy. Of course that happened in 1948. Those who have observed this have all been in agreement that the major fulfillment of Bible prophecy in the 20th Century is the establishment of the State of Israel."

And what is the scriptural basis for that belief?

"There are just a number of scriptures," Stearman replied. "Of course, Ezekiel Chapters 36 and 37 speak of the nations' coming together in a particular way in which a global world order would be established. The prophet Jeremiah speaks of the re-gathering of Israel. In Jeremiah 31:31, 'Behold the days come, saith the Lord, that I will make a new covenant with the House of Israel and the House of Judah.' And all of this is set in the context of Israel being re-gathered back into the land in the latter days.

"I suppose there must be over one hundred major scriptural passages that speak of Israel being re-gathered and established as a nation in the latter days. And along with that establishment, prophecy says consistently that Israel would suffer opposition of every sort from the moment it became a modem state until the return of Jesus to this world. Israel would struggle against all odds for its very existence. Which we see today of course."

UFOS, ARMAGEDDON AND BIBLICAL REVELATIONS

THE EVENTS OF SEPTEMBER 11, 2001

One question I was eager to ask Stearman concerned just how the terrorist attack of September 11, 2001, fit into the general scheme of prophecy.

"Well," Stearman began, "if you look at the parties that are contesting each other, you discover that the real battle began in the Middle Ages when the Crusaders and the forces of Islam battled over the Holy City. For a few years, the Crusaders actually captured Jerusalem until they were run out by the forces of Saladin approaching the 13th Century. When that happened, the Crusaders retreated for a while and the forces of Islam actually began to move into what had been the territory of Western Civilization. If you examine the current Islamic drive for jihad, you discover it's a battle that's been fought back and forth across European soil since 1100 or so. It's an ancient battle—the Crusaders versus the Islamics.

"In fact, you would hear Osama bin Laden often referring to the forces of the West as the 'Crusaders,'" Stearman said. "They do not regard the battle as having been dropped in any way. For them, it's still an open, raging battle. They see the West – that is Europe and America – as a force that must be eliminated before Islam can rise to its full glory.

"So when they attacked the World Trade Center, they were attacking essentially the centerpiece of the Crusader forces," he continued. "The Twin Towers of the World Trade Center are an edifice of global banking, global merchandise, controlled by European and American banking interests. And these interests are the offspring of the Crusaders, the wealthy leaders of Europe in the Middle Ages. So it's an ancient battle brought right up to the present day."

Stearman went on to explain further.

"There are two things that Islam hates," he said. "They hate the Western merchant-trader and global banking. And they also hate what they call 'Zionism.' They're taking that word directly out of the Bible. Zion is the piece of real estate known as the Temple Mount in Jerusalem. And the Zionist movement, which began really seriously in 1897 and continues to this day, is a movement which desires to center the life of Israel around the Temple Mount, which has been, and still is, the most contested piece of real estate on the face of the Earth.

"Because of our general financial aid to Israel, the West is seen as supporting Zionism. And so the twofold hatred of the modern Islamic movement is against Western business, finance and also against Zionism, which is said to be holding hands with Western business interests."

Stearman also quoted a passage from Isaiah that now seems eerily prescient. "In Isaiah 30, verse 25, there is a word from the Lord," he said, "on the destruction of the enemies of Israel. The verse says, 'And there shall be upon every high mountain, and upon every high hill, rivers and streams of water, in the day of great

106

slaughter, when the towers fall.' And this has been quoted by a number of people as possibly referring to the Twin Towers, and it may.

"Generically, I think it refers to the towers of global power. The great skyscrapers, you know, and the accumulation of power in the West. And then the next verse says, 'Moreover the light of the moon shall be as the light of the sun, and the light of the sun shall be sevenfold,' and so forth, which is speaking of the great and terrible day of the Lord. It puts the falling towers in the same context as the day of the Lord. So I think that's a fascinating prophecy."

WAS GLOBAL WARMING PREDICTED IN THE BIBLE?

When I asked Stearman for any specific predictions about the near future that he could offer, he referred back to the prophecy he had just been quoting.

"I think number one," he said, "the thing that people need to look for, particularly in the light of that prophecy I just read in Isaiah 30:26, where it talks about the variability of the light of the sun and moon—over and over again in scripture, we see that there is going to be a cataclysmic variability in the sun. At one point, it apparently causes people to seek shade because the sun is burning their skin, indicating that the light of the sun is seven times brighter than usual. In another place, it's so dark that men can't find their way around for want of light.

"So I think we can look for solar, terrestrial disturbances," he said. "Now it's fascinating that in the last year, we have seen exactly this. The number of magnetic storms on the sun has reached record levels in the year 2001, and is continuing right on to the present. And it's affecting the weather on Earth and possibly the other planets. By the way, this is available on public record.

"'The New York Times and The New York Post, for example, have noted that not only is the Earth's climate warming up, but also the climate of Mars is warming up, and they're noticing that the Martian polar cap is disappearing at a rapid rate. And the only explanation for this that they've been able to come up with is that the sun is getting hotter. So global warming is perhaps not caused by manmade pollutants, but may be an extraterrestrial event.

"Now with these solar magnetic flares, these magnetic storms, come violent changes in the weather. A lot of people have been predicting abnormally large hurricanes, tornados, unusual and out of place weather fronts, etc., and we're beginning to observe those. So in terms of what the Bible predicts in the immediate future, wild excursions in the weather, perhaps variability in the sun and solar storms, I think that's something we can definitely be on the lookout for."

Stearman said that the Day of the Lord is described by some of the prophets of the Bible as "a day of darkness" or "a day of gloominess," which may be characterized by strange instabilities in the weather the likes of which have never been seen before. He also quoted Isaiah 24, verses 19 and 20: "The Earth is utterly broken down, the Earth is rent asunder, the Earth is shaken violently, the Earth shall stagger like a drunken man – the transgressions thereof shall be heavy upon it, and it shall fall and not rise again.'

"So with the upcoming tribulation," he concluded, "I look for geomagnetic solar terrestrial difficulty, perhaps abnormally warm weather in Canada and abnormally cold weather in the tropics – all sorts of upheavals that cause mankind to become very afraid."

WHY IS SUCH HARSH JUDGMENT NECESSARY?

At one point, I broached the question that bothers many people who believe in the fulfillment of apocalyptic prophecies, no matter the source. Why is such harsh judgment necessary to God's plan for mankind?

"Why does the tribulation feature such horrors for the planet Earth?" Stearman asked, echoing my question. "Why such harsh judgment? Going back to the Old Testament, all of the Old Testament prophets, including Moses, speak of a humanity which has fallen to such severe depths of apostasy that it has to be judged severely. The story of the Bible, in my opinion, is the story of God giving humanity a number of chances to make the right choices, but in every case humanity makes the wrong choice and always opts for power and wealth over godliness. This is basically the prophetic story of the Bible.

"And so by the time you come through the age of the great rulers," he went on, "the Caesars in the days of Jesus, by the time you come through the era of the churches to the present day, you have the world turning progressively away from God and toward pleasure and paganism. And God says he must judge this. That judgment is based upon covenantal promises that he made in the Old Testament. For example, to Abraham he made a promise. To Moses he made a promise. To the kings of Israel, beginning with King David, he made promises concerning the Kingdom. And those promises all have to be worked out.

"And in order for them to be worked out, the powers of the Earth must be overthrown. So when you get to the tribulation period, the first thing you see is the Antichrist moving forward into a final position of control of a world government. You see war, famine, you see the saints of God persecuted, and you see a global rule set up under ten kings.

"A third of the Earth is destroyed," he continued. "One third of the salt water is destroyed, one third of the fresh water is destroyed, and one third of the heavens are destroyed. The sun is made dark. A great hole or cave is opened in the ground which allows demon spirits to come out and torment humans. And they manage to kill one third of the population of the Earth, according to Revelation, and that of course would amount to over two billion people given the present population."

As if that weren't mind-boggling enough, there is more, according to Stearman and his interpretations.

UFOS, ARMAGEDDON AND BIBLICAL REVELATIONS

"Then there is a second wave of difficulties," he explained. "There is another world war. Men are excoriated with various kinds of insults that eat their flesh, and with sores. All of the sea life in the salt water is utterly destroyed, followed by another cataclysm in the bowl judgments in which all the fresh water is made foul. The heat of the sun is increased sevenfold, followed by a blackout of the sun. And you can just go on and on this way. What you end up with is an amazing picture of God's righteous judgment.

"That is to say," Stearman said, "that his judgments are not arbitrary. They follow a specific pattern, and that pattern was set forth back in the days of the Exodus, when the ten plagues were meted out upon the Egyptians under Moses. Those plagues freed the Israelites to move to the Promised Land. Likewise, in the latter days, the plagues of Revelation will free the Israelites once again to move into the Kingdom. So this is judgment with a purpose."

JUDGMENT VERSUS CHASTENING

Next I asked Stearman if he felt that the terrorist attack of September 11 or the current problems Israel is having fit into the patterns of judgment we were discussing. His answer was very interesting.

"There's a difference," he said, "between judgment and chastening. I believe that you see in the Bible that the nations, the pagan forces of the Earth, are judged. But Israel is chastened. That is to say, Israel is cleansed. And the purpose of the tribulation, by the way, is ultimately to restore Israel to the land. That's something that must never be forgotten."

Stearman went on to say that God has promised three reasons for the tribulation, giving chapter and verse, which seems to come very easily to him.

"Number one," he began, "to make an end of wickedness, Isaiah 13:9. Number two, to bring about a worldwide revival, Revelation 7:1. And number three, to break the power of the holy people, as in Daniel 12:5-7. The holy people are Israel, who have been very proudly subsisting as a nation in their own right. God's ultimate purpose is to break their self-confidence and bring them into godly submission to his rule. So that is chastening, as opposed to judgment with a vengeance, which is meted out on the nations."

A WARNING IN THE PRESENT TENSE

Stearman offered a final warning, one that he feels even the secular mind should understand and take to heart.

"If I wanted to point the secular mind to something," he said, "that is absolutely present tense and very powerful, I would point to Zecheriah 12, the burden of the Lord for Israel. 'Sayeth the Lord, who stretches forth the heavens, who lays the foundations of the Earth and formed the spirit of man within him, "Lo, I am about to make Jerusalem a cup of trembling,"' or a cup of poison, it reads in Hebrew, "unto all people round about when they shall be in siege both against Judah and Jerusalem. And in that day I shall make Jerusalem a burdensome stone for all people.' That has already come to pass right now. 'All that burden themselves with it shall be cut in pieces. So all people of the Earth shall be gathered against it.' That's happened right now."

Stearman next quoted from that same chapter in Zecheriah, the sixth verse.

"The very next prophecy that comes out of that," he explained, "is 'In that day will I make the governors of Judah like a hearth of fire among the wood, and like a torch of fire in a sheave, and they shall devour all of the people roundabout, on the right hand and on the left. And Jerusalem shall be inhabited again in her own place, even in Jerusalem.' So you have a very clear prophecy here: that the nations will be in siege against Jerusalem, and that in that day the governors of Judah will be like a hearth of fire among the wood. In other words, they're going to set fire to their enemies. Which has a very nuclear ring to it."

So Israel will eventually be victorious?

"Yes, but in the process," Stearman replied, "I think Israel goes through some precipitous times. War is never fun for either side. By the way, these 'governors of Judah' in verse six are the Hebrew word for 'secular leader.' We know this is a latter day prophecy because only since 1948 has Israel had secular leaders – Knesset [parliament] members. So this is specifically a prophecy that applies to our day."

Stearman offered one final prophecy, again about Israel and her enemies.

"We read in Psalm 83," he said, "that 'They have taken crafty counsel against thy people, and consulted against thy hidden ones. They have said, "Come, let us cut them off from being a nation, that the name of Israel may be no more in remembrance," for they have consulted together with one consent.' In other words, all of the descendants of Israel's traditional enemies are gathered together to cut Israel off from being a nation. We have that in Psalm 83. And 1983 just happens to be the year that Yassir Arafat reformed the PLO after it was dissolved in 1982. And from that day to this, there has been a continuous assault on Israel. So I believe there are a number of present, active prophecies in the Bible."

BEFORE THE RAPTURE: WHITE HORSES, CHARIOTS OF FIRE
AND A POSSIBLE DIMENSIONAL SHIFT
MORE FROM GARY STEARMAN

The "catching away" of the Church could happen at any moment. Are 2000 years of waiting almost over?

Does the re-establishment of the national state of Israel, which many regard as a crucial fulfillment of Biblical prophecy, point the way to the fulfillment of other prophecies, such as a Battle of Armageddon over the skies of Jerusalem?

UFOS, ARMAGEDDON AND BIBLICAL REVELATIONS

Will the coming of the New Jerusalem be a kind of real-life science fiction, heralding a kind of paradise totally and completely alien to our world today?

Gary Stearman's interest in UFOs began in the 1960s, when he had several personal sightings that were part of a larger flap going on at the time.

"That wave of sightings," he said, "was correlated, at least in my opinion, to the Six Day War of June of 1967 in Israel. I've subsequently noted and have written about the subject, the fact that many of the UFO waves seem to be coordinated with events that happen to national Israel. Which, by the way, shouldn't be too surprising, since national Israel is the centerpiece of God's prophetic program.

"I saw a number of UFOs," Stearman continued, "while I was standing with several other witnesses, and this, needless to say, really opened my eyes to a brand new way of thinking. I started studying UFOs and I've been doing so ever since."

STEARMAN AND THE TROUBLESOME VERSES

Stearman was asked his opinion on the Bible verses in which Jesus told his followers that some of them would not taste death before the coming of the Kingdom of Heaven.

"I would answer it this way," Stearman replied. "When Jesus uttered those words, he was talking to Peter, James and John. And he said that some of you standing here will not die until you see the Son of Man coming in his Kingdom. Well, that's in Matthew Sixteen. And the very next chapter, Matthew Seventeen, features the Transfiguration, in which Jesus took the disciples up to the mountaintop and they saw Moses and Elijah, and Jesus was transfigured before their eyes.

"So one answer to this question," he said, "about when will the Kingdom come, is that it's already come figuratively at the Transfiguration. It was kind of a preview of the Kingdom."

Which leads Stearman to the second part of his answer.

"If the Transfiguration happened as described in the Bible," he said, "and I believe it did, then it presents us with absolute affirmation that the Kingdom itself will come in due time. That due time has been the subject of much prophetic speculation."

Stearman next began to describe something called "The Year/Day Theory."

"I think at the center of the speculations," he said, "about the timing of the Kingdom, is that many people, including Jews, including the First Century apostles, have stated what they call 'The Year/Day Theory,' in which they say that God created the world in six days, and he rested on the seventh. These seven days are symbolic of the coming of seven thousand years of future history. There would be six thousand years during which time the notable events of the Bible transpired, including the lives of Abraham, Moses, David, the prophets, Jesus and then the

111

church. That would take six thousand years, corresponding to the six days of Creation. Then the seventh day would be a thousand year millennium. So that millennium, that Kingdom, is foreshadowed by the Creation pattern."

Stearman said that that particular interpretation of the timing of the Kingdom is backed up by some verses from Psalm Ninety.

"Psalm 90 gives the documentation," he said, "for that belief system. It says, and this was written by Moses, Psalm 90, verse four, 'For a thousand years in thy sight are as but yesterday when it is past, and is a watch in the night.' That Psalm goes on to lay out the Millennial/Day theory, in which the seven days laid out in Genesis become seven thousand years of timing of human history, the seventh of those thousands being the millennium. So what we have in the Transfiguration is a preview of the millennium."

LINKS TO THE RAPTURE

Stearman said that the Apostle Paul later expounded the same Year/Day Theory.

"When Paul writes to the church," Stearman said, "he describes a brand new idea to them. That brand new idea is seen in First Thessalonians, Chapter Four, verses 16 and 17: the catching away of the church. 'For the Lord himself shall descend from heaven, with a shout of the voice of the archangel, with the trump of God. The dead in Christ shall rise first, then we which are alive and remain shall be caught up together with him in the clouds, to meet the Lord in the air, and so shall we ever be with the Lord.' Now, when Paul wrote that, it was a brand new idea. There had never been expounded the idea that the Lord would take a group of people to heaven, en masse, and in a single event.

"Paul wrote this," Stearman continued, "and to Paul and Paul only is given the full and detailed description of that event. But what's interesting about it is that in Second Thessalonians, he links that seven thousand years to the catching away of the church. In Second Thessalonians, Chapter Two, he says, 'Now we beseech thee, brethren, by the coming of our Lord Jesus, by our gathering together unto him, that ye be not shaken in mind. Be troubled neither by spirit nor by word nor by letter as from us, as that the Day of Christ is at hand.' And the 'Day of Christ' is another name for that seventh thousand-year period. In other words, the millennial day being one thousand years is called various things. Here it's called the Day of Christ. Throughout the Old Testament and in other places in the New Testament, it's called The Day of the Lord.

"It begins with a terrible judgment," Stearman said, "and it culminates with the re-establishment of paradise. Paul makes it very clear that the church will be removed from the world prior to that seventh millennium. And so Bible-believing Christians, that is the ones who believe this, are called 'Pre-Millennial,' because they believe in the pre-millennial catching away of the church."

UFOS, ARMAGEDDON AND BIBLICAL REVELATIONS

IT COULD HAPPEN ANY MOMENT

Stearman moved on to discuss something called "the doctrine of imminency."

"Imminency being the idea," Stearman said, "put forth by the apostles, including John, James, Peter and especially Paul; the idea that the Lord could come back for his body of believers, the church, at any moment. The apostles left their followers with the idea that Christ could come at any moment. They did this for one reason: so that believers would live in the constant state of expectancy, which would stimulate them to higher faith. If you stop and think about it, this is a very interesting departure from the Old Testament prophets. The Old Testament prophets spoke literally. They gave timings. In many cases, such as the case with the prophet Ezekiel, the Lord actually gave him numbers of years and days to speak in his prophecies.

"But the New Testament prophecies are always based on the idea of imminency. They're not laid out in terms of years or days, but they're laid out in terms of the imminent return of Christ. And in fact Paul makes a statement in First Thessalonians, Chapter Five, verse one, 'But of the times and seasons, brethren, you have no need that I write unto you, for yourselves know perfectly that the Day of the Lord shall come as a thief in the night. For when they shall say, "Peace and safety," then sudden destruction comes upon them as the travails of a woman with child, and they shall not escape.'"

Stearman also believes the imminent return of Christ and the Rapture are related to events in Israel.

"There was a great man," he said, "a 19th Century statesman, novelist, named Benjamin Disraeli. He was a Jew, actually, baptized into the Anglican Church, and was twice made Prime Minister of England. Once, while he was in Parliament, he was asked if he knew of any infallible proof of God's existence. And the answer he gave is a classic. He said, and I quote, 'The Jew, sir. The Jew.'

"And what he is saying is that the existence of the Jew is the ultimate proof of God's existence. That brings us to the re-gathering of Israel. We mentioned earlier that in the modern era, UFO waves seem to be tied to Israel's entrance into the land and to Israel's wars. This goes all the way back to 1897, which was the year of the first Zionist Congress. It was at this time that Theodore Hertzel and others gathered in Basel, Switzerland, to discuss bringing Israel back as a nation. This event in 1897 actually coincided with the very first UFO wave, which was the appearance of the so-called 'airships.'

"It was exactly fifty years later," Stearman continued, "in 1947, that the United Nations, in a special session, granted Israel the right to proclaim statehood. And wouldn't you know it, in 1947, there was another incredible UFO wave. The 1947 UFO wave is said to be demonstrably the greatest UFO wave of the 20th Century, and included the Roswell Incident and so forth. So when you look at modern prophecy, the number one sign is the Jew and the rebirth of the nation of Israel."

DRIFTING AWAY FROM PROPHECY?

The question remains, however, as to why, after two millennia, do people still have the steadfast faith in Christ's return? According to Stearman, that has not always been the case.

"It's interesting," he said, "that shortly after the death of John, the apostle, which ended the apostolic age right at the end of the First Century, it was not long after that, going into the second, third, fourth and fifth centuries, that teaching drifted away from prophecy. The teaching of the post-apostolic fathers, as they are called, turned to church hierarchy and became preoccupied with establishing a large and authoritative church and became less preoccupied with matters prophetic. It wasn't until about 1000 A.D. that people began to revive the Year/Day Theory and became very, very excited that Jesus might return in 1000 A.D.

"Well, 1000 A.D. came and went," he continued, "and Jesus had not returned, so there was a general cooling off again of the teaching of Bible prophecy. It was not until about 1830, with the teaching of John Nelson Darby, who began to say we must take literally the prophecy that Israel would be reborn as a nation. Darby was the first man to state publicly this principle and to preach it. Others began to follow his lead. At the end of the 19th Century, during the so-called Age of Missionary Activity, when the great missionary movements were established, Darby's teaching had become well-accepted by others. Then, many preachers in England and the United States began to say that Israel would once again be re-founded as a nation.

"Well, there was not even the slightest thought of this happening. Israel had lay dormant for years, millennia actually. Nevertheless, Darby's followers began to preach that Israel could be reborn as a nation, and by the early decades of the 20th Century, this teaching became a standard part of fundamental church doctrine among pre-millennial believers. About the time that Israel became a state, on May 14, 1948, pre-millennialists began to openly teach that we were living in the Last Days as shown by Israel's rebirth, and that the Coming of Jesus couldn't be far behind."

Along with the re-gathering of the Jews in modern Israel, Stearman pointed out another fairly recent phenomenon—the large number of bestselling books on the subject of the End Times.

"Probably, other than the Bible itself," Stearman said, "the bestseller in history was Hal Lindsey's book, 'The Late, Great Planet Earth,' which espoused the idea that since national Israel had been reborn, the Second Coming of Christ would follow soon after. There have been literally dozens of other similar books that have sold in the hundreds of thousands if not millions of copies. All made possible by one thing—Israel's existence as a nation."

TWO FORMS OF RE-GATHERING

"The Bible speaks of two re-gatherings of Israel," Stearman continued. "The first one is a re-gathering of Israel in unbelief, in which the people would come back as a political measure, that is to preserve their lives politically. The Jews, after World War II, were openly stating, 'We must

become a nation in order to stand up for ourselves politically, because if we don't, nobody else ever will.'

"And the Bible also predicts a second re-gathering of Israel in belief. So those who are watching these events develop believe that Israel has first been gathered in unbelief—that is to say, there's no temple. There is no active priest-hood. The accoutrements of national Israel's religious activity are still dormant. The Bible tells us they will remain dormant until the church is taken out of the way, physically removed from the Earth, allowing Israel then to move to the center of the prophetic timeline."

EVENTS PRECEDING CHRIST'S RETURN

Along with the re-gathering of Israel, Stearman pointed to other events that the Bible says must precede Christ's return, using the Book of Revelation as a guide. He spoke of the first six of the famous "Seven Seals" and their dire impact on the future world.

"The first seal," Stearman said, "exposes the antichrist. The second seal is the seal that begins a global war. The third seal represents an economy that's completely and utterly destroyed. The fourth seal represents a siege of death by pestilence. The fifth seal is the seal of those souls who are martyred. And the sixth seal is the beginning of divine judgment.

"The Book of Revelation has the antichrist being revealed as a world leader along with a global conflagration in which billions of people die. No one knows when this is going to happen, but it will happen—that is, relatively in time. Christ returns in Revelation Chapter 19, and is received at last by national Israel. They failed to receive him on his first coming. Revelation 19:11, which is called the Second Coming of Christ, says, 'I saw heaven opened, and behold a white horse. He that sat upon him was called Faithful and True, and in righteousness he does judge and make war.'"

But let's backtrack a moment. Why are horrors like the antichrist and global warfare scheduled to precede the long awaited Second Coming?

"The horrors of the Tribulation are monstrous indeed," Stearman replied. "What you have in Revelation 6:8, 'Power was given to them over the fourth part of the Earth to kill with the sword and with hunger and with death and with the beasts of the Earth.' That would be about one and a quarter billion people, if a quarter of the Earth's population died. We have in Revelation, Chapter Eight, a third of the remainder of the Earth's population dying. Some have suggested that of the six billion people now on Planet Earth, perhaps only one and a half billion or so people would be left after these conflagrations.

"The question is, why does this have to happen concurrent with the raising again of Israel to power? The reason is that there are two functions of the Lord in the Book of Revelation. One function is to chastise Israel and to expose to national Israel all the wrongs that they have ever done. They were supposed to have been the nation that God held as an example for other nations. The second function is to judge all those nations that have attempted down through the last 5000 years or so to destroy Israel.

"From the time of Abraham to the present," Stearman continued, "there have been numerous attempts to annihilate the Jews. The Persians, under Ahasuerus, attempted to destroy the Jews. That's the story in the Book of Esther. The Babylonians attempted to destroy the Jews under Nebuchadnezzar. Multiple attempts have been made. Antiochus Epiphanes, the Selucid leader, attempted in 167 B.C. to destroy the Jews. The Romans attempted to destroy the Jews in 70 A.D. And right up to the present day, in which Hitler and his group attempted to destroy the Jews. It's been a truism among Gentile world leaders that Israel must die.

"And in recompense for all of these assassination attempts, the Lord is going to judge the Gentiles in a way that was prophesied all the way through the Old Testament. The larger population of the world does not believe that this judgment will take place literally. Those who read the Bible literally, who are pre-millennialists, who believe that we are living in the time before the millennium, believe that these judgments are literal and that God has a good reason for the judgments, namely recompense and vengeance for all the assassination attempts ever made on national Israel."

STEARMAN ON UFOs

After that fascinating but dark look at the coming wrath of God, the subject of UFOs again presented itself. Stearman was asked how the UFO phenomenon relates to the Second Coming.

"People who read the Bible," he answered, "believe in the literal existence of angels, that angels come and go, day by day, in our world, but they are not seen in general. They have some sort of an ability to be present without revealing themselves to human eyes.

"And in Second Kings, Chapter Six, there's a wonderful example of that in which the prophet Elisha went out with his servant, and they were camped out. It was a time when the Syrian army was coming against Israel. They woke up the next morning, and Elisha and his servant discovered themselves to be surrounded by the Syrian army. And the servant said,

'What in the world are we going to do?' Then Elisha prayed and said, 'Lord, I pray thee, open his eyes that he may see.' The Lord opened the eyes of the young man and he saw, and behold, the mountain was full of horses and chariots of fire round about Elisha. In other words, these chariots of fire are the way the Bible describes what I regard as UFOs.

"If a chariot of fire makes itself visible," Stearman explained, "such as the time when the prophet Elijah was taken to heaven in a chariot of fire, or in the first chapter of Ezekiel, when a chariot of fire came across the plain and landed right in front of Ezekiel, when these chariots of fire become manifest, they resemble nothing quite so much as what we call UFOs in the modern era. The servant of Elisha was simply allowed to see these fiery chariots, which means they're not far distant from us. There is perhaps a dimensional shift that allows them to conceal themselves."

The conversation returned to the verse from Revelation 19 about Jesus appearing on a white horse and leading the armies of heaven.

"I don't believe Jesus will be riding a white horse as we think of a white horse," Stearman said, "because all through the Bible, horses and chariots are the figures used to describe these celestial transportation vehicles. Jesus is said to lead a heavenly army in verse 14 of that same chapter of Revelation. 'And the armies which were in heaven followed him upon white horses.' I don't believe those were literal white horses. I think they are some sort of celestial transportation vehicle that if they could be rendered visible to the eyes of most people on Earth today, those people would say, 'There goes a UFO.'"

In a manner similar to Dr. Barry Downing's remarks, Stearman argued that the method by which Jesus ascended into heaven in the early pages of the Book of Acts will likely be the same method by which he returns. Stearman quoted Acts One, verses 9-11, saying, "And when he had spoken these things, while they beheld he was taken up and a cloud received him out of their sight. And while they looked steadfastly toward heaven as he went up, behold two men stood by them in white apparel, which also said, 'You men of Galilee, why stand you gazing into heaven? This same Jesus which is taken from you unto heaven shall so come in a like manner as you have seen him go into heaven.'"

"Here we see a couple of angels," Stearman said, "describing to the apostles that Jesus would come in the same way that he left. The way he left is that a cloud received him up, and that cloud departed. I take it that this cloud was some form of celestial transportation vehicle. Therefore, that white horse that we see him riding must be the same sort of vehicle as the cloud into which he was received. So to me, that explains much of what modern man sees when he is looking at UFOs. He's really seeing a glimpse of the spirit world when he sees the UFO."

UFOS, ARMAGEDDON AND BIBLICAL REVELATIONS

WILL THE ANTICHRIST ALSO HAVE A UFO?

Stearman next gamely tackled the question of whether the antichrist is similarly equipped with a UFO.

"The antichrist," he said, "as described in Revelation 13: 11-18, has the ability to display supernatural power. And in Revelation 13:13, it says, 'He doeth great wonders, so that he makes fire to come down from heaven on the Earth in the sight of man.' Now you can interpret that in many ways, but one of the ways that it's most often interpreted is that some sort of celestial display will be brought down from heaven to Earth. I take that to mean a dimensional change of some sort, that something from beyond human sight, perhaps just beyond the barriers of our dimension, is brought into this dimension and made visible to the people of the Earth. That could be fire. It could be a fiery chariot.

"Therefore, I think by inference, that the antichrist will receive much of the power of these fiery chariots that have been seen down through the ages. Many of these fiery chariots are attributed to dark forces. Many are attributed to angelic forces. That is seen in Revelation, Chapter Twelve, verse seven. 'There was a war in heaven. Michael and his angels fought against the dragon, and the dragon fought, and his angels.' That speaks of an aerial battle. I think that to a certain extent, that is going on today. And it involves the celestial transportation vehicles we've been talking about, which at times become visible and at other times remain veiled beyond the dimensional wall so that they can't readily be seen.

"But the antichrist has this power to call down fire from heaven. It probably means that he has the ability to call into this dimension the fiery chariots to do his work."

NOTHING IN THE PRESENT WORLD

When Stearman was asked if he could point to anything in the here and now that might offer a foretaste of a post-Second Coming paradise, he said, "There is nothing in the present world that suggests the kind of perfection that's promised in the Kingdom Age. The only clues we have are the very few allusions to paradise that we have in the account of Adam and Eve. We know that their Earth was perfect in its climate. Its weather was very mild. The distribution of moisture was perfect. The distribution of solar radiation was perfect. Many say that the Earth, instead of being tilted on its axis, was revolving on a zero-degree plane relative to the sun, meaning that the seasons were constant.

"Unlike today, with the twenty-three and a half degree tilt of Planet Earth, with which we have the changing seasons. These seasons changing bring about ensuing weather violence of all kinds, tornadoes, hurricanes, etc."

Stearman quoted from the Book of Isaiah, Chapter 24, verse 19: "The Earth is utterly broken down. The Earth is clean dissolved. The Earth is moved exceedingly. The Earth shall reel to and fro like a drunkard, shall be removed like a cottage, and the transgressions thereof shall be heavy upon it, and it shall fall and not rise again. It shall come to pass in that day that the Lord will punish the host of the High Ones that are on high, and the kings of the Earth upon the Earth."

According to Stearman, "This is clearly speaking of that period in the Day of the Lord when the nations will be judged, but notice that the Earth is said to reel to and fro like a drunkard. Many people have said that this is the process of returning the world back to its ninety-degree position relative to the plane of the ecliptic, and the weather once again will return to perfection. And let's face it, if you can have perfect weather and the atmosphere of the Earth is restored, that's half the battle right there."

There are also predictions in Isaiah Chapter 65 that imply to Stearman a perfect society.

"No more shall there be in it an infant," Stearman read aloud, "that lives but a few days, nor an old man that hath not filled his days, for the child shall die a hundred years old, but the sinner being a hundred years old shall be accursed."

"In other words," Stearman said, "people will live to great old ages and their labor will not be in vain. In the classic passage in Isaiah, 65:25, it says, 'The wolf and the lamb shall feed together, the lion shall eat straw like the bullock, dust shall be the serpent's meat, and they shall not hurt or destroy in all my holy mountain, says the Lord.' So you'll have a restored Earth. The kingdom and the throne of God will be in Jerusalem, physically. The weather will be back in balance, and health will be restored, and people will live to a very great age, as they did prior to the Flood and the destruction of the Earth the first time. And finally there will be domestic peace and peace in the animal kingdom——the wolf and the lamb shall feed together and so forth. With that domestic peace, you'll have a perfect Earth."

A SCIENCE FICTION PARADISE

The discussion returned to the Book of Revelation, this time focusing on Chapter Twenty-One and what seems like a future technological paradise.

"Chapter Twenty-One takes place," Stearman said, "after the creation of a new heaven and a new Earth in the far future. If there is a place in the Bible that reads like science fiction—although it's not fiction, it's fact—it's the place where we find apparently a huge city, orbiting around the restored Earth, and called the New Jerusalem. It's going to be fifteen hundred miles on a side, which is a very large orbiting body, more like the moon in size. And this is said to be the home of the saints forever. But the world will also be perfected during that time, and that perfection will apparently include breathtaking constructions. We see things built out of some sort of gold that's as transparent as glass. I can't even imagine what that's going to be like.

"You can see things fabricated out of materials," Stearman continued, "that we don't use for building right now, like emerald and diamond and sapphire. If you could take a motion picture of this place and bring it back, people would think they were watching science fiction. An absolutely marvelous world to come. Totally regulated, completely peaceful, wars having been ended, and the source of evil having been at last judged and put away."

Google "Prophecy Watchers" for latest episodes.

SUGGESTED READING - BOOKS AND PAPERS BY GARY STEARMAN

BLOOD ON THE ALTER

MYSTERY OF THE MENORAH

PROPHECY BEHIND THE CROWN OF THORNS

AND GOD CREATED OIL

Stearman covers a multitude of topics, most of them related to prophecy as outlined in the Scriptures.

A UFO at first hovers and then shoots skyward from the Temple Mount in Jerusalem.

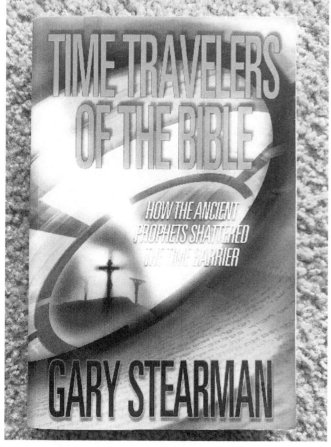

Not only has Gary Stearman investigated UFOs from a Biblical approach, but time travel is another one of his interests, as can be seen by the release of this new book.

Upon seeing the New Jerusalem coming down, some might think it is a three-mile wide UFO known as the "City Ship." Art by Carol Ann Rodriguez.

The war between the Christian Crusaders and the Ottoman Empire has been ongoing for centuries upon centuries.

453

A vivid depiction of the Wrath of God.

"And I saw the holy city, the new Jerusalem, coming down from God out of heaven like a bride beautifully dressed for her husband" (21:2 NLT).

New Jerusalem, in the clouds.

UFOS, ARMAGEDDON AND BIBLICAL REVELATIONS

11

UFO RELIGION - A NEW SPIRITUAL AWAKENING
By Tim Swartz

Brad Baker of Hartford City, Indiana, was reluctant to talk about his UFO experience. Even though his encounter had occurred in 1985, Baker's fear of ridicule induced him to remain silent. That is, until a mutual friend, to whom he had confided his incredible tale, suggested that his story may be of interest to me.

What Baker told me was not very different from the thousands of other "close encounter incidents" that have been reported over the years. What made his story interesting was his opinion that the strange being he saw standing beside a landed disc-shaped object was none other than God himself.

"If it wasn't God, then it was Jesus," said Baker. "I know it sounds crazy, but the figure I saw looked just like those paintings you see of Jesus. He was wearing a long white robe and had long hair and a beard. He was standing in front of a bright-white light that looked to me to be somewhat shaped like a disc or an egg. What was really crazy is that when the light suddenly went out, there was nothing there. It was as if someone had turned off a television and the picture disappears."

Baker confessed that while he had never been a "church going kind of guy," after his incident he found himself interested in religion and spirituality. "Seeing what I did convinced me that there is more going on than what we see in front of us," said Baker. "That figure looked so much like God that I am convinced that there is life on other planets and they could be messengers from God."

Incidents such as that experienced by Brad Baker are just the types of UFO-related reports that send most western UFO researchers heading for the door. The extraterrestrial hypothesis (ETH) has been singled out by many investigators as the most likely explanation for UFO sightings. However, what disturbs some researchers to the point that they exclude such reports is the fact that a substantial number of UFO encounters involve what can be best described as spiritual or metaphysical experiences.

UFOS, ARMAGEDDON AND BIBLICAL REVELATIONS

THE NATURE OF UFOs

Anyone who takes the time to diligently study the phenomena of UFOs will eventually discover that there are no easy answers to be found. The research of UFOs has resisted all attempts to pigeonhole them into any one category. Since 1947 the belief has developed that UFOs are spacecraft operated by extraterrestrial visitors to our planet. This idea has become so predominate in our society that it is almost impossible to avoid the constant media influence that UFOs are being flown by extraterrestrial creatures.

Peter Davenport of the National UFO Reporting Center recently told MSNBC that reports of UFOs probably involve spacecraft whose technology is beyond our current understanding. When asked his opinion of the nature of the visitors, and the purpose behind the visitations, Davenport replied: "Those are the things that keep us motivated." However, he added. "I don't think there's any UFOlogist who has the answers to those questions. And if they do, you should probably reject their information."

After more than seventy years of investigation and research, no one has managed to offer a satisfactory explanation on the true nature of UFOs. However, UFOs and their associated phenomena continue to be reported. The skeptics have failed to convince those who have experienced UFOs that they were somehow mistaken. To these people, their experience was real and nothing can convince them otherwise.

Many UFO experiencers report that their encounter led to a complete change in their lives, often in a spiritual sense. Some have received additional visits by strange beings claiming to be highly advanced extraterrestrials who are here on Earth to save mankind from imminent danger. A few of these people have even been told that they were chosen by the Space People to act as a mouthpiece, or even a Messiah, to lead the population to an eventual communion with the benevolent aliens.

Popular literature is full of such stories. These tales of gods and angels from outer space make most "nuts and bolts" UFO researchers uncomfortable, and sometimes even a little hostile. Some UFO investigators scorn the contactees who claim to have a psychic link with the Space Brothers. Walter Andrus of the Mutual UFO Network says such claims sound "a little bit like channeling, and we don't take much stock in channeling." Yet the recent history of UFOs seem to show that there have been deliberate attempts to connect the belief in otherworldly entities with spirituality and even religion. We could be now experiencing the birth of a new religion – a religion that combines scientific rationalism, spiritual beliefs and a hierarchy of semi-divine beings allegedly from other planets.

SCIENCE AS RELIGION

In ancient times God and his spiritual minions were everywhere...the daily rising and setting of the sun, in the thunderous lightning that split the sky in two, in the forests and glens that supplied an infant mankind with provisions and a sense of place in the world. Man walked the Earth and God existed in the heavens above.

These were all the answers that were needed when the curious asked about the nature of the Universe and the secrets contained within. Before long, these explanations were not enough and the inquisitive nature of man sought to unravel that which only God understood. Science was born and it quickly replaced God with the cold equations of mathematics. The old religions were dead, replaced by the new religion of Science.

However, science as a religion for the masses left a lot to be desired. Science preached an "It All Just Happened" philosophy that left no room for spiritual beings and a divine Creator. This belief system directly conflicted with the millenniums-old doctrines of a universe filled with Heavenly denizens. These deity-based beliefs were effective because they appealed to an instinct buried deep within all of us that seemed to acknowledge the basic reality of God.

Since the Nineteenth Century, science has enjoyed a tremendous following and has rewarded its believers with exciting discoveries and incredible technology. But it is devoid of any spirituality or purpose. Organized religion resisted the temptations by branding new scientific discoveries as evil or heretical. Both faiths demanded total loyalty, there could be no middle ground, one or the other must be chosen.

To the average person this separation between science and spirituality made little sense. It seemed more realistic that the two were actually connected, eternally intertwined, one working with the other. A Creator made the Universe along with the laws of science to sustain it. It was obvious that reality was governed by scientific principles, but how did these principles arise in the first place? The Universe seemed a little too orderly to have all happened just by chance.

Unfortunately, religion and science remained unconvinced. Organized religion refused to change with time. It was becoming increasingly difficult to interest a modern audience in religious beliefs and dogmas that were developed by nomadic tribesmen thousands of years ago. And science was too busy enjoying its new found prestige to admit that there could be room for new and radical ideas.

This conflict was the perfect catalyst for the creation of a new belief system. A system that took both science and religion to blend them into a new structure.

THE COMING OF THE GODS - AGAIN

People have asked why we don't see miracles today like those referred to in ancient religious writings. These old texts are filled with tales of angelic beings, strange wonders in the skies and divinely inspired prophets and their prophecies.

UFOS, ARMAGEDDON AND BIBLICAL REVELATIONS

However, these events are still occurring today on a daily basis throughout the world. Now, the wonders in the sky are silvery discs recorded on home video cameras. And rather than angels from God, we have spacemen from the Pleiades who are here to deliver prophetic messages of doom or salvation. The gods and goddesses of old have not gone away; they have merely traded in their long white beards and togas for spacesuits and helmets.

When UFO contactees in the early 1950s began to tell of their alleged encounters with the pilots of UFOs, their stories seemed too fantastic for most to believe. Yet the tales of angelic Space Brothers – here to help guide mankind away from its evil ways – struck a chord with those who were raised with scientific materialism.

Since science had supposedly proven that there was no place for God and angels in the universe, here instead were beings from another planet whose appearance and philosophies seemed more divine then physical. It was the perfect melding of spirituality and science…superior beings from other worlds that were not only advanced technologically, but also spiritually.

The appearance of entities claiming to be from other worlds is not new to history. However, it was not until after 1947 that the belief in UFOs and extraterrestrials started to develop beyond a few individuals and science fiction novels.

In a little more than seventy years we have seen a rapid evolution in the acceptance of alien creatures visiting our planet. This development is similar to past events that led to the creation of all major religions known today. It is therefore clear that we could be experiencing the genesis of a new spiritual system based on the belief in highly advanced, spiritual beings from outer space. The Space Age Religion.

HOW REAL ARE THE EXTRATERRESTRIALS?

In his book "Report on Communion," author Ed Conroy writes: "Students of the paranormal have often seen that UFO reports are known to have occurred during periods of other extremely unusual events that include poltergeist-like phenomena, reports of spontaneous human combustion, an upsurge in popular religious fervor and even – quite controversially – anomalous animal mutilations and disappearances."

It is true that many UFO cases involve reports that seem to be more ghost-like than real. UFOs and their occupants appear to be solid one minute and then vaporous the next. The alleged extraterrestrials have often seemed to be unduly concerned with the spiritual affairs of mankind. If anything, the UFOnauts act more like guardian angels than astronauts visiting for scientific explorations.

To those who have experienced the UFO phenomenon, the event often begins by being struck by a blinding beam of light. John Keel writes in "The Eighth Tower": "All great religions and countless cults began with the exposure of a single person to this phenomenon. Saul, Daniel, and other Biblical personages saw luminous phenomena at the outset of their adventures. They usually received messages and accurate prophecies. Later, when they passed the prophecies onto their friends and followers, those predictions usually came true. Because of this, they felt the holiness of their condition had been proven. The ranks of their followers grew. It was this process that inspired the spread of Christianity. In other ages the same process spawned the pagan religions and the myths of demonology."

Like the old religions, the Space Age religion has its hierarchy of divine and demonic beings. The angels are now played by the blond, Nordic Space Brothers. While the devil and his demons are the big-eyed "Greys" that are believed responsible for an epidemic of UFO-related abductions that has dominated the UFO culture for over forty years. It is amazing how quickly the mythology that now surrounds UFOs has grown and developed over the years. This is what will ground and sustain the Space Age religion over the rest of the millennium.

"This grounding and founding is maintained through the elaboration of particular ceremonies and rituals, especially the repetition of the content of the myth; the creation story. Each repetition of the foundational myth recreates those primary distinctions (such as 'flying saucer' or 'alien abduction') that bring a particular world into view; each successive re-creation holds the world in place," writes Keith Thompson, in his book "Aliens and Angels." This is echoed by Holger Kalweit who states: "Perhaps the otherworldly journey motif is 'camouflaged' in the modern lore of space travel which, like the fantastic voyage legends of the past, exemplifies what might be called the lure of the edge."

MISSIONARIES FROM THE STARS

Over the centuries, thousands of books have been written by people who claim to be channeling spirits, angels and even extraterrestrials. More than likely all of our great religious writings can be traced in part to messages received while in an altered state of consciousness. All of these trance state communications read disturbingly the same, no matter if the source claims to be a divine being or alien entity from another galaxy. It has often been noted that channeled communications from supposed extraterrestrials sound so much like the messages received from angels and spirits that the two could be interchanged with little disruption.

Channeled communications from friendly extraterrestrials are given just about as much credence from researchers as tales of Santa Claus or the Easter Bunny. However, there are many reports of physical close encounters with UFO entities who seem interested in preaching their form of spirituality to witnesses, missionaries from the stars if you like.

On January 30, 1965, Sidney Padrick was taking a walk along Manresa Beach in California. Suddenly he heard a loud humming sound and saw a strange machine shaped like "two real thick saucers inverted." Padrick started to run away but was stopped by a voice that came from the object inviting him aboard. At the voice's urging, Padrick entered through a door that appeared in the side of the now landed saucer. Inside he was greeted by a medium-sized man with very pale skin, a sharp nose and chin and unusually long fingers. When Padrick asked for the man's name, he was told, "You may call me Zeeno."

Mr. Zeeno gave Padrick a quick tour of the craft which came with its own "chapel." Padrick remembered, "The color effect in that room was so pretty that I almost fainted when I went in. There were eight chairs, a stool, and what looked like an altar. Zeeno said: 'Would you like to pay your respects to the Supreme Deity?' I didn't know how to accept it. I'm forty-five years old, and until that night I had never felt the presence of the Supreme Being, but I did feel him that night."

In 1952, Cecil Michael of Bakersfield, California, observed a flying saucer at close range. He subsequently had encounters with alleged aliens who took him away to their home planet. Michael claimed that the planet was orange in color, very hot and home to a strange creature that he called "the Devil."

"As I stood looking fearfully at the devil there was suddenly a bright white light that appeared besides me," recalled Michael. "In the middle of the light, Christ appeared in plain view... I turned to the Devil and, pointing my hand to the light, said, 'If you don't let me go, He will send for me.' The Devil responded: 'Yes, He is always interfering.'"

After spending almost three weeks on the alien planet, Michael was returned to Earth. Upon returning, the two extraterrestrials asked him to write the story of the incident with the Devil and Christ. "This is for the benefit of humanity," the aliens said. "We want the world to know about the great cosmic struggle between good and evil in which your planet is unknowingly involved."

Dr. Leopoldo Diaz of Guadalajara, Mexico, says that in 1976 he had two contacts with beings who said they were from another planet. In the course of the visits the aliens told Dr. Diaz to proclaim the truth far and wide. His message was that "God is everywhere, all religions you profess on Earth are only roads to the same purpose – to know God."

These stories are just a few out of the hundreds of UFO close encounters that had religious undertones. The witnesses are often given the task by their contacts to deliver a message to the world, a message usually steeped in spiritual/religious connotations. Individually, none of these messages of salvation from the stars had much of an impact. But, collectively, over time, these stories serve to reinforce the UFO idea...the promise of hope from divine beings in the sky.

CARL JUNG ON UFOs

Shortly before his death, Carl Jung was one of the first to try and analyze UFOs in a symbolic way. In a 1951 letter to an American friend he wrote, "I'm puzzled to death about these phenomena, because I haven't been able yet to make out with sufficient certainty whether the whole thing is a rumor with concomitant singular and mass hallucination, or a downright fact."

In 1958, Jung concluded that it was more desirable for people to believe UFOs exist than to believe they don't exist. One of his final works, "Flying Saucers," was an attempt to answer why it was more desirable to believe in their existence.

Jung thought that UFOs were examples of the phenomena of synchronicity, where external events mirror internal psychic states. For Jung the UFO images had much to do with the ending of an era in history and the beginning of a new one. In his introductory remarks to "Flying Saucers" he wrote:

"As we know from ancient Egyptian history, they are manifestations of psychic changes which always appear at the end of one Platonic month and at the beginning of another. Apparently they are changes in the constellation of psychic dominants, of the archetypes, or 'Gods' as they used to be called, which bring about, or accompany, long-lasting transformations of the collective psyche. The transformation started in the historical era and left its traces first in the passing of the aeon of Taurus into that of Aries, and then of Aries into Pisces, whose beginning coincides with the rise of Christianity. We are now nearing that great change which may be expected when the spring point enters Aquarius."

In a manner similar to that which the medieval alchemists projected their psyche into matter, Jung felt that modern man projected his inner state into the heavens. In this sense, the UFOs became modern symbols for the ancient Gods which came to man's assistance in time of need.

Like the ancient visitations, the modern UFOs and aliens appear to be just as real and tangible, possessing intelligence and will that seem to go beyond mere projections of the inner psyche; a force that is independent of human existence, yet somehow influenced by it on an intimate level. In other words, if you believe in gods, demons, witches, fairies or flying saucer people, some intelligence, unknown by modern science, will adopt these roles and exist as long as there are believers. When the belief structure becomes outdated or forgotten, the entities will simply assume some other guise to continue their existence.

A DRIVING FORCE

This could be the driving force of religion and other spiritual beliefs since the beginning of time. In the past, some unknown intelligence wanted us all to believe in the gods. When monasticism became all the rage, the phenomena changed with the times and produced beings such as angels, the Virgin Mary and other holy entities. Now they have traded in their chariots for sleek futuristic flying saucers. However, there are still plenty of old religious beliefs around to keep visitations by figures like the Virgin Mary busy appearing to children and other believers.

UFOS, ARMAGEDDON AND BIBLICAL REVELATIONS

The modern belief in extraterrestrial visitors springs not from the presentation of concrete evidence but from the repetition of the extraterrestrial "line" through thousands of contactees over the past seventy years or so. All of our religious beliefs have a similar basis, prophets who have allegedly talked with supernatural beings have spread the beliefs to the masses of people who have had no direct experiences with the phenomenon but are willing to accept the word of those who have.

It seems odd that aliens would be interested in our spiritual well-being. Richard Thompson writes in "Alien Identities" that extraterrestrials could be deliberately invoking mythological trappings to influence contacts. Thompson also theorizes that "UFO humanoids are not as alien to us as one might suppose. This is based on the argument that beings with humanlike form, humanlike emotions, and humanlike paranormal powers might be related to humans on a fundamental level."

The debate remains on just who or what is formulating this grand experience. From John Keel's mindless "Ultraterrestrials," Budd Hopkins big-eyed "Greys," Jacques Vallee's faceless "control group," Gordon Creighton's "Jinns," to Carl Jung's "projected collective psyche." All of these theories, on the surface, seem to offer viable explanations. Yet, none can totally claim to be the absolute truth. Perhaps portions from each can best explain the true nature of the phenomena.

Some have argued that the spiritual aspects of certain UFO contacts are nothing more than an intellectually superior race using our superstitions to hide their true intent and purposes. Barbara Marciniak, who claims to be channeling messages from Pleiadians, reports that the creatures told her: "We refuse to be your answer. Just when you think you have us pinned down, we'll tell you something else. No one belief system can encompass all of reality in a complex universe."

John Keel has often stressed the significance of belief structures as related to UFO phenomena. "The phenomenon is dependent on belief," Keel writes in "The Mothman Prophecies:" "As more and more people believe in flying saucers from other planets, the lower force can manipulate more people through false illumination. I have been watching, with great consternation, the worldwide spread of the UFO belief and its accompanying disease. If it continues unchecked we may face a time when universal acceptance of the fictitious space people will lead us to a modern faith in extraterrestrials that will enable them to interfere overtly in our affairs, just as the ancient gods ruled large segments of the population in the past."

While Keel may be overly alarmed about the process, his idea that there is a developing "faith" in extraterrestrials is almost certainly correct. Whether or not this faith is being postulated by true extraterrestrials, supernatural beings who mimic extraterrestrials, or our own unconscious minds, the fact remains that we are seeing an ancient process unfolding before us, with the creation of a new belief system, a new religion, as its ultimate goal.

THE WAR OF RELIGIONS

Since the early 1950s, a number of authors have postulated that UFOs may have connections to certain Christian beliefs and mythologies of the end times. The idea that UFOs and their occupants may actually be either angels or demons has captured the attention of many interested in religion and the UFO phenomena.

Either side of the debate can offer up substantial evidence to prove their point on the true nature of UFOs and their occupants. Christopher Montgomery in his manuscript "The Angel UFO Hypothesis," states that: "Many ministers believe that aliens are not actually from another planet, but are demons disguising themselves as aliens in flying saucers. What a nefarious plot; I can think of nothing more sinister. That they are devils and nothing good could come from a UFO. But what if I told you of an even more diabolical plot than that one. That would be that the fallen angels should try to convince us that they are from other planets, using UFO sightings to underscore their sincerity! This while knowing that the UFO is the only thing separating us from Satan's insatiable wrath. The Bible says that the fallen angel, Satan; '...walketh about, as a roaring lion, seeking whom he may devour.' Many people know that verse. But few are they that remember the rest of this famous passage. It says 'whom resist, steadfast in the faith!' We could take that one step further and say that UFOs are in fact angels, and further that this is just another example of the mysteries of the UFO and the Holy Bible paradigm."

Researcher John Thompson writes, "There is a definite God connection. As someone asked me, 'How do you know that 'they' don't come from an extraterrestrial dimension instead of a demonic one, I told him, I don't. But the truth is it does not really matter as nearly all alien reports fit with what religious writings have warned of for centuries. The aliens behind abductions are evil and the calling for help from God, if one believes in God, stops alien activity in the household or certainly brings it to a crawl.

"The fact that many modern Biblical scholars look upon UFO phenomena with mistrust should come to no surprise. Most religions exist in a state of perpetual hostility with each other, all believing that only their beliefs are the true path toward the Creator and salvation. It has been recognized by some experts that certain aspects in the belief of extraterrestrial UFOs have taken on a religious perspective. These emerging belief structures are seen as a threat to the current religious hierarchies and are thus attacked for being in league with Satan and unclean spirits – a not so dissimilar situation that greeted a newly-created Christian religion that suffered bloody attacks from the ruling government in Rome."

Early Christians were thought to be necromancers and demon-worshipers. It was widely reported that they conducted secret ceremonies that involved infanticide, blood sacrifices and cannibalism. This smear campaign was so successful that a persecuted Christianity was forced to essentially remain a "secret society" for centuries, conducting their religious ceremonies in secret caves and tombs. A condition that did little to improve their already tattered image among the pagan population.

Later, this same campaign of accusing other religions of demon-worshiping along with distasteful ceremonies was eagerly used by the Church to force their newly found dominance over the pagan religions. We can see this time honored tradition today as some religious writers express their viewpoint that UFOs and their occupants are actually demons under the guise of helpful space brothers.

A good example of the "Satan Flies the Saucers" belief can be found in the article "The Great Flying Saucer Myth" by Kelly G. Seagraves who writes: "What are these beings from outer space? I truly believe that we are being visited by beings that are extraterrestrial. I do not believe beings live on other planets. I believe that these visitors are fallen angels who have come to prepare the kingdom of the Antichrist on this planet. I believe these are the same sons of God who came to have relationships with the daughters of men either physically or through some type of possession in Genesis 6, and produced a race of people who did not believe in the true God. I believe the same signs and wonders contributed to the great destruction in the past, and perhaps the men of renown who were born of fallen angels, the mighty men and giants described in Genesis 6, helped contribute to the unbelief of multitudes before the flood. I believe this explains why when God judged and destroyed the race in the great flood these giants and mighty men of renown were no more.

"I believe this illustrates the fact that angels as revealed in the Bible, even fallen ones, have many powers, including the power of deception and others that we do not ordinarily attribute to them. Already Satanism is on the rise. The church of Satan worships openly, using the Satanic Bible. The belief in UFOs and aliens is simply another way of believing in and worshiping Satan."

ANGELS OR ALIENS

So could this all be true? Are UFOs and their occupants fallen angels who have taken on the guise of friendly space brothers – claiming to be here to help us, while actually after our immortal souls? Or is this merely disinformation from people fearful of different beliefs and religions, looking for ways to counteract the inevitable changes that take place as the centuries roll by?

The term "flying saucer religion" can be applied to a number of religious groups which invest alien contact with religious significance. Such contact is most often made on a psychic level with a member of an advanced alien race. Generally the benign aliens bring to the human race doctrine concerning spiritual advancement and eschatology. The beliefs of flying saucer religions are characteristically eclectic and often dovetail eastern and western traditions. This ecumenical feat is accomplished by identifying historic religious figures such as Jesus Christ and the Buddha Gautama with advanced alien beings. The New Testament is a key eschatological influence for most of these new religious movements, and both pre-millennial and post-millennial groups exist.

Flying saucer religions are new religious movements born of a common American history. Similar to other religions in their infancy, these new religious movements are formed as one or two leaders attract a small following. The leaders of these religions, termed contactees, are those who have established a steady contact with their space brothers. Through these contactees, followers have access to spiritual instruction which in turn prepares them for their cosmic eschatological expectations; replacing the role of contactee with that of a channeller results in a religious phenomenon analogous to spiritualism. This is no coincidence, since nearly all flying saucer religions are heavily influenced by Theosophy.

In this light, UFO religions, their origins, and their predecessors are relevant to modern religious history. These beliefs are of interest, because they reflect the more diverse manifestations of religious pluralism in the world.

Samuel Eaton Thompson was one of the first to take the flying saucer phenomenon to a new level. On March 28, 1950, Thompson claimed to have physically encountered and communicated with several Venusians in their spacecraft. While this encounter did not receive nationwide publicity, Thompson's encounter closely resembles later contact phenomena. The aliens told Thompson of the Second Coming of Christ in the year A.D. 10,000. These Venusians would arrive once again to enlighten the corrupt earthlings so that the path of Christ might be prepared. Such apocalyptic messages, whether pre-millennial or post-millennial, are a common feature of most contact accounts.

The most influential of the early contactees was George Adamski, a California occultist. Adamski made physical contact with his first Venusian on November 20, 1952, in a California desert. Adamski later wrote several popular books which detailed his contact experiences and included drawings of aliens and spacecraft. Adamski's books borrowed heavily from the works of the Theosophist Madame Blavatsky. The Theosophical interpretation of alien contact is an approach used by most flying saucer religions.

Shortly after Adamski published his first book, many other contactees appeared on the scene. Some contactees communicated with aliens while in their physical presence, although most channeled messages from the aliens through telepathy or automatic writing. Possessing a steady contact with the alien entity, the channellers were the contactees most likely to gather a following.

The earliest influential flying saucer group was the Heralds of the New Age founded in the 1950s and located in New Zealand. It was Gloria Lee, backed by the Cosman Research Foundation, who really launched the extraterrestrial channeling movement in the U.S. Lee relayed the messages of J. W., an alien from Jupiter, through frequent newsletters and two highly Theosophical books titled "Why We are Here" and "The Changing Condition of Your World."

Having received spacecraft construction plans from J. W., Lee traveled to Washington in 1962 so that she might present them to the U.S. government. Until she heard from the government, J. W. instructed Lee to fast while locked in a hotel room. After sixty-six days, Gloria Lee lapsed into a coma and died several days later. Gloria Lee's death was, however, far from insignificant. Many new flying saucer groups were inspired to organize shortly thereafter, and existing ones began to channel her spirit.

DEMONS FROM THE STARS

Why have UFOs and the belief in extraterrestrials garnered so much interest and concern in this day and age? Strange, glowing objects flying about in the sky are nothing new as most surviving ancient writings will attest. So why should we now suddenly start paying attention to something that has been occurring apparently since the beginning of time?

Some Biblical scholars speculate that interest in UFOs is at an all-time high because of what is referred to as "the end-time delusion." That "non-human" intelligences, disguised as space people, are infiltrating our society with the intention of placing the "Antichrist" in a position of world power sometime in the near future. This viewpoint is predominately embraced by fundamentalist Christian groups in the United States who eagerly look for any evidence that the end of the world will happen soon. These groups, certain of their own perfection over the rest of the world, have even gone as far as to fund terrorist operations in the U.S. and Israel in order to speed up the process of Armageddon.

One website that advocates the belief in Satanic UFOs glibly states: "The spiritual development of mankind has been guided by nonhuman intelligences whose agenda has been to infiltrate, and even instigate, religious traditions in all cultures. These nonhuman intelligences are now pretending to be enlightening aliens. Legends of cultures ranging from Babylonian to Hindu to Native American are laden with beings who possess superior technology, spiritual beings enjoying worship and reverence in exchange for distributing wisdom."

Guy Malone in his book "Come Sail Away: UFO Phenomena & The Bible" (1998 Seekye1.com), writes that any belief system other than the Bible is inherently Satanic in nature: "The true issue at hand here is not whether UFO and 'visitor' happenings are real or not. I believe that they are. The issue is whether they really are extraterrestrial life forms, here to help us, or demons, with the express purpose of deceiving multitudes. Jesus said that we could recognize a tree by the fruit it bears (Matt 7:15, Sermon on the Mount) ... there are, all over the Bible, descriptions of demonic forces that have the specific task of 'blinding the minds of unbelievers (2 Cor 4:4, earlier)' so that they will not be able to believe the gospel when it is preached to them. Almost all the books on UFOs are found in the New Age section of your local bookstore. Examine the fruit of the UFO culture. Does it lead people to Jesus? Do you know of any strong adherents to the UFO culture, who believe aliens are among us, that are also Bible-believing Christians? If you have a strong interest in UFOs, are you a Christian? Generally, those who have a strong faith in UFOs also have a non-Christian belief system that would be described as New Age."

What these writers fail to realize is that UFOs and UFO sightings enjoy a rich tradition in the Bible that was embraced by the writers and readers alike as evidence of God's rich tapestry of creation. These Biblical miracles were not considered to be Satanic, but instead were seen as evidence of God's true love for us and the ultimate mystery of life.

THE NEW MILLENNIUM RELIGION

I almost hate to use the term "New Millennium" since it has already been used to such excess that it has become clichéd. However, it best describes what may be in store for future generations: A religion that uses a belief in space people as its divine emissaries. If you look back at the creation of all of the world's religions you will find striking similarities in their development and the growth and belief of UFOs and aliens.

All major religions generally start out as another religion's heresy. The Hebrew faith was a heresy from the earlier pagan religions, and Christianity was certainly considered a Jewish heresy. The new religions developed from the roots of the old, and they carried with them various doctrines of belief to insure their continued existence.

This process is propagated by the visionary experiences of prophets and their contacts with divine beings. These entities deliver messages of spiritual teachings and prophecies for the ever growing faithful. This system occurs rapidly at first, but then tapers off to a slower but sustained growth that may take hundreds of years to fully develop. This is exactly what we have experienced this century with the UFO phenomena. The next several centuries will show whether the UFO religion will be able to sustain itself. Its disciples, due to their faith in friendly space people awaiting us in the cosmos, may be responsible for the scientific developments that will finally propel mankind off the planet and into the universe…something that may be the ultimate goal of whatever is controlling the process.

The day will come when somewhere out in space mankind will finally run across another civilization. At that time we may ask them why they have been flying around in our skies all these years with their flying saucers. Their response could very well be: "Us? We thought it was you flying around our skies!"

Tim Swartz traveled to the Middle East to explore the pyramids and scope out the existence of UFOs in ancient and modern times in this part of the world.

UFOS, ARMAGEDDON AND BIBLICAL REVELATIONS

Brad Baker said he saw Jesus inside and later standing beside a UFO. He might have been teleported onboard.

Jesus in the clouds in Argentina. To some the Second Coming has already begun!

UFOS, ARMAGEDDON AND BIBLICAL REVELATIONS

New Jersey-based Howard and Connie Menger were at the forefront of the 1950s and 60s contactee movement, which involved UFO beings who were very "Godlike" in appearance.

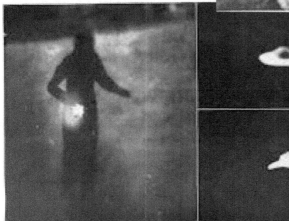

The Mengers took many photos of the space ships and their friendly occupants in the apple orchard behind their rural home in Highbridge, NJ.

Left: Space woman walks toward the author. Just after she reached thisy gadget on belt she disappeared. A space man standing near her said she had returned to the craft. Upper and lower right: Spacecraft in flight at night.

Carl Jung did not dismiss the existence of UFOs out of hand.

To many, the occupants of UFOs are seen as the "space gods," as depicted by inspirational artist Carol Ann Rodriguez.

12

RETURN OF THE SON OF MAN IN THE CLOUDS
By Professor G. C. Schellhorn

The number of references in the Old and New Testament to clouds and the return of the Son of Man is surprising, even startling. Once we have become aware of the close relationship between clouds and spacecraft found in the scriptures, and add to that realization the fact that the Son of Man is prophesied to return "on the clouds," the implication becomes stunning, to say the least.

These references begin in the Old Testament. For instance, in the Book of Daniel:

"I saw in the night visions, and behold, with the clouds of heaven there came one like a son of man, and he came to the Ancient of Days and was presented before him. And to him was given dominion and glory and kingdom, that all peoples, nations, and languages should serve him; his dominion is an everlasting dominion, which shall not pass away, and his kingdom one that shall not be destroyed."

Daniel 7:13-14

We are told not only that "with the clouds of heaven there came one like a son of man" but that this son of man "was given dominion and glory and kingdom." This dominion "is an everlasting dominion" and it "shall not pass away" and "not be destroyed." Here we have, as Bible scholars well know, an obvious reference to the messiah, either to Jesus, if one is a Christian, or to a messiah yet to appear for the first time, if one is Hebrew. If one is Buddhist, Hindu or Hopi, it is also a repeat of an earlier phenomenon. Some Moslems likewise look forward to the appearance of a special Mahdi to set aright a confused and increasingly godless world.

That this messiah will not (again) come tenderly is made quite clear in Isaiah:

"For behold, the Lord will come in fire, and his chariots like the storm wind, to render his anger in fury, and his rebuke with flames of fire. For by fire will the Lord execute judgment, and by his sword, upon all flesh; and those slain by the

Lord shall be many."

Are these "chariots like the storm wind" unfamiliar? We have already seen so many examples of them associated, as here, with "fire." The remaking of the Earth this time is not by water but fire. Aren't we quite logical, then, under the circumstances, in wondering if this fire might not be atomic fire unleashed by our own hand and precipitating a nuclear holocaust?

In Matthew we are told how Jesus leads Peter, John and James, his brother, up a high mountain:

"And he was transfigured before them, and his face shone like the sun, and his garments became white as light. And behold, there appeared to them Moses and Elijah, talking with him. And Peter said to Jesus, 'Lord, it is well that we are here; if you wish, I will make three booths here, one for you and one for Moses and one for Elijah.' He was still speaking, when lo, a bright cloud overshadowed them, and a voice from the cloud said, 'This is my beloved Son, with whom I am well pleased; listen to him.' When the disciples heard this, they fell on their faces, and were filled with awe. But Jesus came and touched them, saying, 'Rise, and have no fear.' And when they lifted up their eyes, they saw no one but Jesus only."

Matthew 17:2-8

Several things about this passage should give us pause for thought. No wonder the disciples are filled with "awe." What they are seeing is extraordinary. The "bright cloud," it makes sense to assume, is reference to a hovering spacecraft. The commander of the craft communicates with ground level by means of a loud-speaker. Undoubtedly those at ground level who had never seen a spacecraft reflecting the sun and heard a voice emanating from it would be very impressed, even overwhelmed. The disciples surely are. They "fell on their faces." Not only is the man they follow extraordinary, but he leads them literally and figuratively to extraordinary, out-of-this world experiences.

Now, we have got to ask, just where in the world did Moses and Elijah come from? This is the same Moses who talked directly with "God" well over a thousand years before Jesus was born. This is the very same Elijah who also talked with "God" and who was translated (transported) at last out of this world, perhaps aboard a spacecraft, just as Enoch had been. The easy answer is to say, God can do anything. The skeptic might say the disciples are experiencing an optical illusion or a mass hallucination – that the bright sun got to them this particular day.

I don't pretend to know for sure all the answers to the questions this puzzling scene raises. But I have some ideas. They have to do with the dilation of time effect at high speeds, which is an accepted fact among our scientists today. We need to understand that as speeds approach closer to the speed of light, such as in a fast moving (or orbiting) spacecraft, the passage of time, as we know it on Earth, slows. A living physical body traveling at, say, 100,000 miles per second in a spacecraft ages less quickly, much slower than the same body or a like body left on Planet Earth. All of this can be calculated mathematically, of course, according to formulae. Time is a variable product, it would seem, depending upon the mix of energy, speed and distance. So what are we really saying, then?

The time dilation effect can lead to some startling results. Our children may fly off someday to visit stars and planets many light-years from Earth. When they return, only a few years or decades older, Earth will have aged tens of thousands of years. It would indeed be a different world, unrecognizable perhaps, with no chance of seeing past acquaintances and loved ones. In a way, Thomas Wolfe, the novelist, was far more accurate than he himself knew for our space travelers when he titled one work, "You Can't Go Home Again."

What does all this have to do with Peter's and James' and John's experience? Simply this. It is scientifically possible that they were actually looking at the original Moses and Elijah. If Moses and Elijah were transported in body aboard a spacecraft more than a millennium before, and that craft had been flying at speeds close to the speed of light, or even beyond it, they would only be a few years older at the most than they had been when first taken aboard ship. And Jesus Christ, if he returned today or in the near future as commander of a space fleet come to usher in a New Age and sweep out the old, could have, if he chose to, the same body he had two thousand years ago and it would have aged only slightly.

The same could be said of Viracocha, an ancient astronaut who visited the Incas, or Buetzalcoatl, probably another extraterrestrial visitor, who influenced the Mayas and Aztecs greatly before taking his leave. The same principle would apply to any space visitor from our ancient past. Theoretically, any one of them could return to us today only slightly older and, one assumes, as fit and in as fine fettle as of yore.

The scene on the mountain suggests even more. Moses and Elijah and Jesus are working together, as if there is a plan, as if details and strategies are being worked out. And things are being done in the sight of these three disciples, who will record the vision and spread it over the world with the passage of time. Even to us, today. Once again we have evidence that extraterrestrial activity is the guiding hand for much of what transpires on Earth, certainly for much of what happened in biblical times.

The idea of Jesus as an ancient astronaut, an enlightened entity from here or elsewhere who embodied as a human to live as an example to men and to teach and preach the potentiality within man, the kingdom to come that is realizable and which is the destiny of man if he wishes to be – that idea is supported by more evidence than many people, including theologians and governments, would like to believe. Didn't the Master say after all, "You are from below, I am from above; you are of this world, I am not of this world"? (John 8:23)

UFOS, ARMAGEDDON AND BIBLICAL REVELATIONS

That "coming with the clouds of heaven," as Mark quotes the Master as saying, (Mark 14:62) threatens too many vested interests, just as it called into question the lifestyle of the masses and the theological and governmental practices of the era in which he walked the Earth. He was preaching the kingdom to come, the style of life of a future New Age. He was not preaching himself, making himself into a cultish ritual as churches are wont to do with him today. The focus has been shifted and dangerously so. The governments of men, no matter how pathetic they may be, do not wish to relinquish their power over the destiny of men's lives. The churches, long corrupted, preach guilt and fear mixed with ritual, not real new life through the perfection of the mind and spirit of man under the tutelage of wiser, cosmic intelligence. The vision that present day popular government and popular religion hold out for man, amidst their squabbling, is a rather nebulous materialistic present, supported by false advertising and an inferior product, wedded to a future lacking spiritual growth and personal responsibility. The Master knew what man's true potential was and came to remind him in spite of what false priests and false governments might tell him:

"Truly, truly, I say to you, he who believes in me will also do the works that I do; and greater works than these will he do, because I go to the Father."

John 14:12

It would appear that man's true potential is to develop mind and spirit to the degree that he can "do the works that I do; and greater works than these." There is no magic here.

Cosmic laws are inviolable. Miracles happen when someone does something, using his greater knowledge of cosmic law, and it astounds the less knowledgeable in his presence. When man has reached the spiritual growth level that makes him capable and worthy of such knowledge, he will be the total master of the material world, capable of doing things that he thought formerly impossible or the doings of gods only:

"For truly, I say to you, If you have faith as a grain of mustard seed, you will say to this mountain, 'Move hence to yonder place,' and it will move, and nothing will be impossible to you."

Yes, even move mountains. "Nothing will be impossible to you." That is the promise. In fact, the Master Jesus of Nazareth made additional reference to the potentiality of developing man when he said: "Is it not written in your law, 'I said, you are gods.'"

John 10:34

He is quoting the 82nd Psalm ascribed to the seer Asaph, companion to David:

"They have neither knowledge nor understanding, they walk about in dark-

145

ness; all the foundations of the Earth are shaken. I say, 'You are gods, sons of the Most High, all of you; nevertheless, you shall die like men, and fall like any prince.'"

Psalms 82:5-7

The great message to men, who have been developed and guided by enlightened extraterrestrials whose mission was to help a fledgling species rise out of savagery, that great message is the destiny of their own godliness, equaling the spiritual and mental development even of those who nurtured them. It is a destiny with potential seemingly without limit. One recalls again the words of the "Lord" in Genesis:

"And the Lord said, 'Behold, they are one people, and they have all one language; and this is only the beginning of what they will do; and nothing that they propose to do will now be impossible for them.'"

Genesis 11:6

But there are certain conditions. There is danger along the way. The psalmist says, "nevertheless, you shall die like men, and fall like any prince." Like any mortal prince. It appears that man is seen by the psalmist as yet an imperfect creation, a transitional being, and at his present state of development, he is heir to his human mortality. He is not guaranteed everlasting life, as are the true Sons of God. The Master in his references to the 82nd Psalm does not contradict him. But he offers the vision, the future. The danger is ego and selfishness.

The "serpent" in the Garden of Eden knew the potential of man:

"But the serpent said to the woman, 'You will not die. For God knows that when you eat of it your eyes will be opened, and you will be like God, knowing good and evil.'"

Genesis 3:4-5

Ah! To be like God'! To know so much! The danger to man is double pronged. He can be slothful and lazy, a Russian Oblomov who sleeps his life away and his opportunities for mental and spiritual growth. Or, like Goethe's Dr. Faust, he can insist on learning things which are counterproductive or which he is not mentally and spiritually developed enough to cope with successfully. Thus we have the extraterrestrial commander in Genesis putting a break to man's premature attempt to reach the heavens:

"And the Lord said, 'Behold, they are one people, and they have all one language, and this is only the beginning of what they will do; and nothing that they propose to do will now be impossible for them. Come, let us go down, and there confuse their language, that they may not understand one another's speech.' So the Lord scattered them abroad from there over the face of all the Earth, and they left off building the city."

Genesis 11:6-8

UFOS, ARMAGEDDON AND BIBLICAL REVELATIONS

But man insists on reaching for the heavens. He will not long be put off. There is something innate in him that makes him reach out and upward to understand the world, the universe and its Creative Force, to imitate creation and emulate his God. Perhaps no one has written better of this relentless urge of man's spirit to strive upwards than the fourteenth century German mystic, Meister Eckhart:

"Even so the mind, unsatisfied with infernal light, will press through the firmament and press through the heavens to find the breath that spins them. Yet this does not satisfy it. It must press farther into the vortex, into the primal region where the breath has its source. Such a mind knows no time nor number: number does not exist apart from the malady of time. Other root, the mind has none save in eternity, it must surpass all number and break through multiplicity. Then it will be itself broken through by God, but just as God breaks through me, so I again break through Him. God leads this spirit into the wilderness and into the oneness of its own self..." (Translated by C. de B. Evans)

The New Testament is filled with references to the enlightened messiah coming "on the clouds" to set man's striving, which has lost its direction, back on course:

"Immediately after the tribulation of those days the sun will be darkened, and the moon will not give its light, and the stars will fall from heaven, and the powers of the heavens will be shaken; then will appear the sign of the Son of man in heaven, and then all the tribes of the Earth will mourn, and they will see the Son of man coming on the clouds of heaven with power and great glory; and he will send out his angels with a loud trumpet call, and they will gather his elect from the four winds, from one end of heaven to the other."

Matthew 24:29-31

In the Gospel of Matthew, after a description of great Earth changes, perhaps even an axis shift, the messiah is seen "coming on the clouds of heaven with power...." Is it presumptuous to suggest that the gathering of "his elect from the four winds" has not already begun? The increased UFO activity of the last few years which is worldwide in scope makes this idea distinctly possible, if not probable.

The Gospel of Luke also speaks of the messiah coming out of the clouds:

"And there will be signs in sun and moon and stars, and upon the Earth distress of nations in perplexity at the roaring of the sea and the waves, men fainting with fear and with foreboding of what is coming on the world; for the powers of the heavens will be shaken. And then they will see the Son of man coming in a cloud with power and great glory. Now when these things begin to take place, look up and raise your heads, because your redemption is drawing near."

Luke 21:25-28

UFOS, ARMAGEDDON AND BIBLICAL REVELATIONS

First we have another indication of great Earth changes preceding the event. Then the Son of Man comes "in a cloud." Must we be so literal as to suppose, as so many theologians do, that this particular day is simply overcast or that the clouds somehow represent a metaphor for "great glory"? It seems as likely or more likely that the "cloud" is biblical language for either extraterrestrial craft or the cloud cover they manufacture or use to veil themselves, evidence of which is plentiful from both past and present.

When Paul writes in I Thessalonians, he uses similar language to Matthew and Luke:

"... then we who are alive, who are left, shall be caught up together with them in the clouds to meet the Lord in the air; and so we shall always be with the Lord."

1 Thessalonians 4:17

The traditional explanation for these statements is vague and unsatisfying, usually a sketchy idea of some kind of divine supernatural levitation about which we aren't supposed to ask too many embarrassing questions. However, the ability of present-day extraterrestrial craft to transport or levitate physical bodies, including cows, cars and men, from ground level into a hovering craft has been witnessed or experienced by more than one person. (See Andrews' "Extraterrestrials Among Us" and Hopkins' "Intruders.") It makes sense to view this kind of scene in a new light. Then we can visualize the apotheosized Adam, Jesus Christ, arriving with his extraterrestrial friends to aid the elect and the "first fruits" in the extremity of the moment. These individuals are to be saved not only because of their spiritual attainment but also possibly to help reestablish, and repopulate, a better new Earth. They are "caught up together in the clouds to meet the Lord in the air." The "Lord in the air" is the messiah, the Christ. And he is aboard a spacecraft, with other spacecraft hovering near to carry out the plan, to bring to fruition the Great Experiment.

Finally, we need to take a look at Revelation and what it tells us about the messiah coming out of the clouds. It will serve as a kind of capstone to our discussion of Jesus Christ, messiah and astronaut.

St. John gives us the most dramatic pictures of the returning messiah. Early on in Revelation, we get our first glimpse: "Behold, he is coming with the clouds, and every eye will see him, everyone who pierced him; and all tribes of the Earth will wail on account of him. Even so. Amen."

Revelation 1:7

The "clouds" will be with him. Here again we have the use of a plural. There is more than one craft. There is a fleet. "Every eye will see him." Already, a large number of human beings have seen UFOs with their own eyes. The Gallup polls taken in the past are quite revealing about the public attitude toward the "phenomenon." The 1966 poll indicated that 40% of the population believed that UFOs are real. By 1984 the figure had jumped to 80%. We might suppose that with the increased exposure the population has had to UFOs – and a planned one, it would seem, like a gradual acclimating – that the appearance of a fleet of spacecraft during the calamitous happenings of an "end time" situation would be not only awe inspiring but also something that the eyes and minds of the masses would recognize as being biblically related and then draw the appropriate conclusions.

"Then I looked, and lo, a white cloud, and seated on the cloud one like a son of man, with a golden crown on his head, and a sharp sickle in his hand."

Revelation 14:14

The description gets more specific now. The "cloud" is a "white cloud" and one "like a son of man," an extraterrestrial follower of the messiah, is actually "seated on the cloud." Seated in the "cloud," in the craft would be a more accurate translation, but the meaning seems clear enough, unless someone wishes to maintain that the "man" is sitting on fleecy billows of wispy air just before he helps clean up Mother Earth's house.

Revelation continues with its own description of the "end time" and the Earth changes accompanying the moment. Then in chapter nineteen we are given a final striking account of the descent of the messiah himself to earth:

"And the angel said to me, 'Write this: Blessed are those who are invited to the marriage supper of the Lamb.' And he said to me, 'These are true words of God.' Then I fell down at his feet to worship him, but he said to me, 'You must not do that! I am a fellow servant with you and your brethren who hold the testimony of Jesus. Worship God' For the testimony of Jesus is the spirit of prophecy. Then I saw heaven opened, and behold, a white horse! He who sat upon it is called Faithful and True, and in righteousness he judges and makes war."

Revelation 19:9-11

Notice that the angel-crewman accompanying the messiah cautions John not to worship the crew members themselves, which man was so accustomed to doing in biblical times, making gods out of extraterrestrial craft commanders and crewmen alike. He is only a fellow servant, like John and his brethren. "Worship God," he advises. This "God" of which the "angel" speaks is not an extraterrestrial spaceship commander, I take it, but the real thing, the Greater God of both earthlings and extraterrestrials alike. And one of his servants is the man who overcame the most adversity on Earth, perfected himself so well that he achieved a greater oneness with this Greater God in his Earth life (lives) and perhaps existences elsewhere than any entity who has walked the paths of this world – this Jesus the Master who became the Christ.

"Behold, a white horse!" The "heavens opened" and he who is called "Faithful and True," the messiah, descends. The "white horse" analogy, which I take to be another attempt to describe and make acceptable the spacecraft idea to an earlier mankind, is repeated in Indian scriptures (in Krishna's, the Kali avatar's, return), the Maitreya Buddha's appearance, the Mazdean savior Sosiosh's appearance and others. Could it be that it is not accidental that these various religions have so much in common in the descriptions of the return of their avatars, of the appearance of their messiahs? The temptation is to say that the cultural impetus to believe in such returns is not accidental but has a distant though similar factual base from which to build the existence of extraterrestrial visitors who paved the way for their return.

SUGGESTED READING

WHEN MEN ARE GODS

DISCOVERING THE LOST PYRAMID

BALD EAGLE BOOK

SURVIVING CATASTROPHIC EARTH CHANGES

THE WHITE SANDS INCIDENT - DAN FRY STORY

PSYCHIC AND UFO REVELATIONS FOR THE TWENTY FIRST CENTURY

PROF. G. COPE SCHELLHORN

When not hunting for UFOs and waxing philosophical on scripture, Prof. G. C. Schellhorn is an author and publisher and professional bird photographer. Schellhorn has launched a website named Bird Photos Gallery Bank. The site features over 300 digital bird photos taken over a period of 14 years and sets a high standard for the growing field of bird photography...

G.C.'s most popular book – "Extraterrestrials in Biblical Prophecy."

Daniel 7:13, New International Version (NIV). 13 "In my vision at night I looked, and there before me was one like a son of man, coming with the clouds of heaven."

Some see Ashtar, the commander of a fleet of UFOs sent here to save the Earth, as comparable to the Second Coming of Jesus. Some proclaim him to be the Earthly embodiment of the Christ.

Many channeled works proclaim the coming of friendly "Space Brothers," and some believe they stand with Jesus in a parallel dimension.

13

THE HOPI PROPHECIES
By Timothy Green Beckley

I have visited the Hopi reservation several times with my dear friend Chris Franz Dickey, who unfortunately is now deceased.

I first met Chris at the University of Wyoming at Laramie while lecturing there for Dr. Leo Sprinkle's UFO and abduction group. His was an annual event and people from all over the western states attended. I had to drive from God knows where because the local airport is so small that planes only fly in and out of the town several days a week and none would work into my schedule.

I sat at the bar after unpacking as I wanted to relax and get the lay of the land. Turns out two ladies next to me were talking about the forthcoming program and mentioned my name. What an ego booster. Of course I introduced myself. What would you have done?

Jackie Blue ended up living on my property in Colorado for several years while Chris managed the place since I was an absentee owner. But this isn't about real estate. This is about prophecy and all things related.

After shaking hands and ordering us all a round, I asked Chris why she was attending the conference. She explained that she had been placed under hypnosis by Dr. Sprinkle to recall certain "things" that had happened to her. Chris, on several occasions, had seen UFOs land on the ranch of Pat McGuire outside Bosler, Wyoming. Pat was your typical cattle rancher until he came across a couple of mutilated cattle. Later he had an ongoing series of UFO contact experiences and his visitor friends had told him where to drill for water, which he successfully did. The press said it was like he had located "an underground river."

Chris said a UFO had even hovered right above the hood of her car while out driving near Pat's property. She had begun to have a series of dreams in which an eagle had appeared and she had been led to the Hopi reservation to talk with a shaman as to the meaning of her nocturnal vision. You can find her full experience in "The American Indian Star-Seed Connection," which I edited with additional contributions by Brad Steiger and Diane Tessman – two of our faithful "regulars."

Later on, I returned to visit with Chris and we drove together out to Second Mesa, which I found out firsthand is located on a rather desolate part of the Hopi Reservation, atop the 6000 foot mesa with a population of just around a thousand who reside in three isolated villages, Musungnuvi, Supawlavi, and Songoopavi. The Hopi Cultural Center on Second Mesa. is the hub of activity, attracting visitors looking primarily for Native American jewelry. I got a wonderful silver bracelet made by one of the local craftsmen that is so spectacular and one of a kind. The Kachina Dolls that some say look like "aliens" also are a must if you are a fan of ancient astronauts. During certain ceremonies, the residents don costumes like the Kachina and if you are lucky you might be welcome to one of their powwows, like I was. Chris had already established contacts on the reservation as she was part Native American.

There had been a scad of UFO sightings around the Mesa in the early 1970s. And some predictions made that the much heralded "Purification Day" was to come soon, being ushered in by the "True White Brother's" arrival from the sky. They were coming, it was said, to warn and save the "Faithful Ones" from the "purification to come." Some of the shamans claimed that they were successfully making contact with the "sky people" as they were best known among tribal members. One of the elders, "Chief Dan," who was said to be over one hundred, was a spokesperson for this group.

We did a bit of sky-watching at night. Ate at a local Indian restaurant adjacent to the Hopi Cultural Center (love that Indian corn meal bread), and visited with one of the medicine men who gave us the most wicked tasting "cure all potion." I was told I had to drink it on the spot or it would be insulting to the shaman. Down the hatch it went! I guess what doesn't kill you cures you. That seems to be the best philosophy to go by under the circumstances.

I did learn about the prophecies of the Hopi, both from Chris and from Brad Steiger, who, though of Scandinavian heritage, was initiated into the Seneca tribe as a medicine man, thus becoming one of the few "non-blood brothers" so honored.

HOPI PROPHETS ATTEMPT TO GO BEFORE THE U.N.

As we have repeatedly tried to communicate throughout this book, it is not one particular sect, cult or religious denomination that is responsible for these forecasts of doom. Just about every culture on Earth seems to realize that we are treading on very dangerous ground, and that the future looks quite bleak.

For example, the Hopi feel strongly about this subject. Several years ago the Hopi Indian prophets attempted to get inside the United Nations in New York, where they hoped to present their findings regarding the End Times (based upon

UFOS, ARMAGEDDON AND BIBLICAL REVELATIONS

a sacred stone tablet which the tribe has had for many generations) to the General Assembly, and ask that the White Man's ways be mended before it is too late. Said Chief Dan Katchongva, "Many people, living at this time, will live to see the White Brother return to the Earth, and when they do they will live to consider what they could have heard if they had permitted the original inhabitants of these, the Americas, to give a message to that great body of people."

Chief Katchongva was not allowed to deliver his End Times message to the U.N. delegates, and for this he voiced his sad concern. The following Hopi prophecies are given as signs by this American Indian tribe that we should all be aware of:

1. A SERIES OF EARTHQUAKES WILL BE FELT THROUGHOUT THIS LAND, AND WILL COME AS WARNINGS TO THE PEOPLE TO REPENT, IF THEY DO NOT HEED THESE WARNINGS AND REPENT BEFORE IT IS TOO LATE, A BAD EARTHQUAKE WILL STRIKE, DEVASTATING MANY CITIES AND RESULT IN THE DEATH OF LARGE MASSES OF PEOPLE.

2. FLOODS WILL BE SEEN IN PLACES WHERE THEY HAVE NEVER BEEN SEEN BEFORE.

3. THERE WILL BE A GREAT CLIMATE CHANGE WORLDWIDE; HOT/COLD, DRY/WET, IN EACH CASE IT WILL BE THE WORST IN RECORDED HISTORY.

4. THERE WILL BE FAMINE, PESTILENCE, DISEASE, AND PLAGUE THROUGHOUT THE LAND.

5. THE HOPI WERE WARNED NEVER TO DEPEND UPON GREAT INVENTIONS THAT WOULD BE BROUGHT TO THEM BY THE WHITE RACE, THEY WERE TOLD THAT A LIGHTING SYSTEM WOULD BE ESTABLISHED THROUGHOUT THE LAND, AND ALL ONE HAD TO DO WAS TOUCH THE WALL TO LIGHT THE ROOM, HOWEVER, ONE DAY, WE WERE TOLD, THIS SYSTEM WOULD BE CUT OFF AT ONCE, AND THE PEOPLE WOULD BE LEFT IN PANIC. WE WERE ALSO WARNED AGAINST RUNNING WATER THAT WOULD COME INTO OUR HOMES. THIS WATER WILL BE POLLUTED AND ANYONE DEPENDING ON IT WILL DIE OR GET TERRIBLY SICK.

6. THERE WILL BE TERRIBLE FIGHTING ALL OVER THE LAND, CITY AGAINST CITY, VILLAGE AGAINST VILLAGE, AND FAMILY AGAINST FAMILY, THE HOPI WERE WARNED TO STAY ON THEIR RESERVATION.

7. THE MOON WILL TURN TO BLOOD, AND THE SUN WILL HIDE ITS FACE WITH SHAME.

8. THE SEASONS WILL CHANGE, AND ICE WILL FLOW FROM THE NORTH COUNTRIES.

The Hopis believe that a messiah, a true white brother wearing a red cap and red cloak, will return to the Earth and will try to straighten out our affairs for us. Apparently, the Hopis are quite familiar with UFOs, and have seen them many times hovering over their hunting grounds and later near their reservations. Their legends take into consideration the fact that we are not the only intelligent beings to reside in God's universe. Many great American Indian leaders have developed as spiritual leaders in the last few years, and there are an ever-increasing number of New Agers who are starting to accept the idea that the American Indian may at least be in part responsible for the safety of many during the coming turbulence.

Sun Bear and Rolling Thunder have spoken widely on this theme and their writings have become very popular. Harley Swiftdeer has lectured widely on the theme of the Red Man in prophecy and the increasing role of the medicine man - or shaman. A true visionary, Swiftdeer has, along with other Native American seers, put together a picture of what is to occur between now and the year 2000.

"These prophecies," says Harley Swiftdeer, "are a dream that is potential reality. It is not an ultimatum. But it is ours to behold and to create if we only dare to dream it together."

THE VISION

"The next few years are critical. And the reason for this is that for three years seeds of light have been planted and we are starting to grow and the teachings are starting to come out and all those ones inside each of the Eight Great Powers who have taught partial truths, who have taught deliberate lies in myth, who have used the power of wheels to gain control of people to gain followers, to gain disciples, to gain devotees, are going to be very threatened by the awakening of the consciousness of the Rainbow People because the Rainbow People exist in every country, in every nation, in every land.

"In other words, the Sun Dancers are going to be strong enough. The dark forces will be extremely threatened and they will use their power and their power exists in technology. We are going to see some of the strongest technological advances known to humanity, and these very technological advances are going to be a tremendous threat as well as a blessing to the survival of humanity. Now, what is also a Heyoka (trickster) is that we must establish balance and harmony between the light and the dark forces. It's going to be interesting and that's why we have this sense of urgency because it is getting short.

"Grace Walking Stick is the head seer and visionary of the Black Widow Society. She said there will be a major crisis to put us on the brink of nuclear war and the only thing that will stop it – that is, that the dark force is trying to create an artificial sun nuclear war – that we must exert the influence, the Sun Dancers, the Rainbow People, by smoking our pipes, of gathering together and of sharing our medicine for solar power, for world peace. And, whatever else happens, we MUST NOT give energy in protesting or being against something, because, if you take the amount of energy you spend marching, talking, writing letters against things and instead put an equal amount or double amount of energy with what you are for, we can change it. Example: Instead of protesting uranium, promote solar.

"If we get through this period, then there will be more teachers, and more teachings brought out to open view than has ever been seen on this planet in the first fifty thousand years. Because then we will reestablish contact in a very knowledgeable way with our ancestors from the stars. So mark that down, because it will happen. The first wave will come from Pleiades and will be totally acknowledged and will be known by all the world powers. The second wave will come from Sirius.

"Ruby Morning Star was the head seer of the Crystal Skull Society. She said that you will see a total change in the concept of what we call the United Nations. Instead of political opposition and struggle it will change names and become the new circle of law- the Eight Great Powers.

"When Tagashala and the enlightened teachers begin to open the veil of the crack between the worlds, we will see our memory circles. All Kivas and sacred power spots will come alive and be totally awakened. The inner room of the Great Pyramid will be opened. The Order of the Golden Dawn will have ceremonies there again for the first time in 20,000 years. The Temple of the Sun in Palenque will be refurbished, reawakened, and ceremonies will begin. The old traditional ceremonies that are still applicable for today's world will be renewed. Many of the ceremonies that are performed by so-called 'traditionalists,' who are trying to keep us locked in the past and will not function today, will fall. It will be hard for some of the people of the medicine societies because they don't know any other way. They're going to have to change or die. Many teachers who have been seen as great teachers, who have literally kept us in the dark as worshippers of the sacrament orders, will physically die and go over because it's the only way they can find the light in 1986. Many teachers will be seen for what they were and they will be the farmers, the laborers, and the gas station attendants and they will be seen as the real teachers because the Tagashala will be fully awakened.

ENLIGHTENED TEACHERS

"At this point, 144,000 Sun Dance enlightened teachers will totally awaken in their dream mind-bodies. They will begin to meet in their own feathered serpent or winged serpent wheels and become a major force of the light to help the rest of humanity to dance their dream awake. A Sun Dance teacher is any human being who has awakened, who has balanced their shields. Who has gained the dream mind-body and who honors all paths, all teachers, and all ways. I look for the day when I can sit down with my pipe and the Buddhists with theirs. You will see me sit down with my dagger and my Sufi drum, with my sword, my Shinto way, and my pipe, my Indian way.

"We're going to put our Soul out on the table and say 'I love you all.' This is a sacred dance. That's what 1987 is about. That's a Sun Dancer. You cannot say that you have the only true way, for all ways are true. In 1987, 144,000 enlightened Souls will sit down in gathering together circles saying 'Here it is, Brothers and Sisters. Openly, totally. Come and receive it.' A lot of these are going to be so-called common people and not the teachers you see up there now. On August 17, 1987 the various winged serpent wheels will begin to turn, to dance once again and when they do the Rainbow Lights will be seen in dreams all over the world and those Rainbow Light dreams will help awaken the rest of humanity.

"We will sit in a new circle of law. Civil and social law will tumble. All civil and social laws by whatever governments will have to be in conformity with natural law or the people will not accept them, and they will have the enlightenment necessary to reject the laws. Science will once again become metaphysics, will once again become magic. They will discover four laws that will help them jump from natural to magical law and transcend the time/space continuum which is the limitation of the age. And once again we will begin to take our power and to work with rules and laws that are magical laws and cosmic laws.

"We will once again see the way to continue a new dream. We will be given the roadmap back to the stars and will see the star people come out of the illusion of their two-legged form and into their actual Great Sleeper-Dream form. And so you will see some very, very powerful, totally enlightened Masters and the Second Coming of the Christ spoken of in the Book of Revelation and it will be the awakening of a new circle, a new design of energy movement for humanity. Christ means a circle. So the second coming of the sacred circle is all enlightened humans dancing as one consciousness."

FUTURE TIMES

Here is Swiftdeer's breakdown, year by year, of events that she believed were possibly going to affect us all, rich or poor, young or old. You can judge how these "predictions" turned out against the news events of the day. We did not alter the dates that were given to us and they were not necessarily fixed in time. We have learned from previous experiences that the future can be changed.

1990 – "A powerful year and it's really hard for me to talk about it. I am a great dreamer but I don't know if I dream that large. We will see a real shift in planetary consciousness. Many of the enemies of the humans shall begin to drop away. In 1990 you will see the Twelve Sacred Driver Wheels of each of the Eight Powers stored and put together to create the figure 8 of infinity sign. And 1990 will begin through the Feathered Serpent Medicine Wheels, those groups of seventeen Great Sleeper Dreamers. The first migration to the next world will begin, leaving behind on this planet another world of enlightened humanity to join the many already on other planets throughout our universe. When you speak of this migration to other planets, are you speaking of a creation of a new race? Another dream, another dance, another series of dances in another dream in another world. What's the difference between this world and the new creation? It is those that go on ahead that are the pathfinders.

1991 – "For those who stay here on Grandmother Earth, they will totally gain the light of the Great Light Wheel. That there will be one humanity, one planet composed of all the different ways of dancing in complete harmony in the great gathering together circle. In 1991 all the seeds will be planted.

1992 – "The Earth will have its true reality formed. It will join the sisterhood of planets, the Daughters of Copperwoman, and it will create within itself all forms of all things in harmony with the everything.

1993 – "We will see a whole new way of perfection. There will be plants on this Grandmother Earth that will give life and sustenance as never before seen. Starvation on the earth – all those things will be gone.

1994 – "There will be total balance and harmony. All human beings will be balanced fives or enlightened fives – a six. And they will still be in their physical bodies.

1995 – "The new race of humans will begin to design their new reality of life on this planet as they intended it to be when they came from the stars.

1996 – "The second migration to the new world will occur leaving behind on Grandmother Earth those who are choosing to continue to hold the power on this planet within the space of all the Sacred Twelve. All of these people who choose to remain after the second migration will begin to establish this planet and use the collective unconscious to hold the power of this space in harmony with the Great Circle of Twelve, all the planets, and there is a whole lot I don't even know. There is more that I am not supposed to talk about yet.

1997 – "The dream will be actualized and this planet will hold its space in the great Council of planets and become part of the Universal enlightened Brotherhood and Sisterhood of humanity, because there is an organization that is intergalactic that is known as the Great International Brother and Sisterhood of Humanity and Keepers of the Light Circles. It's happened on many planets and it's expected to happen on a lot of other planets.

1998 – "There will be a moment in 1998 when the population will be the population. The Circle of Law will hold the image of fast thought necessary to allow this planet to become a starship. (Is this fun? Not bad for a bunch of ignorant savages).

1999 – "The Third migration will leave this planet for the other new world and this planet will now be a starship, a spaceship, have its design of energy movement guided by all of humanity that's living here because, see, it's been a starship all along floating around a central sun but not in harmony with sister planets.

UFOS, ARMAGEDDON AND BIBLICAL REVELATIONS

2022 – "In the year 2022 the Great Spirit will have left its seed and the egg of the everything here on this planet and it will create itself twenty times over at the speed of light. And thus the prophecy ends, as I have been given it by the Grandmother and that I share with you now."

*****

So we leave the prophecies with a cliffhanger. I am sure there is more to come. Both Chris Franz and Brad Steiger have passed and, as I am getting up there in age, I am not able to wander around the villages on the Hopi reservation, especially as related to Second Mesa.

The last time I was there, the streets, where there were streets, were somewhat difficult to walk along as there was little pavement and lots of stones that the wind had blown around.

But those who crave a bit of adventure should surely travel to the reservation. Check online with the Cultural Center to see when events are being held that visitors might attend. The Powwows are really very colorful – and, hey, buy your wife or significant other a silver bracelet or a large squash. Guaranteed it will work on your behalf, if you know what I mean. She will love you for it and you will be helping the tribal crafts people out.

UFOS, ARMAGEDDON AND BIBLICAL REVELATIONS

Publisher/researcher Tim Beckley traveled with Chris Franz Dickey to Second Mesa where there were continuing reports of encounters by tribal members with the "Sky People," as they are referred to.

Those interested in finding out more about the "American Indian Starseed Connection" may find the book with the same name to their liking as it tells of Chris's prophetic visions in detail.

Chris had her first encounter with a UFO on property owned by rancher Pat McGuire, who claimed contact with ETs.

Pictographs portray discs, giants and possible spaceships.

As messenger and translator for Hopi elders since 1948, Thomas Banyacya, Sr. (1909-1999) traversed the globe trying to help people understand the warnings passed down from generation to generation among the Native American tribes.

Kachina Dolls represent the Sky People to some shamans living on Second Mesa.

Going on spiritual inspiration, as time rolled by, Chris Franz became adept at taking photos of unexplainable objects on a regular basis. This photo was taken over Grande, AZ.

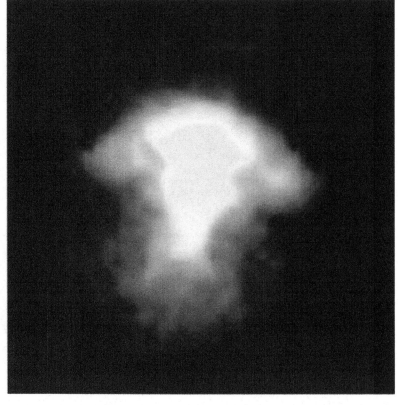

14

SAINT MALACHY'S PROPHECIES OF THE POPES, AND THE "GLORY OF THE OLIVES"
By Arthur Crockett – Updated by Tim Beckley

These Catholic-based predictions could foretell the end of the world as we know it (look all around you). Some U.S. Senators say you have a Constitutional right to go back to church in the middle of a pandemic. So you might ask your local parish priest as you stand a safe distance from him wearing a mask.

Did he hear you right? Saint who?

Well, regardless if you recognize his name or not, one of the most startling sets of prophecies to be found in religious history concerns itself with St. Malachy and the predictions he made for all of the Popes starting with Celestine II and ending with the final Pope and the end of the Catholic Church. Some scholars have interpreted this to mean the Pontiff who currently resides in Vatican City, but it's not a sure bet.

St. Malachy was born in 1094 in the town of Armagh, Ulster, Ireland. His real name was Mael Maedoc ua Morgair. Apparently he was born to the priesthood because even in school he surpassed his teachers in knowledge and in saintliness. Still a boy, he joined the Ismar Armagh, a small cloistered religious community. It had its center in the cell of the hermit. St. Malachy's devout studies brought him to the attention of the Bishop of Armagh, Celsius, who ordained the young man a priest and a deacon at a rather young age for such an important position.

Malachy rose quickly in the service of God. In no time at all he was made Abbott of Bangor. The job was not an easy one. The monastery had grown neglected and Malachy had a rough job in order to put it back into shape. But he did, and did it so well that God conferred on him the dual gift of miracles and prophecy. Eventually, Malachi became the Archbishop of Armagh. In later years he visited Rome, where it was said that he wrote some exceedingly strange prophecies, many of them dealing with the Popes.

UFOS, ARMAGEDDON AND BIBLICAL REVELATIONS

THE STORY BEHIND ST. MALACHY'S PROPHECIES

Oddly enough, the holy man's work remained unpublished for nearly 500 years. According to legend, a Dominican friar named Arnold de Wion published a book of prophecies that were said to be the work of the Irish monk. Wion said that Malachy completed the manuscript in Rome and that he showed it to Pope Innocent II, who approved of it and placed it in the Vatican archives. Wion published it in 1595, five hundred years after Malachi's birth. Wion merely dragged the script out of its dusty niche, brushed it off and set it in print.

MALACHY'S LATIN MOTTOES

The old manuscript consists of one hundred and eleven brief Latin mottoes allegedly identifying each Pope in succession, starting with Celestine II, who lived during Malachy's time.

The last pope, perhaps still in the future, was described as "the time of the end." While this is heavily debatable, some insist that Francis is the last pontiff based upon the dire nature of Malachy's warnings.

Indeed St. Malachy ends his long list of prophecies with the following words: "During the last persecution of the Holy Roman Church, there shall sit the Roman Peter, who shall feed the sheep amid great tribulations, and when these are passed, the City of the Seven Hills shall be utterly destroyed and the awful Judge will judge the people."

Will the real Nostradamus please stand up?

FACT OR FORGERY?

There are some Malachy scholars who believe the above passage is a forgery, and even that the entire manuscript is a hoax. Their contention is that the work was written by Dominican friars. Their theory is that the prophetic mottoes were strangely accurate between 1095 and 1595, when the work was published, but that accuracy fails after that latter date.

What these scholars fail to take into account is the fact that even after the work was published, Malachy's mottoes seemed to fit. Admittedly, in a few cases the references made by the Irish monk are rather vague, but there are enough of them which do appear to have pinpoint accuracy. Examine them for yourself.

****

POPE LEO XI

Malachy dealt early with Pope Leo XI. The Spanish Pope's real name was Alessandro de' Medici-Ottaviano. He was a patron of the arts and was a son of a niece of Leo X. Malachy's motto for Pope Leo XI was "Wave-man: Like the wind he came, and like the water he went."

The prophecy could not have been more accurate. Pope Leo XI reigned for only 27 days. He was Pope from April 1, 1605, to April 27,1605. His election had been approved on all sides and there was great sorrow when he died. It's also interesting to note the dates. Leo XI died 600 years after Malachy was born.

****

POPE PAUL V

Pope Paul V succeeded Leo XI and sat on the Throne of St. Peter from May 16, 1605, to January 28, 1621. Malachy's prophecy for him was two short words: "Perverse People."

The phrase may sound obscure until you realize that Paul V had problems with certain people at the very beginning of his pontificate. There was a sharp dispute with Venice. A state church was created and persecutions were taking place. A war was threatened, with English and German Protestants ready to fight on the side of Venice. Henry IV of France stepped in and offered a compromise which saw the Pope and the Church defeated. The situation worsened when Henry IV was murdered in 1610. Pope Paul V was accused by England of hatching the Gunpowder Plot, a desperate plan of persecutions which was actually denounced by the Church. Persecutions spread all the way to Ireland. The Pope then saw the outbreak of the Thirty Years' War.

Malachy certainly appears to have come close when he suggested that Pope Paul V would have to deal with "Perverse People."

****

POPE ALEXANDER VII

This Pope's real name was Fabio Chigi and he headed the church from April 7, 1655, to May 22, 1667. He had a coffin and skull made and placed in his room to remind him of human frailty.

Malachy's motto for him was "Guardian of the Hills." How could the Irish monk know, 150 years later, that a Pope would reign whose family arms portrayed three hills watched over by a star?

****

POPE CLEMENT X

Clement's pontificate lasted from April 29, 1670, to July 22, 1676, only six years. Malachy's motto for him was "Concerning the Mighty River." Prophetic? It certainly was! When Clement was a baby he nearly drowned when the Tiber overflowed its banks and flooded his home. He was almost swept away by the rushing water. The quick action of his nurse, who grabbed him at the last instant, saved his life.

Malachy must have had a real vision with Clement because the Pope's family arms depicts the Milky Way. The Latin name for Milky Way is "magnum flumen," or "great river."

UFOS, ARMAGEDDON AND BIBLICAL REVELATIONS

****

POPE INNOCENT XIII

Innocent came from an extremely religious family. He was educated by the Jesuits. His character was irreproachable. Innocent was one of the most religious of all Popes to that time.

Malachy's motto for him was "Of Good Religion."

****

POPE BENEDICT XIII

Benedict's family produced only soldiers. His pontificate lasted from May 29, 1724, to February 21, 1730, and although he was a saintly man himself, he was surrounded by evil men who enriched themselves through corruption.

Malachy's motto for Pope Benedict XIII was "Soldier in Battle."

****

POPE CLEMENT XII

Clement headed the church from July 12, 1730, to February 6, 1740. During his pontificate he purchased the busts of the emperors from the collection of the well-known Cardinal Alessandro Albani. He laid the foundations of the Capitoline Museum, which was the first archeological museum in Europe. He also built the Fontana Trevi and the facade of the Lateran Basilica. One of the most beautiful chapels in the world—the Capella Corsini—was built by Clement XII.

Malachy's motto for him was "The Column is Raised Up."

****

POPE CLEMENT XIII

At times St. Malachy was uncanny in his prophecies, and describing Clement XIII was one of them. The Pope reigned from July 6, 1758, to February 2, 1769, and his real name was Carlo Rezzonico. He was the 94th Pope. Before his pontificate began he lived in Umbria. Umbria's symbol was a rose.

Malachy's motto for Clement was "Rose of Umbria."

****

POPE CLEMENT XIV

Malachy's accuracy was shown again with Clement XIV. This Pope headed the church from May 19, 1769, to September 22, 1774. A persistent rumor suggests that he died by poisoning, but it has no basis in fact. Clement's escutcheon or Family Arms shows a running bear. Malachi wrote of him, "Ursus Velox," or "Swift Bear."

****

UFOS, ARMAGEDDON AND BIBLICAL REVELATIONS

POPE PIUS VII

Pius VII headed the church for only a short time—March 31, 1829 to November 30, 1830. When he was a Bishop, Pius VII predicted that he would be Pius VIII. Only one encyclical was attributed to Pius VIII and it dealt with laxity in religion.

Malachy's words for him were: "Religious Man."

****

POPE GREGORY XVI

This Pope came from a religious order in Etruria. He specialized in archaeological research. He was particularly interested in the "balnea," or ancient baths, for which the province was famous.

Somehow, Malachy was aware of that fact even though Pope Gregory lived 300 years after Malachi's death. The Irish monk wrote of Pope Gregory XVI: "Concerning the Baths of Etruria."

****

POPE LEO XIII

This Pope's pontificate lasted from 1878 to 1903. His crest was a comet on an azure field. Malachy knew it would be because his motto for Pope Leo XIII was a "A Light in the Sky."

****

POPE BENEDICT XV

It was with this Pope that St. Malachy really hit the nail on the head.

Benedict was the 104th Pope. His pontificate began on September 3, 1914 and ended on January 22, 1922.

The year 1914 saw the outbreak of World War I. For the next four years, millions of Christians would die on the battlefields. Then, in 1917, the start of the Russian Revolution was another strong setback for Christians. At that time more than 200 million people turned away from Christianity to embrace the new "religion" in Soviet Russia.

****

POPE PIUS XI

Pius XI's most pressing problem was the struggle against Communist purges in Russia, Spain and Mexico. These purges zeroed in on the Catholic Church. The bloody persecutions of the Catholics in Germany started in 1933 and lasted until the end of World War II. Pius XI was so furious with Adolph Hitler that when the German dictator visited Rome in 1938 the Pope refused to see the murderer of thousands of innocent people. Pius XI closed the Vatican and left Rome. He died in 1939, still trying to stop the madman in Germany from denying freedom to thousands of people.

Malachy's motto for him was "Intrepid Faith."

****

POPE PIUS XII

We said earlier that Pope Pius XII was a visionary Pope, a faith healer and a clairvoyant. We also said that many people, even non-Catholics, regard him as a saint.

Malachy's motto fit him perfectly: "Angelic Pastor."

****

POPE JOHN XXIII

"Papa John" as he was lovingly called is a mystery to proponents of Malachy's prophecies. The monk's motto for John XXIII was "Pastor and Sailor." However, there is nothing in his background or his time as pope to indicate that he was a sailor.

****

POPE PAUL VI

Paul VI is the 108th Pope. Malachy described him as the "Flower of Flowers." The prophecy is rather vague. So far, Malachy appears to have missed his mark. Nevertheless, that does not mean that he was wrong. Something yet may turn up about Paul VI that will have some significance.

****

POPE JOHN PAUL II

The world knows much about John Paul II. Apparently, so did St. Malachy. Shortly after 5:00 p.m. on May 13, 1981, Pope John Paul II was shot while riding in a white jeep through St. Peter's Square.

The man who shot him was Mehmet Ali Agca, a Turk.

Malachy's brief words for Pope John Paul II were: "Concerning the Crescent Moon." Many have taken that to mean a threat from the Arab or Moslem World.

But it was a Turk who caused the Pope injury. And if you look at the Turkish flag you will see a crescent moon and a star on a red field!

****

AS FAR AS MALACHY WAS CONCERNED, ONLY TWO POPES REMAIN

Malachy's 110th Pope was given the motto: "Of the Labor of the Sun." The motto for the 111th Pope is: "Of the Glory of the Olive." It was the monk's last motto.

Does it mean that the end of Christianity will come when the last Pope closes his pontificate reign? Stewart Robb, a Nostradamus scholar and an expert on the Malachy prophecies, refers to the last prophecy, "Of the Glory of the Olive" when he says: "It could mean the inception of lasting peace, this being the connotation of the olive branch, or since the olive is a symbol of the Holy Land, any glorification of the Holy Land might indicate a resurgence of true Christianity."

THE LAST POPE AND NOSTRADAMUS

Stewart Robb's view is optimistic, and one hopes he is right. But the subject of his intense studies –Nostradamus – has a more frightening prophecy in store for us.

And we can apply a Nostradamus quatrain which is quite alarming: In the year (to be determined) in the seventh month,

A great king of frightfulness will come from the skies

To resuscitate the great king of Angoumois,

Around this time Mars will reign for the good cause.

Qualified interpreters read this to mean that a horrendous war will take place at that time. Angoumois refers to France, and that she will not engage in such a war without her traditional allies beside her. Having a king come from the skies won't be unusual now because interplanetary travel will be commonplace. The appearance of the king, however, will greatly help the cause of the allies.

"OF THE GLORY OF THE OLIVE" – IS FRANCIS THE FINAL POPE?

One point we have to take into account is Malachy's detailed description of the last Pope. He said more about this one than about any other. The phrase, "Of the Glory of the Olive" was expanded on by the Irish monk. He added:

"During the final persecution of the Holy Roman Church, there will sit upon the throne Peter the Roman, who will pasture his flock in the midst of many tribulations; with these passed, the city of the seven hills will be destroyed; and the awful Judge will then judge the people."

Pope John Paul II (1978-2005) is said to match the 110th phrase on the list, "from the labor of the sun," because he was born and entombed on days when there were solar eclipses. That makes Benedict XVI number 111, "the glory of the olive." A monastic order founded by the saint from whom Benedict took his name has a branch known as the Olivetans, though Benedict himself is not one of them.

That passage certainly ties in with the quatrain of Nostradamus. It is not at all optimistic, and it does not supply us with any hope that the olive in this case refers to lasting peace.

ANOTHER EXPLANATION

In his book, "The Story of Prophecy," Henry James Foreman writes: "The prophecy of St. Malachy regarding the last of all the Popes is more explicit than most; Peter, the Roman, will lead his sheep to pasture in the midst of numerous tribulations; the City of the Seven Hills will be destroyed. The twilight settles –

indeed, the depth of night – before the promised dawn! "The End of the Ages will be upon the world and the last persecution, the most terrible of all, will afflict the church. The tribulations will be as great as those which overtook the Jews at the end of the destruction of Jerusalem by Titus. So devastating indeed will they be, that, in the words of St. Matthew: 'And except be no flesh saved; but for the elect's sake those days shall be shortened.'

"But not Peter the Roman, nor any number of just men, shall avail to save the Eternal City!

"Many commentators do not like to believe, in spite of the prophecies, that this Peter is actually to mark the end of the papacy. They believe that only a sort of hiatus will ensue, and then a glorious recrudescence. Mostly, however, this prophecy is taken literally, in common with all others bearing upon the predecessors of Peter the Roman. And that being so, does it mean that the End of the Ages, as prophesied in the Gospels, and in many other places, is actually at hand?

"With only seven more Popes (now two more Popes since Foreman's book was written), after the present one, that dreadful period looms ominously near. St. Malachy's prophecy begins with Pope Celestin II in the 12th Century. Since then in a period of 779 years there have been 94 Popes (up to the time this book was written), up to Pius XI, giving an average of eight years for the reign of each Pope. Even if we increase the average to say nine years, owing to greater statistical expectation of life in more recent times, only sixty-three years of .the papacy would remain after the present Pope (Pius XI). We know, of course, that some Popes have had long reigns. Pope Leo XIII, for example, sat in the Vatican for a quarter of a century, and Pius IX ruled for thirty-two years. We are now, however, considering averages. Sixty-three years is the equivalent of but two generations. One generation of this century has already more than passed. Two more generations bring the time to the end of the century, or roughly to about the year 2000."

Stuart Robb maintained that Nostradamus fixed the year 1999 as the time for an attack – so he was wrong as far as the date goes, but we know that "No one knowest the time!" – and of the terrible destruction of the city of Paris, by a strange people coming from the north, perhaps Asia. St. Malachy and the monk Padua predict the burning of Rome at the end of the papacy, which seems to fall at about the same period. Many other prophecies point to the "End of the Age" as falling within the present century. One cannot but recall the words of the Gospel according to St. Mark: "Verily I say unto you that this generation shall not pass till all these things be done."

****

JEANE DIXON'S PROPHECY OF THE ANTICHRIST

Jeane Dixon, was a businesswoman, having amassed a fortune along with her husband in Washington DC real estate. She was also an author, and, without a doubt, the best known of modern psychics before her death in 1997. Being very religious, she relied on visions from God, but also received premonitions in dreams. She occasionally used a crystal ball. She says she was able to see the future to 2037.

She did talk about the birth of someone of great renown who would change the world. We will have to see if this individual ever emerges.

Reading along she seems to refer to this person in terms of the Antichrist.

"A child was born somewhere in the Middle East shortly after 7:00 a.m. (EST) on February 5, 1962, and will revolutionize the world. He will bring together all mankind in one all-embracing faith. This will be the foundation of a new Christianity, with every sect and creed united through this man who will walk among the people to spread the wisdom of the Almighty Power.

"This person," continues Dixon, "though born of humble peasant origin, is a descendant of Queen Nefertiti and her Pharaoh husband; of this I am sure. There was nothing kingly about his coming – no kings or shepherds to do homage to this new-born baby – but he is the answer to the prayers of a troubled world. Mankind will begin to feel the great force of this man in the early 1980s and during the subsequent ten years the world as we know it will be reshaped and revamped into one without wars or suffering. His power will grow great until 1999, at which time the peoples of the Earth will probably discover the full meaning of the vision."

Jeane Dixon tells us that this man in Rome will prove to be a "false prophet of evil." Whatever evil he does will be corrected when Jesus Christ will be seen bodily in the Holy Land, at which time all Jews will proclaim him the true Messiah.

This intriguing man coming from the Middle East undoubtedly won't be Peter the Roman, the last Pope, but it is easy to speculate that he might bring about the end of Christianity, and the line of Popes.

Dixon also had a vivid vision while worshiping at St. Matthew's Cathedral in Washington DC.

"Suddenly the very air seemed rarefied. A glorious light shown again from the dome of the cathedral, and before me stood the Holy Mother. She was draped in purplish blue and surrounded by gold and white rays which formed a halo of light around her entire person. In a cloudlike formation to the right and just above her I read the word 'Fatima' and sensed that the long-secret prophecy of Fatima was to be revealed to me.

"I saw the throne of the Pope, but it was empty. Off to one side I was shown a Pope with blood running down his face and dripping over his left shoulder. Green leaves of knowledge showered down from above, expanding as they fell. I saw hands reaching out for the throne, but no one sat in it, so I realized that within this century a Pope will be bodily harmed. When this occurs, the head of the Church will thereafter have a different insignia than that of the Pope. Because the unearthly light continued to shine so brightly on the papal throne, I knew that power would still be there but that it would not rest in the person of a Pope. Instead, the Catholic Church would blaze the trail for all peoples of every religion to discover the meaning of the Almighty Power; to grow in wisdom and knowledge."

Many of Jeane Dixon's prophecies have come true; we can only wait and see if this prediction was accurate. She is deceased now so we can't pin her down any further. Anyone who missed out on Mrs. Dixon's rise to power in the psychic community can probably find a beat up copy of Ruth Montgomery's "A Gift of Prophecy," to fill in the gaps. It was a New York Times bestseller when it was first published. She was even welcome on the Johnny Carson Show, and everyone knows that Johnny was a dyed-in-the-wool skeptic who once tried to turn Uri Geller "out" when the Israeli psychic failed to perform because of "bad vibes," he later claimed.

THE STRANGE STORY OF POPE JOAN

One Pope is missing out of Saint Malachy's list. The reason being that this Pope was a woman. This is one Pope you are not likely to find any reference to as "he" was a definite she. Pope Joan has been excluded from all religious history books, especially those published by the Catholic Church.

HistoryChannel.com sparked our interest with this fascinating account:

"The Vatican's official records state that all of the Catholic popes have been men, but according to a medieval legend, a lady pontiff may have reigned for a brief period in the ninth century. As the story goes, this 'Pope Joan' was a young woman who disguised herself as a man and entered into religious training. After distinguishing herself as a scholar, she rose through the church ranks and was elected Pope John VIII in the year 855. She went on to rule for more than two years, her gender always carefully concealed beneath her flowing holy robes. Her secret was only revealed in 858, when she unexpectedly went into labor during a papal procession. Some accounts allege that she died in childbirth, while others claim her enraged followers dragged her behind a horse and stoned her to death.

"The forgotten Pope first planted herself in the medieval imagination in the 13th century, when her story appeared in chronicles by the Dominican friars Jean de Mailly and Stephen of Bourbon. She was later christened 'Joan,' and went on to become a widely-accepted part of Catholic history. The 14th century writer Giovanni Boccaccio mentioned her in a book about famous women, and her image graced paintings, sculptures and tarot cards. She was even briefly included in a collection of papal busts in Italy's Siena Cathedral."

The Catholic Church – sanctioned or not by its hierarchy – has always been associated with End Times predictions, probably because of the visions recorded

UFOS, ARMAGEDDON AND BIBLICAL REVELATIONS

at Fatima and elsewhere of the "Lady in White," which followers of the faith have interpreted as the Virgin Mary, mother of Jesus, returned to scold her children and set the world right with her blessings.

SUGGESTED READING

SCANDALS OF THE POPES

PROPHECIES OF THE POPES

DVD – SECRETS OF THE VATICAN – Produced by Tim Beckley and Tim Swartz.

St. Malachy's "Last Judgement" as seen circa 1648

UFOS, ARMAGEDDON AND BIBLICAL REVELATIONS

At a very young age Malachy was made Abbot of Bangor Abbey.

St. Malachy's calamities on Earth – rough times ahead!

Jeane Dixon predicted future events up to 2037. One doesn't know how many of us will be around to check them all out.

Nostradamus wrote in the year 1551 this! There will be a twin year (2020) from which will arise a queen (corona) who will come from the east (China) and who will spread a plague (virus) in the darkness of night, on a country with 7 hills (Italy) and will transform the twilight of men into dust (death), to destroy and ruin the world. It will be the end of the world economy as you know it.

Nostradamus is a prophet for all seasons. Born Jewish, he converted to Catholicism.

"The future has been shown to me to the year 2037."

So writes Jeane Dixon, whose extraordinary gift of prophecy has helped her predict many great events that have come to pass. What sort of future awaits us? A world of glory or Hell on earth—the choice is ours, the prophetess insists. Here, in her most inspiring and urgent book to date, Jeane Dixon describes her startling and awesome vision of life without God and sounds a joyous call for revolution, revival and rebirth—a revolution of belief, a revival of faith, and a rebirth of man's affinity with his creator.•••••••••••••••••••••••

The Call to Glory
Jeane Dixon
Speaks of Jesus and Prophecy

The last Pope and the current Pontiff play a vital role in Malachy's predictions.

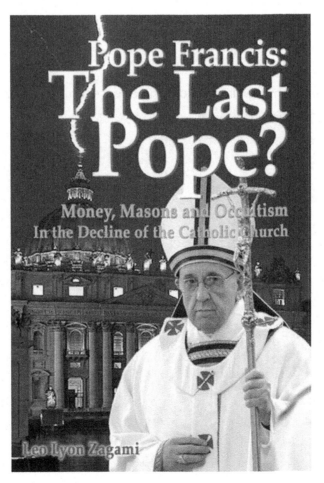

Vatican archives – treasure trove of hidden mysteries.

According to St. Malachy, it will all be coming down soon enough inside Vatican City.

UFOS, ARMAGEDDON AND BIBLICAL REVELATIONS

St. Malachy predicted the coming of the Popes and the End Times.

Numerous books have been written on Malachy's futuristic vision – there are varying interpretations.

Much has been written about the only female Pope. There is even a video about her.

No one might have known that the Pope was a woman until she went into labor during a papal procession

15

AMERICA'S SPIRITUAL DESTINY – FROM UFOS
TO PROPHECIES OF THE PRESIDENTS
By Sean Casteel
PRESIDENTIAL UFO ENCOUNTERS

As we have seen, UFOs play an integral role in our search to find out what the future may have in store for us, in both Biblical and non-Scriptural terms.

The presidents have had their share of UFO contacts along with matters more directly occult. The fact that Jimmy Carter saw a UFO in October 1969 and stated so publicly in 1973 is generally known among UFO enthusiasts, as is Carter's unfulfilled campaign promise to unlock the government's secret files and open the subject to public scrutiny.

But "Prophecies of the Presidents," a book by Timothy Green Beckley and the late Arthur Crockett, actually reprints the official report that Carter filed with the now-defunct National Investigations Committee on Aerial Phenomena (NICAP) as well as quoting comments from Carter's press secretary, Jody Powell, who told reporters: "I remember Jimmy saying that he did in fact see a strange light, or object, at night in the sky, which did not appear to be a star or plane or anything he could explain. If that's your definition of an unidentified flying object, then I suppose that's correct. I don't think it's had any great impact on him one way or the other. I would venture to say that he probably has seen stranger and more unexplainable things than that during his time in government."

Perhaps less well known is the story of President Dwight D. Eisenhower's meeting with beings from outer space said to have taken place on February 20, 1954. Beckley and Crockett say the story has been confirmed for them by a member of the British Parliament of their acquaintance, among others. Eisenhower was vacationing in Palm Springs when he was summoned to Murdoc Airfield by high-ranking military officials. Murdoc was later renamed Edwards Air Force Base and served as the landing field for the space shuttle. Eisenhower canceled a scheduled news conference to go to Murdoc with the official explanation being that he was at the dentist.

Eisenhower and a handful of U.S. officials watched as five alien craft landed and the aliens disembarked, appearing something like humans but by our standards "misshapen." The aliens asked Eisenhower to begin a public education program about them for the American people and eventually the entire Earth. Eisenhower allegedly replied that the world was not ready for such an announcement and the aliens agreed to contact only isolated individuals until the people of Earth got used to the idea of their presence.

After demonstrating some of the capabilities of their spacecraft – and making the entire presidential contingent quite nervous by showing that they could become invisible at will – the aliens boarded their ship and departed. It is a generally-accepted theory that we are currently experiencing a cultural conditioning program intended to help us gradually accept the fact that aliens are real and already among us, as the aliens requested that day at Murdoc.

Although Robert F. Kennedy never became president, he was a politician with enormous clout and influence whose political star was very much in the ascendancy when he was assassinated in 1968. The reader may not be aware that he had a definite belief in UFOs. In a personal letter to publisher Gray Barker of the Saucerian Press, Kennedy noted that he was a card carrying member of the Amalgamated Flying Saucers Club of America and indicated that he accepted the stories of those who claimed to have encountered aliens from other planets.

Kennedy wrote: "Like many other people in our country, I am interested in the UFO phenomenon. I watch with great interest all reports of Unidentified Flying Objects and I hope someday we will know more about this intriguing subject. Dr. Harlow Shapely, the prominent astronomer, has stated that there is a probability that there is life in the universe. I favor more research regarding this matter and I hope that, once and for all, we can determine the true facts about flying saucers."

What is important about stories like these, especially the Carter and RFK stories, is that they place the UFO phenomenon in a real-world setting where our leaders grapple with the unknown the same way we do and also burn with a curiosity they long to see satisfied. We are comforted that UFOs are not just a fixation of the fringe elements of society but are of genuine concern to even our most highly placed officials.

FIRST THINGS FIRST

Along with that fascinating sojourn into presidential UFO lore, Tim Beckley and Arthur Crockett declared in their book "Prophecies of the Presidents," that America has an important role to play in the coming New Age, what the authors call "an age of reason and enlightenment which is soon to engulf the entire planet we live on." Nothing in human history happens by chance, they believe, and so

UFOS, ARMAGEDDON AND BIBLICAL REVELATIONS

God intended the U.S. to help lead the entire world in the direction of freedom, love and perfect balance for all mankind.

"There is every reason," the authors write, "to believe that many of our Founding Fathers were reincarnated philosophers from Greece and Rome (and perhaps other planets) who originally lived in the time of Atlantis and had reentered physical shells in order to help reshape the history of the planet for centuries to come. Their main objective was to steer humans on the proper course and to see that this great nation got off on the right foot."

Reading this for the first time, I was struck by what an ingenious combination of various ancient spiritual ideas this concept was. When the authors speak of the Founding Fathers voluntarily being reincarnated to the physical plane to help guide America's birth, one is reminded of the Buddhist concept of the Bodhisattva, enlightened spirits who forego nirvana and willingly incarnate to happily share in the miseries of the world. Meanwhile, the authors' belief that our leaders are not selected by mere chance recalls the words of Saint Paul from the book of Romans, Chapter 13:1: "Let every person be subject to the governing authorities. For there is no authority except from God, and those that exist have been instituted by God."

GEORGE WASHINGTON'S VISIONS OF FUTURE AMERICA

Having mixed for us this heady cocktail of spiritual optimism and patriotic fervor, the authors next tell the story of George Washington, whom they say was supernaturally implanted with an indomitable faith in this country that saw him through the darkest parts of the Revolutionary War. Later in his life, Washington wrote a letter to the governor of Connecticut in which he stated that it was "almost possible to trace the finger of Divine Providence through those dark and mysterious days which led the colonists to assemble in convention, thereby laying the foundation for prosperity when we had too much reason to fear that misery and confusion were coming too rapidly upon us."

There had been moments in the war when Washington could be seen to openly weep, especially during the difficult winter of 1777, when his forces had suffered severe reverses on the battlefield and were close to starvation and freezing to death. He made a daily habit of going into a thicket, out of sight of his troops, to drop to his knees in prayer and ask for aid and comfort from God.

One day Washington gave strict orders that he not be disturbed in his headquarters so that he could draft an important dispatch without interruption. At one point he looked up and was startled to see a lovely young woman standing before him. She was by far the most beautiful creature he had ever seen, yet she had violated his privacy, so he asked her why she was there. After he had repeated the question four times, with no reply, he began to feel strange sensations and found himself unable to rise to his feet in the normal way of a gentleman greeting a lady. The room began to glow and Washington wondered if he was now dying.

UFOS, ARMAGEDDON AND BIBLICAL REVELATIONS

Finally, the woman raised her arm to the east and said, "Son of the Republic, look and learn." There followed a series of visions in which Washington was shown that the American nation would one day spread from the Atlantic to the Pacific Ocean. Another vision seemed to forewarn Washington about the Civil War to be fought less than a century hence. A third vision prophesied an invasion of America by the combined forces of Europe, Asia and Africa, which the authors link to the book of Revelation, Chapter 9:13-16. Those verses speak of troops that will be 200 million in number and wage war in the Last Days. Washington's visions concluded with the promise that America will emerge victorious from that future conflict and that her union will stand as long as there are stars in the sky.

WASHINGTON APPEARS IN A VISION
TO GUIDE THE NORTHERN ARMY

Washington is said to have appeared in a vision to Union General George B. McClellan at a point in the Civil War when the prospects for a northern victory seemed bleak. Washington warned McClellan that Confederate troops were set to descend on the nation's capital and score a decisive victory.

"General McClellan," Washington's voice spoke with amazing clarity, "do you sleep at your post? Rouse you, or ere it can be prevented, the foe will be in Washington! You have been betrayed, and, had God not willed it otherwise, ere the sun of tomorrow had set, the Confederate flag would wave above the Capital and your own grave. But note what you see. Your time is short."

As Washington spoke, McClellan beheld a "living map" which showed all the various troop positions. He took up a pen and copied down everything he saw. When Washington was assured that McClellan understood the military situation, he then spoke to the general about the 20th century, when other perils would beset the country even as America took its place as a leader among the nations of the world. McClellan would later write that the country would become "a Messenger of Succor and Peace from the Great Ruler, who has all nations in his keeping."

THE PRESIDENTS DENOUNCE ECONOMIC INEQUALITY

But not all the messages from the next world are so cheery and hopeful. "The Prophecies of the Presidents" also deals with information obtained through 19th century mediums like Lucy Brown, quite renowned in her day. She, too, felt she was in contact with the spirit of George Washington, who "predicted fascist dictatorship and its threat to America's destiny," according to Beckley and Crockett.

"Clouds in the horizon that are looming up to overcast the future of America," Washington allegedly spoke through Brown, "becoming very dense, dark and foreboding ill, will burst in an unexpected moment upon the heads of her people. The mutterings of discontent, engendered by a sort of incipient, despotic rule, mild, perhaps, at present in its hold over the masses, and swelling into vaster

184

proportions and power, is breeding discontent and disharmonies in the ranks of all classes of minds who labor diligently for a subsistence and gain a small and inadequate pittance of their hourly needs and daily bread."

This economic unrest among the working classes is due to the "widespread and desolating schemes of the robbers of the people of their rightful inheritance to life, land, home and pursuit of happiness." This financial chicanery does not go unnoticed by the hosts of spirits who dwell above the mortal sphere and can see into the secret workings of the minds and motives of the oppressors.

After Washington spoke, Thomas Jefferson added to the indictment by saying, "If the American people ever allow the banks to control the issue of currency, first by inflation and then by deflation, the banks and corporations that will grow up around them will deprive the people of all their property until their children will wake up homeless on the continent their fathers conquered."

President James Madison spoke even more frankly: "We are free today, substantially, but the day will come when our republic will come to impossibility because its wealth will be concentrated in the hands of a few. When that day comes, then we must rely upon the wisdom of the best elements in the country to readjust the laws of the nation to the changed conditions."

Abraham Lincoln confessed that he trembled for the safety of future America because, "As a result of war, corporations have been enthroned and an era of corruption in high places will follow. The money power will endeavor to prolong its reign by working on the prejudices of the people until all the wealth is aggregated into a few hands and the public is destroyed."

It was presumably a later medium that channeled Woodrow Wilson, who grimly charged that, "The masters of the government of the United States are the combined capitalists and manufacturers of the United States. The government of the United States at present is a foster child of the special interests. It is not allowed to have a will of its own. The government, which was designed for the people, has gotten into the hands of bosses and their employers, the special interests. An invisible empire has been set up above the forms of democracy. America is not a place of which it can be said, as it used to be, that a man may choose his own calling and pursue it as far as his abilities enable him to pursue it. American industry is not free as it once was free; American enterprise is not free."

THEIR WORDS FROM BEYOND THE GRAVE FULFILLED

I have quoted this section of "Prophecies of the Presidents" so carefully and extensively because it strikes me as being genuinely prophetic. The spirit voices of this small grouping of American chief executives are addressing what would in fact become a major issue for dissent in this country, as expressed by the Occupy Wall Street movement that began in September 2011. The movement's unforgettable slogan, "We are the 99 Percent," neatly summarizes the present condition of social and economic inequality suffered by the American people that has resulted from the greed, corruption and undue influence of corporations on government.

In 2012 and 2014, the media uncovered proof that the FBI and the Department of Homeland Security had monitored Occupy Wall Street through its Joint Terrorism Task Force despite labeling it a peaceful movement. Declassified documents showed extensive surveillance and infiltration of OWS-related groups across the country. Perhaps the wary suspicion of the two law enforcement agencies was also fueled by corrupt corporations seeking to guard their financial empires from a change in the national temperament.

Whether or not the "messages" spoken through the mediums were truly sent from the departed souls of some of our late presidents, or even if Beckley and Crockett made them up from whole cloth, they were nevertheless FULFILLED. One should realize that "Prophecies of the Presidents" was initially published in 1992, a full 19 years before the Occupy Wall Street movement first entered New York's Zuccotti Park.

Someone somewhere did indeed see the future and managed to get it written down in Beckley and Crockett's book. Some unknown power wanted it etched in stone and on the record. To me, that's a little uncanny. But, given my many years of writing for Tim Beckley, I guess I shouldn't be too surprised. He has always seemed to occupy some kind of publishing netherworld unto himself where books like his updated "America's Strange and Supernatural History" with its "Prophecies of the Presidents" bonus reprint just come with the territory.

SUGGESTED READING

THE SUPERNATURAL HISTORY OF AMERICA by Tim Swartz

AMERICA'S STRANGE AND SUPERNATURAL HISTORY

THE BELL WITCH PROJECT

COSMIC REVELATIONS TILL THE END OF TIME

DARKNESS OF THE GODS AND THE COMING OF PLANET X

UFOS, ARMAGEDDON AND BIBLICAL REVELATIONS

Artist Jon McNaughton voices his opinion on present day revelations: "The Vision of George Washington is not so well known by most Americans, but it is worth consideration as our country stands in peril of losing everything we hold dear. At a time when our financial solvency and our national security are more vulnerable than they have ever been, what will save us from the doom that lurks at our doorstep? I chose to paint this vision at the triumphant moment when the Angel of Liberty bursts upon the scene. Whether or not the vision is authentic is debatable, but the message it contains is timeless." Fine lithos are available and can be found on the web.

UFOS, ARMAGEDDON AND BIBLICAL REVELATIONS

President Eisenhower greets Kenneth Arnold while running for governor of Idaho. Arnold helped coin the term "flying saucer" following his sighting of nine UFOs over Mount Rainier, Washington, on June 24, 1947.

Just about everyone realizes that President Jimmy Carter had a UFO sighting while Governor of Georgia. But few realize that a UFO followed his helicopter taking off after a conference in Panama. The photo is actually from the Carter Library. And Tim Beckley interviewed the photographer – so it's the real thing!

Did Eisenhower meet aliens at Edwards Air Force Base? His encounter has grown into an urban legend. Read "America's Secret UFO Treaty" by Commander X to follow up.

The Incredible Story They Tried to Hide for 28 Years

Ike Met Space Aliens

President Dwight D. Eisenhower met with beings from outer space almost 30 years ago, a British high government official reveals.

EISENHOWER met with space aliens in 1954 and saw their advanced UFOs operate.

UFO EXPERT
Lord Clancarty

ROBERT F. KENNEDY
NEW YORK

United States Senate
WASHINGTON, D.C.

May 9, 1968

Mr. Gray Barker
Publisher, Saucer News
Box 2228
Clarksburg, West Virginia 26301

Dear Readers:

As you may know, I am a card carrying member of
the Amalgamated Flying Saucers Association. Therefore,
like many other people in our country I am interested
in the phenomenon of flying saucers.

It is a fascinating subject that has initiated
both scientific fiction fantasies and serious scientific
research.

I watch with great interest all reports of unidentified flying objects, and I hope that some day we will
know more about this intriguing subject.

Dr. Harlow Shapley, the prominent astronomer,
has stated that there is a probability that there is other
life in the universe.

I favor more research regarding this matter, and
I hope that once and for all we can determine the true facts
about flying saucers. Your magazine can stimulate much
of the investigation and inquiry into this phenomenon
through the publication of news and discussion material.
This can be of great help in paving the way to a knowledge of one of the fascinating subjects of our contemporary world.

Sincerely,

Robert F. Kennedy

Robert Kennedy's letter to the late Gray Barker regarding his membership
in a contactee-oriented UFO group.

Are the days of tribulations upon us? Inspirational artist Carol Ann Rodriguez depicts how an angel could usher in the last days.

UFOS, ARMAGEDDON AND BIBLICAL REVELATIONS

DID PRESIDENT RONALD REAGAN HAVE AN ENCOUNTER WITH ALIENS AND A UFO?

WERE HE AND NANCY ABDUCTED WHILE ON THEIR WAY TO A PARTY AT THE HOME OF WILLIAM HOLDEN?

Ronald Reagan, Former U.S. President, is one of the most well known UFO believers out there, often mentioning the phenomena in his speeches. It is rumored that Reagan and several other people, including his pilot watched a UFO for several moments from his plane.

Both of Reagan's UFO sightings occurred when he was the 33rd Governor of California (1967 – 1975). The first occurred on the night that Reagan was invited to a party that actor William Holden was having in Hollywood. A number of key personalities were invited. Two of them, comedian Steve Allen, and actress Lucille Ball both told the story of Reagan's UFO encounter.

Reagan was missing when the party began and the party was held up until he and Nancy arrived nearly an hour late. According to both Allen's and Ball's version of events the Reagans were ashen and shaken.

Reagan said that he and Nancy had seen a UFO while coming down the coast highway to Los Angeles and stopped to watch the event. After examing the landed craft, they continued on to the party but were unable to account for the missing hour.

The other Reagan sighting occurred in 1974 just before Reagan ended his second term as governor. The story was told by Air Force Colonel Bill Paynter who became the pilot of Reagan's Cessna Citation jet plane following his retirement from the Air Force.

It is a story Ronald Reagan told to Norman Miller, Washington Bureau Chief for the Wall Street Journal, Reagan's plane was making an approach to land in Bakersfield, California.

It was during the descent that Reagan noticed a strange light behind the plane. "We observed it for several minutes, Reagan told Miller. "It was a bright white light. We followed it to Bakersfield and all of a sudden to our utter amazement it went straight up into the heavens." Paynter, the pilot, stated. "It appeared to be several hundred yards away and it was a fairly steady light until it began to accelerate. Then it appeared to elongate. Then the light took off. It went up a 45 degrees angle at a high rate of speed. Everyone on the plane was astonished."

16

VISIONS AND PROPHECIES OF THE LADY IN WHITE
By Timothy Green Beckley
AS FIRST REVEALED IN THE BOOK OF REVELATION

She goes by various names in various cultures

She is known as "The Woman of the Apocalypse" or the "Lady of the Sun." (Rev 12:1-6,)

The apparition of a beautiful woman adorned in white is first thought to have been seen in a series of visions early in the Twentieth Century, and we have come to associate her with three shepherd children and the town of Fatima, Portugal. But the truth is "she" has been appearing throughout history. In fact, the Book of Revelation identifies her in prophetic terms as being in association with a "great red dragon, with seven heads and ten horns." In Biblical days, as now, visions of this lady are often a precursor to an "act of God" and eventually to the end of all time, the destruction of humanity by godless forces who will roam the earth.

"And a great sign appeared in heaven: a woman clothed with the sun, with the moon under her feet, and on her head a crown of twelve stars. She was pregnant and was crying out in birth pains and the agony of giving birth. And another sign appeared in heaven: behold, a great red dragon, with seven heads and ten horns, and on his heads seven diadems. His tail swept down a third of the stars of heaven and cast them to the Earth. And the dragon stood before the woman who was about to give birth, so that when she bore her child he might devour it. She gave birth to a male child, one who is to rule all the nations with a rod of iron, but her child was caught up to God and to his throne, and the woman fled into the wilderness, where she has a place prepared by God, in which she is to be nourished for 1,260 days." (Rev 12:1-6)

WHAT AND WHERE IS FATIMA?

Fatima is a small city in central Portugal where the landscape is dry and rocky. For centuries, people made their living there raising sheep and other animals. In May 1917, three shepherd children — two girls and a boy — claimed they saw an apparition of the Virgin Mary. The children described Mary as "a lady dressed all in white, more brilliant than the sun." Mary told the children that praying the rosary would end what was then called The Great War — World War I— which left 17 million dead.

According to the children, Mary appeared to them six times that year. In one appearance, Mary said a miracle would occur on Oct. 13, 1917. Initially the children were scolded and even threatened with death for spreading what were considered baseless stories. But pilgrims from all over the world gathered in Fatima on that date and awaited Mary's appearance. In what came to be called the "Miracle of the Sun," many reported seeing visions in the sky while others reported miracles of healing. A newspaper of the day reported: "Before their dazzled eyes, the sun trembled, the sun made unusual and brusque movements, defying all the laws of the cosmos, and, according to the typical expression of the peasants, 'the sun danced.'"

After much contemplation, in 1930, the Catholic Church declared the events at Fatima "worthy of belief," and chapels, sanctuaries, shrines and other memorials to the events popped up.

WHY HAS FATIMA BECOME SUCH AN ATTRACTION?

When the church declared the Fatima apparitions worthy of acceptance, it is said pilgrims who travel there may obtain a special blessing as well as pray for healing and spiritual guidance. Today it is one of the most popular shrines in the world. The largest numbers come dutifully on May 13 — the anniversary of the first apparitions.

What is not well known is that Marian apparitions, as they have become popularly known, is not just an historical event of monumental proportions, but a growing phenomenon that has swept the world during the course of the decades since the three young shepherds bore witness to this series of ongoing events. Their experience pitted them and those who held fast in their beliefs against a rigid communist dictatorship who had officially declared themselves an atheistic state.

Even if only on a subconscious level, there are signs all around us that such illuminated manifestations have had an impact on our culture. Who would ever think that the Beatles, for instance, would write a song in which Paul McCartney croons, "When I find myself in times of trouble, Mother Mary comes to me, speaking words of wisdom, Let it Be, Let it Be." Truly, there can be little doubt in anyone's mind upon reading through the maze of available literature that something utterly profound happened at Fatima, Portugal, on October 13th, 1917, when thousands gathered for a miracle which had been promised by three local children. Peering up into the dark, cloud-filled sky, the throng witnessed a spectacle that has deservedly gone down in history as one of the greatest spiritual events of modern times. There is no disputing this!

MIRACLE OF THE SPINNING SUN

The events that transpired on that dreary day, weather-wise, in October 1917 can be attested to by newspaper accounts throughout Europe, and not just in the Catholic press, which was censored in Portugal at the time, the Church being continually attacked by the country's godless rulers

In that rain soaked field, tens of thousands of true believers and the just plain curious, standing about, literally fell to their knees as they observed the sun – or what they perceived to be the sun – spin from its lofty orbit and come so close to the ground that beams of colored light could be seen radiating in all directions upon the Earth.

Some described the "Miracle of the Falling Sun" as a whirling wheel of fire that scorched the soil, drying up the muddy land within moments of its descending from the heavens. Others spoke of nearly being blinded by the brilliant shafts that seemed to fly off the surface of the sun right into their eyes and onto their bodies. Not one person – believer or skeptic – went away feeling that he or she had not been touched by something supernatural.

Indeed, many among this heavily atheistic crowd were converted overnight to the ways of the church from their previously strong communistic viewpoint on God and creation. Today, more than a hundred years later, millions continue to flock yearly to Fatima to be cured of all manner of physical, mental and emotional ailments. Many say that the air around Fatima still seems to be filled with unknown energies which can, of their own volition, bless and heal saint and sinner alike. That three, wide-eyed, innocent children could stir up such passions of faith, hope and charity that have lasted for a century, is just about proof enough that their vision of a lady engulfed in a blinding light was not a group fantasy or a mass hallucination, but was a subjective reality based on what their individual senses told them was really happening.

Even the most religious of the flock can see the obvious connection between the apparitions at Fatima, combined with the anomalous spinning "sun," as having a likely relation to the appearance of UFOs, "spacemen" and "spacewomen" and other paranormal occurrences. To a large degree, it would appear that one's cultural and sociological backgrounds play an important role in how they determine the nature of the events being witnessed.

But one doesn't wish to dwell any further on the prophecies associated with this once isolated town. as there are now a bevy of similar apparitions of what I prefer to call the "Lady in White," yet is best known, because of the heavy duty Catholic influence on the apparitions, as "Marian Phenomena."

For it is an established fact that sightings and interactions with the Lady have come from all over the world and from individuals of all faiths and backgrounds.

We have already mentioned the Fab Four's musical association with the apparition, but there is another rock-n-roller who I once spoke with who told me about an unusual visionary experience which seems to have had a profound influence on his life.

AN EYEWITNESS ACCOUNT BY DR. JOSÉ MARIA DE ALMEIDA GARRETT, PROFESSOR AT THE FACULTY OF SCIENCES OF COIMBRA, PORTUGAL

"It must have been 1:30 P.M. when there arose, at the exact spot where the children were, a column of smoke, thin, fine and bluish, which extended up to perhaps two meters above their heads, and evaporated at that height. This phenomenon, perfectly visible to the naked eye, lasted for a few seconds. Not having noted how long it had lasted, I cannot say whether it was more or less than a minute. The smoke dissipated abruptly, and after some time, it came back to occur a second time, then a third time

"The sky, which had been overcast all day, suddenly cleared; the rain stopped and it looked as if the sun were about to fill with light the countryside that the wintery morning had made so gloomy. I was looking at the spot of the apparitions in a serene, if cold, expectation of something happening and with diminishing curiosity because a long time had passed without anything to excite my attention. The sun, a few moments before, had broken through the thick layer of clouds which hid it and now shone clearly and intensely.

"Suddenly I heard the uproar of thousands of voices, and I saw the whole multitude spread out in that vast space at my feet...turn their backs to that spot where, until then, all their expectations had been focused, and look at the sun on the other side. I turned around, too, toward the point commanding their gaze and I could see the sun, like a very clear disc, with its sharp edge, which gleamed without hurting the sight. It could not be confused with the sun seen through a fog (there was no fog at that moment), for it was neither veiled nor dim. At Fatima, it kept its light and heat, and stood out clearly in the sky, with a sharp edge, like a large gaming table. The most astonishing thing was to be able to stare at the solar disc for a long time, brilliant with light and heat, without hurting the eyes or damaging the retina. [During this time], the sun's disc did not remain immobile, it had a giddy motion, [but] not like the twinkling of a star in all its brilliance for it spun round upon itself in a mad whirl.

"During the solar phenomenon, which I have just described, there were also changes of color in the atmosphere. Looking at the sun, I noticed that everything was becoming darkened. I looked first at the nearest objects and then extended my glance further afield as far as the horizon. I saw everything had assumed an amethyst color. Objects around me, the sky and the atmosphere, were of the same color. Everything both near and far had changed, taking on the color of old yellow damask. People looked as if they were suffering from jaundice and I recall a sensation of amusement at seeing them look so ugly and unattractive. My own hand was the same color.

"Then, suddenly, one heard a clamor, a cry of anguish breaking from all the people. The sun, whirling wildly, seemed all at once to loosen itself from the firmament and, blood red, advance threateningly upon the Earth, as if to crush us with its huge and fiery weight. The sensation during those moments was truly terrible.

"All the phenomena which I have described were observed by me in a calm and serene state of mind without any emotional disturbance. It is for others to interpret and explain them. Finally, I must declare that never, before or after October 13 [1917], have I observed similar atmospheric or solar phenomena."

ADDITIONAL TESTIMONIALS

From "The True Story Of Fatima," by By John de Marchi, I.M.C, we get the following very typical, for research purposes, accounts. This seems to be a well-balanced look into the overall phenomena written, as it were, by someone in the Church. Many thousands of people in the Cova da Iria and in neighboring villages witnessed the overwhelming signs. Their reports are of intense interest. There are slight variations in their descriptions of the events, though all agreed it was the most tremendous, the most awe-inspiring sight they ever witnessed. Some idea can be had of its effect on the people by reading the newspaper accounts of the day.

"At one o'clock, solar time, the rain stopped," O Dia reported. "The sky had a certain greyish tint of pearl and a strange clearness filled the gloomy landscape, every moment getting gloomier. The sun seemed to be veiled with transparent gauze to enable us to look at it without difficulty. The greyish tint of mother-of-pearl began changing, as if into a shining silver disc that was growing slowly until it broke through the clouds. And the silvery sun, still shrouded in the same greyish lightness of gauze, was seen to rotate and wander within the circle of the receded clouds! The people cried out with one voice; the thousands of the creatures of God, whom faith raised up to Heaven, fell to their knees upon the muddy ground.

"Then, as if it were shining through the stained glass windows of a great cathedral, the light became a rare blue, spreading its rays upon the gigantic nave... Slowly the blue faded away and now the light seemed to be filtered through yellow stained glass. Yellow spots were falling now upon the white kerchiefs and the dark poor skirts of coarse wool. They were spots which repeated themselves indefinitely over the lowly holm oaks, the rocks and the hills. All the people were weeping and praying bareheaded, weighed down by the greatness of the miracle expected. These were seconds, moments that seemed hours; they were so fully lived."

O Século, another newspaper of Lisbon, provided more details of the extraordinary events. "From the height of the road where the people parked their carriages and where many hundreds stood, afraid to brave the muddy soil, we saw the immense multitude turn towards the sun at its highest, free of all clouds. The sun resembled a plate of dull silver. It could be stared at without the least effort. It did not burn or blind. It seemed that an eclipse was taking place. All of a sudden a tremendous shout burst forth, 'Miracle, miracle! Marvel, marvel!'"

BILLY SQUIER – INFLUENCED BY A "VIRGIN"

This was the account related to me by rock guitarist-singer-songwriter Billy Squier who was a teenager at the time of his experience. "I was living in Wellesley, Massachusetts, and one summer afternoon a group of three or four of us guys were out on the golf course, on the 10th hole, about to tee off, when we all noticed a peculiar glow off in the woods."

Initially, Squier thought it might be the sun setting, but he soon realized it was too early in the day. Suddenly, a strange figure appeared out of nowhere in the midst of a glow, and they all saw it at once. "I had to blink twice to make sure I wasn't imagining things," Billy revealed. "The figure was that of a woman, and I would say she looked something like a Madonna – you know, like a holy statue." The talented musician insists that the figure remained stationary for close to half a minute, and then disappeared in front of everyone's eyes as if entering another dimension. He felt it was both "incredible" and "baffling," and he's happy there were others present to verify what he'd seen.

Best known for his popular hits "Stroke Me," "Everybody Wants You" and "Lonely Is the Night," the curly haired pop star hit his stride in the 1980s. While he still tours at seventy, Squier "mysteriously" disappeared from the musical scene for a period of time. Now, I can't say for sure if this had anything to do with his vision of the "Madonna," but we do know from past experience that a high percentage of those who come in close proximity with any sort of para-physical apparition or phenomena, be it a "space person" who emerges from a landed UFO or a visit from a Marian-like figure, find themselves becoming more spiritually involved with the world around them. Some experiencers suddenly become fixated with healing others and perhaps even healing the planet we live on, in an attempt to do what they can to "save the Earth," and make it a better place in which to live.

Squier has admitted that he is not your typical rock musician known for partying and womanizing. He says he likes to spend time alone in "metaphysical contemplation" (my words).

"New York Post" scribe Linda Stasi says she once met up with Billy and he had a 25-foot saw in his hand. He was in Manhattan's Central Park and he was pruning trees.

Stasi explains: "Turns out that Billy ('The Stroke'), who had just gotten back from France where he took 40 of his pals to celebrate his 50th, has taken up the 'aesthetics of plants.' I begged and finally met the wild man, who is now into wild-life, in the lobby of his Central Park West building to find out how he went from playing guitar to pruning plants. First off, he's sexier than hell. I never could resist a man with a sickle."

He revealed to the journalist in a moment of candor, "I'd be walking through 'my front yard,' [that would be Central Park] and I figured it could use some help. So I took pictures of my yard in Bridgehampton to the head of volunteers for the Central Park Conservancy, and she gave me the go-ahead.

"I've an arsenal of my own tools," he said while holding a 25-foot extension saw.

Why does he do this? "I much prefer the company of nature to the poison of the business community. When money enters the aesthetic, it changes the per-spective on it all."

For that reason he remains strictly a cutting volunteer. "I do it because I want to do it. And I play [music] now when . . . (I want to)"

"No, he won't do it for money, so don't think you can hire him to do your terrace," Linda ends her story.

Frankly, I haven't followed Squier in recent years. I'm told he's become somewhat of a famous hip hop celeb whose work has been sampled by the fa-mous of that branch of the musical scene, a scene which I admittedly do NOT fol-low. Rock-n-roll is the only world for me!

Want to rock? Join the Billy Squier Fan Club – www.billysquier.com/

MARY IN ALIEN LANDS

Not being influenced by any one religious persuasion, the Marian phenom-ena are worldwide and not simply associated with the Catholic Church.

Oddly enough, Mary has appeared in countries which are not in accord with Christian beliefs. One of those places is Russia. In 1948, a local secretary of the communist party, a man named Liaret, saw a tall figure in the road ahead of him. He called her the "lady in night."

Also in 1948, in Trieste, a young girl saw a beautiful angel who told her to return to the same spot every day for fifteen days. The girl did so, seeing the same vision on every occasion. At the end of the period the girl was given seven perfect rose petals. A botanist examined the petals and stated emphatically that they had not come from any roses grown on earth. In a Catholic country, Italy, in 1947, a communist sympathizer in Tre Fontane saw an angel-like figure which appeared to be the Virgin Mary. Thousands of people visited the spot, and many of them were communists who later rejected their atheistic beliefs.

The Holy Mother has been seen in virtually every country in the world, regardless of that nation's religious or political beliefs. Apparently, she appears before us not to make converts, but to awaken us to the fact that time may be running out.

JACQUES VALLEE'S POSITION

For many years, French-born Jacques Valle has been at the forefront of UFO and paranormal research. He is highly credentialed, trained in science, and author of a good number of books and papers on unexplained phenomena. While the majority of UFO researchers have been out chasing "UFOs from Mars," Dr. Vallee sees the illusionary phenomena as being more "homegrown," more "earthbound," much more of a conditioning influence by an outside force yet to be determined.

Vallée has contributed to the investigation of the Miracle at Fatima and Marian apparitions. His work has been used to support the Fatima UFO Hypothesis. Vallée is one of the first people to speculate publicly about the possibility that the "solar dance" at Fatima was a UFO. The idea of UFOs was not unknown in 1917, but most of the people in attendance at the Fatima apparitions would not have attributed the claimed phenomena there to UFOs, let alone to extraterrestrials. Vallée has also speculated about the possibility that other religious apparitions may have been the result of UFO activity, including Our Lady of Lourdes and the revelations to Joseph Smith. Vallée and other researchers have advocated further study of unusual phenomena in the academic community. They feel that this should not be handled solely by theologians.

WAYS MARY PRESENTS HERSELF

A Methodist clergyman in Haines City, Florida, Reverend B. W. Palmer, has spent years collecting hundreds of contemporary visions of the Holy Mother. His research on the subject indicates that there are at least 24 methods the Virgin uses to manifest herself. There may be as many as fifty ways, but we list here the 24 most commonly manifested. Brad Steiger first clued me in on Rev. Palmer's fine investigative work, for which I am most grateful, as it adds a great deal to our understanding of the Marian apparitions.

1. The skies appear to open up and Mary with a band of angels appears to descend.

2. In the presence of a viewer, Mary appears to descend in a shaft of light.

3. The Virgin appears or disappears through a solid object such as a door or a wall.

4. A viewer may hear footsteps outside his house. Then a knock on the door. When he opens it he sees the Holy Mother.

5. The Virgin can also appear as though she is in a picture on the wall.

6. A witness may awake because he feels a spiritual presence in the room, or may feel someone's touch. When he opens his eyes he sees the Holy Figure bending over him.

7. An angel or the spirit of a deceased person may appear to the witness first, then lead him to the materialization of the Holy Mother.

8. The witness may see the face of the Virgin or Jesus Christ appear above the person who is desperately in need of help.

9. The witness may hear a voice which tells him or her to go to a certain place and do a certain thing. When he complies, he sees the Virgin Mary.

10. The figure of the Virgin Mary appears in the sky, but greatly magnified.

11. The viewer may be awakened by the light of a very bright moon. At that moment he sees the Holy Mother.

12. Clouds play a part in visions. The Virgin often appears out of a cloud moving toward a person, and she also uses the cloud to make her departure.

13. A cloud or heavy mist may materialize in the viewer's room. And out of the mist the Virgin will appear.

14. During the Fatima miracle, the Holy Mother appeared to the three children in exactly the same way. All three gave the same description of what they saw. In many cases the Virgin appears to several persons at the same time, but each witness gave a different description of what he or she saw. To one witness, the Holy Mother may appear as a ball of light; to another, a flash of lightning; to another, a disembodied voice.

15. The Virgin may appear in a room occupied by several people. But only one person will see her. The others may see the spirits of the dead.

16. The Virgin may also appear in the dreams of a witness. A manifestation like this is usually associated with healing or cures.

17. The Holy Mother may vanish suddenly, or fade away slowly, slipping into a cloud, through the ceiling, doors or walls. She may walk away, fading from view as she gets further and further away from the witness.

18. In most visions of the Holy Mother, only the witness singled out for communications may see her even though there are a lot of people present. This was so in the Fatima miracle in which thousands of people saw the three children talking to an entity they could not see.

19. In many of the visions collected by Rev. Palmer, the Virgin appears in a strange light, one that illuminates the witness as well. In some of these cases, the light appeared first, then the Holy Figure.

20. In some visions, the witnesses said they saw no figures at all, but were

aware of the Holy Presences through the supernatural light and the voices that came to them.

21. Those who have experienced out-of-body incidents have reported seeing the Holy Mother, but that the vision disappeared once the out-of-body experience ended.

22. In other out-of-body experiences, people have claimed to travel through space to visit friends and relatives, and on such excursions have usually seen a Holy Figure, that is, the Holy Mother, a saint, an angel, or other Holy Entities.

23. In still other out-of-body travels, people have claimed to have seen the lower spirit worlds where good spirits attempt to help the lower spirits. In some instances during these lower-plane visits, the travelers have seen Jesus Christ or the Virgin Mary.

24. During near-death experiences, people said they saw Jesus or Mary for a brief moment when their bodies were physically dead.

In the second part of our presentation, we will take a look at some of the more recent apparitions, leaving 1917 Fatima behind.

The book that tells the entire story. Original edition played upon revealing the Third Prophecy to sell a ton of books through the tabloids.

Fatima statue dedicated to the apparition in Valinhos near Cova da Iria.

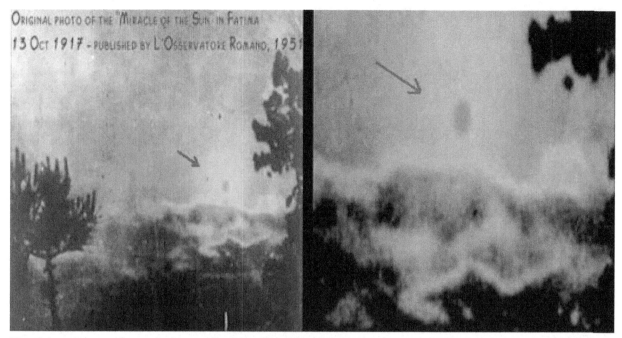

The "dancing sun" as photographed on the day of the main event. It can easily be classified as a UFO!

A dramatic reenactment of the spinning sun phenomenon.

UFOS, ARMAGEDDON AND BIBLICAL REVELATIONS

An artistic interpretation of the event of the dancing sun associated with the final appearance.

An estimated 70,000 stood with umbrellas, with some even on their knees praying in the mud.

"Woman of the Apocalypse" is associated with a child and a dragon with seven heads and ten horns. It seems to forecast the appearance of the Madonna in Fatima in 1917.

Despite dire threats, the shepherd children persisted in telling the same story over and over again.

UFOS, ARMAGEDDON AND BIBLICAL REVELATIONS

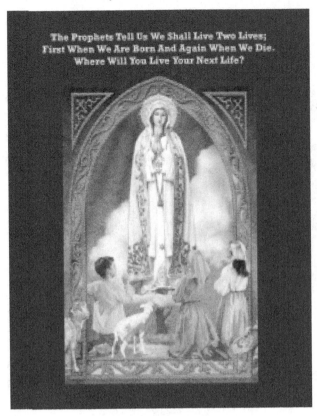

The three children said the apparition appeared on the same day every month as a glowing figure just above a tree.

From the "private sector" (we have no idea of his religious beliefs – if any), rock legend Billy Squier reveals that he had a sighting of the "Madonna" on a golf course in Massachusetts.

17

MARIAN VISIONS AT ZEITOUN, EGYPT
By Timothy Green Beckley

There is no denying the fact that the Fatima apparitions have been covered more than any other Marian encounter. But there are hundreds of other such incidents involving "The Lady," some of which have gotten a certain amount of attention, others which have been reported on pretty much only locally, and a number of which have gotten no attention at all. These are what John Keel used to call the "Silent Contactees" in the UFO community. Basically, a group consisting of those who either frown on publicity for one reason or another, or are paranoid that they will be attacked publically for their beliefs.

I justifiably like the case known as "The Visions of Zeitoun, Egypt" because the sightings of the Lady are more or less a current affair. (i.e., in our lifetime). Furthermore, the apparition has been observed, I hear, by upwards of a million or more eyewitnesses, by those who live locally and by visitors who come to view the phenomenon for themselves. Two things are very attractive about this case – the apparition has been photographed many times and a good portion of those who have seen her are of the Islamic faith. You would think they would be skeptical observers, but as our "guest reporter" Bill Kern will shortly point out, there is definitely a tie-in with those who follow the teachings of Allah.

The visions began in this relatively poor suburb of Cairo on April 2, 1968, and lasted well over three years, before the vision vanished as mysteriously as it had first appeared, only to reemerge from the shadows in the Nineteen Nineties.

The population of the town is mostly Muslim, but there is a fairly large Coptic Catholic minority in the city and it has long boasted of having a beautiful church known as St. Mary's Church of Zeitoun.

Coincidentally – and of course this is a true synchronicity if there ever was one! – the church was christened "the Apparition Church" by its builder Tawfik Khalil Ibrahim, under the supervision of the Italian architect Leomingelli. He built it as a miniature of the famous Agia Sophia church in Istanbul, Turkey, after a vision he had seen in which the Holy Virgin told him that she would appear in her church at Zeitoun after forty years. The church was consecrated during the Holy Mass on Sunday 29 June 1925. According to tradition, the site is one of the locations where the Holy Family stayed during their flight into Egypt

Well, you get the picture. The church was "ordained" from the start as a place where the Madonna was to present herself. We can't say the original architect was behind the appearance of the Lady, that he somehow hoaxed this, as he had long since joined Mary in heaven.

The night of the first occurrence, two mechanics were working in a city garage across the street from the church, which stands at Tomanbey Street and Khalil Lane. The mechanics happened to look over at the church and were startled to see a nun dressed in white standing on top of the large dome at the center of the roof and holding onto the stone cross at the top of the dome.

Their first thought was that the nun was about to commit suicide by jumping to the ground. One of the men ran into the church to get a priest while the other telephoned for an emergency squad.

The priest was the first to recognize the event for what it was – a Marian vision. The figure remained in view for a few minutes, then disappeared. The news of Mary's visit spread rapidly, and crowds formed around the church to see the miracle. But the Virgin Mary did not make an appearance again until April 9th, a Tuesday. Nevertheless, crowds of people saw her standing atop the dome of the church and were awed.

Fortunately, an American priest named Rev. J. Palmer, who we identified previously, rushed to Zeitoun as soon as he heard about the phenomenon and was able to investigate it firsthand.

He learned, for instance, that in the early 1920s the Khalil Family donated the land that St. Mary's Church of Zeitoun stands on. At the time, a revelation was made to one of the family members that the Mother of God would appear in the church for one year.

Rev. Palmer saw the apparition and tells us: "The apparitions of Our Lady are usually heralded by mysterious lights. Not only does the Blessed Mother appear in a burst of brilliant light, so bright the spectators find it impossible in most cases to distinguish features, but flashing scintillating lights, compared by witnesses to fluorescent lights or sheet lightning, precede the appearances by approximately a quarter of an hour. These sheflas appear sometimes above the church, sometimes in the clouds that on occasion form over the church and cover it like a canopy."

Rev. Palmer also talks about the mysterious clouds which accompany the apparition: "One should include perhaps the 'lights' – the mysterious clouds that are sometimes seen hovering over the church, even when the rest of the sky was cloudless. One night, Bishop Gregorius stated, there poured from the sealed, stained-glass windows of the high dome such clouds of incense that it would take millions of sensors to produce a like quantity. The incense cloud settled over the throng standing around the church.

"Another phenomenon witnessed by the spectators is the appearance of bird-like creatures before, during and after the apparitions, and sometimes on nights when there is no apparition at all. These creatures in some ways resemble doves. They are larger than doves, they are larger even than pigeons."

Whence they come or whither they go no one can determine.

It is known, says the keeper of the Cairo Zoo, that pigeons do not fly at night. But these can hardly be any kind of natural bird.

"First of all, the birds fly too rapidly. They fly without ever moving their wings. They seem to glide before, into and around the apparition. They never came to rest on the roof or trees, and on some occasions have been seen to disintegrate in the sky like wisps of clouds."

Rev. Palmer described the birds as being spotless white and emitting light. He said they were electrically-illuminated birds which could be seen in the brilliance of the apparition and also in the darkness of the sky above the vision. They appeared and disappeared without any sound at all.

In Rev. Palmer's work, "Our Lady Returns to Egypt," he documents the various attitudes of the Blessed Mother. "At first, she appeared above the dome of the church in traditional form, wearing the veil and long robes associated with other appearances, such as at Lourdes and Fatima. There is nothing perceptible other than light, and that is described by Bishop Athanasius as bluish white or whitish blue. It is somewhat like the color of the sky on a clear day.

"Mary does not stand motionless, but is seen blowing and greeting the people in silence. She bends from the waist, moves her arms in greeting and blessing and sometimes holds out an olive branch to the people.

"She has appeared between the trees in the courtyard in front of the church; she has appeared under each of the four small domes, through the windows of the larger dome, and has often walked about on the flat church roof so as to be seen by those standing on all sides of the church."

The duration of the apparitions varied greatly. They lasted from a few minutes to several hours. On the night of June 8, 1968, they remained visible from 9.00 P.M. to 4:30 A.M. The visions of the Blessed Mother continued from 1968 through 1970, and many photographs were taken.

MARY REMAINED SILENT

Although there were a great many cures at Zeitoun, the Blessed Mother elected not to speak from her lofty perch atop the church. There were no warnings or admonitions from her this time. There was no individual recipient to whom she could communicate her thoughts. It was obvious that in Zeitoun she hoped to reach as many people as possible by appearing at the church for a period of three years.

DID THE LADY RETURN?

The Lady seems to like Egypt, as she has appeared in this nation time and time again. Sometimes to massive throngs of Christians and Muslims, who seem comfortable with her and welcome her appearances.

Declaration of the Coptic Priests in Assiut Concerning the Marian Apparitions at St. Mark Church El-Keraza Official Magazine of the Coptic Orthodox Church Following is a translation of the original Arabic article that appeared in the last Keraza which is a declaration issued by the Priests' Council in Assiut (Zeitoun-eg.org received this translation on Friday 13 October 2000). The Keraza also includes pictures. "We have received the following declaration signed by the Coptic priests, members of Assiut City Priests Council with photographs that we publish herewith.

"This declaration was issued by the Assiut City Priests Council concerning the crowds witnessing the revelations of the Virgin Mary between the two church towers and domes of St. Mark's Church, which was recently opened for prayer and was rebuilt with the Diocese building.

"It was found that, starting two months ago, the local residents adjacent to the church saw at night spiritual phenomena in the sky which they first thought were something natural and ignored before they were repeated for several times with groups of big and extremely bright doves. This was also accompanied by apparitions of the Virgin Mary at different times from the night of 17 August 2000. Crowds gathered on adjacent buildings' roofs and in streets and passages surrounding the church. The news spread and bigger crowds came from different countries seeking the blessing of Virgin Mary.

"Some visitors who wanted to visit the site inquired about the time of the apparitions of the Virgin Mary and we answered, mentioning that the apparitions and spiritual phenomena are not subject to human desires or time measures. So that some people, seeking to see Her, go and don't see while other people coming afterwards might see Her by coincidence.

"The Church received many questions from overseas concerning the apparitions and we hope this declaration has clarified matters."

ONE MORE TIME

Summary

On the 17th of August 2000, the Blessed Holy Virgin Mary started Her apparitions at St. Mark's Church in Assiut, Upper Egypt, accompanied by glorious lights and big, bright white doves. Those who have witnessed the apparitions have reported seeing dazzling supernatural lights and blue-green flashes over the church. Many residents and pilgrims also recount seeing the Blessed Holy Virgin Mary in a full figure.

While the vision was reported in the media throughout Europe, it did not seem to get much, if any, recognition, in the States, which is not unusual since our papers have become more celebrity-orientated than anything else, gossip certainly more appealing than a religious miracle or two!

Assuit, Egypt (AP) – Thousands of Egyptians and some foreigners have been flocking to this southern Egyptian city in recent weeks, where residents say they've seen an apparition of the Virgin Mary and a flock of exceptionally large, white pigeons in an inexplicable shining light. Since the first reported apparition on Aug. 17 in skies surrounding the dome of Saint Mark's church, villagers and visitors have descended on the neighborhood, waiting in the streets and on rooftops for a glimpse of Mary.

The city's local Coptic Christian synod released a statement on Sunday stating that civilians had reported seeing "spiritual features" on several occasions and at different times since Aug. 17. The statement did not say whether religious leaders had confirmed any sightings personally.

"I haven't seen any light," Father Baki Sedka, head of the First Biblical Church (Protestant), a neighboring church to Saint Mark, told The Associated Press on Monday night. "I stayed up all night and I didn't see anything except a few pigeons.

"The appearance of a few pigeons doesn't justify a miracle," Sedka continued. "This case needs a lot of consideration before we can authoritatively assert these sightings."

Since word of the apparition spread, the synod said thousands of Egyptians and some foreigners have come to Assiut, 180 miles (290 kilometers) south of Cairo, the capital, where they've been singing hymns and reciting prayers while waiting for the next vision to appear.

Copts make up less than 10 percent of the population in Egypt, where Islam is the state religion. Assiut has a substantial Coptic Christian population, but also has been a hotbed for Islamic fundamentalism and the site of violent attacks targeting Christians and tourists.

A PROLONGED APPEARANCE OVER EL-WARRAQ

I don't have a map of the towns around the Nile, but as far as I can tell El-Warraq is a small island of roughly 20,000 located in the Giza governorate, district of greater Cairo. Though mainly Muslims live there, a Christian minority is also noticeably present. There do not seem to be any reported clashes between the two faiths. The one thing they have in common is that both groups are relatively poor.

A miracle did seem to unite them for a period of a year or so, as the number of tourists with money to purchase local goods increased considerably during the visions of who they believed was the mother of Jesus.

She first appeared on December 22, 2009, when a shopkeeper across the way from the Michael Coptic Orthodox Church observed a strange materialization "of great brilliance" over the church's dome. The apparition was of a "glowing nature," so much so that it could be seen miles away. Those that had been at Zietoun when the church had been visited said that the manifestations were almost identical in appearance. People used their mobile phones to make videos of the apparitions and share them via Bluetooth and on YouTube. The full silhouette of the "Blessed Holy Virgin Mary" was dressed in a light blue gown that could be clearly seen over the domes of the church between the church crosses. The apparitions received wide media coverage in Egyptian newspapers and on Arabic television.

Though not "officially endorsed," those that witnessed the "light show," included His Holiness Pope Shenouda III, prompting a statement by Anba Dumadius, Archbishop of Giza:

"The Bishopric of Giza announces that the Holy Virgin has appeared in a transfiguration at the Church named after her in Warraq al-Hadar, Giza, in the early hours of Friday 11 December 2009 at 1:00 A.M. The Holy Virgin appeared in her full height in luminous robes, above the middle dome of the church, in pure white dress and a royal blue belt. She had a crown on her head, above which appeared the cross on top of the dome. The crosses on top of the church's domes and towers glowed brightly with light. The Holy Virgin moved between the domes and on to the top of the church gate between its two twin towers. The local residents all saw her.

"The apparition lasted from 1:00 A.M. till 4:00 A.M. on Friday, and was registered by cameras and cell phones. Some 3,000 people from the neighborhood, surrounding areas, and passers-by gathered in the street in front of the church to see the apparition.

"Since Friday, the huge crowds gathered in the vicinity of the church have been seeing luminous white pigeons soaring above the church during various times of the night, as well as a star which emerges suddenly in the heavens, travels some 200 meters across, then disappears. The huge crowds gathered around the church do not cease singing hymns and praises for the Holy Virgin.

"This is a great blessing for the Church and for all the people of Egypt. May Her blessing and intercession benefit us all."

—Signed Anba TheodosiusBishop-General of Giza

Throngs filled the street nightly to witness the appearance of the "Lady of Light," as she was sometimes referred to.

The Lady appeared just about every night over the dome of St. Mary's Church of Zeitoun.

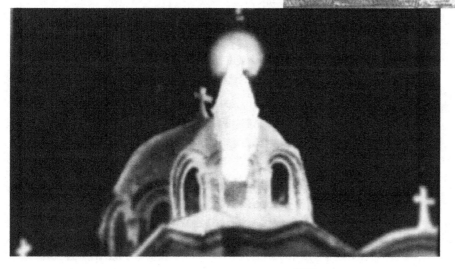

For three years, the Lady in White appeared over the dome of St. Mary's of Zeitoun.

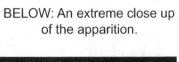

BELOW: An extreme close up of the apparition.

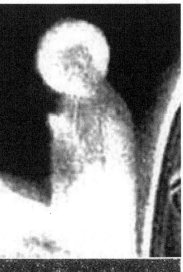

It was debated whether they were doves or angelic forms that appeared over the apparition's head.

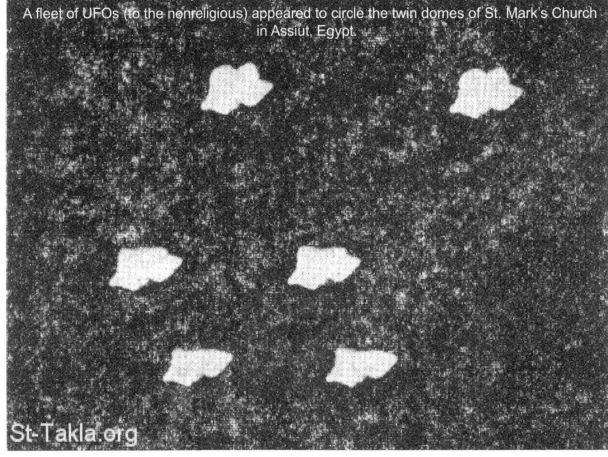

A fleet of UFOs (to the nonreligious) appeared to circle the twin domes of St. Mark's Church in Assiut, Egypt.

St-Takla.org

Sunday World-Herald

OMAHA, NEBRASKA, MAY 5, 1968—244 PAGES, 10 SECTIONS. SECTION A—28 PAGES.

Egyptian Coptics Confirm Vision of the Virgin Mary

By Reuters Agency, Ltd.

Cairo, Egypt—Reports of a vision of the Virgin Mary—which have brought thousands of people flocking to a Cairo suburban church—were verified Saturday by the Egyptian Coptic Church "with full confidence and great joy."

A statement read to newsmen on behalf of the Coptic Patriarch Kyrillos, said the Virgin Mary appeared several consecutive nights for periods as long as 2½ hours on occasions dating back to April 2.

The vision, seen standing with outstretched arms on a parapet of the Church of the Virgin in the suburb of Zeitoun, was accompanied by several medically verified miraculous cures, the statement added.

The road leading to the church has been packed solidly with thousands of persons from Cairo

and foreign tourists from dusk to dawn every night for the last two weeks as reports of the vision spread.

The road on which the church stands is reputed to be part of the route taken by the Holy Family in its wandering through Egypt.

According to those who say they have seen the vision, the image of the Virgin ascended from the church roof into the sky Monday evening and has not been seen since.

The church's statement said the vision sometimes appeared life-size—surrounded by a halo and accompanied by a bright light around the church dome—bowing and blessing the crowd.

At a celebration of the Coptic Easter April 21, scores of persons in the church reported seeing the vision in the form of an intense light.

The apparition was front page news in the European press.

The apparition lit up the sky for miles around St. Mark's Church.

The Lady in White drew thousands to the church in El-Warraq. She was seen to hover over the church towers with their trio of crosses. She floated and moved from side to side. Was she "real" or a hologram?

At times she floated away from her pedestal as if she were levitating or floating in space.

The clerics of St. Mary's verified the presence of the manifestation.

18

THE LADY WEARS WHITE, THE VISIONS AT GARABANDAL, AND THE "WEEPING VIRGIN" PREDICTIONS
By Timothy Green Beckley

We travel next to Peru to visit with the Lady of the Mountains, who is a miniature version of the Madonna. Though it may seem strange, we have verified numerous cases now where UFOs and the occupants have changed shape or morphed into a different being or craft altogether. See "UFOs Deja Vu," for complete validation.

Actually the region of the Andes has a long history of veneration of the Lady.

We bring your attention to the fact that Spaniards arriving in sixteenth-century South America encountered a rich and complex indigenous tradition of gold working that had developed over the course of millennia. Many, if not most, Pre-Columbian works in gold were melted down in the sixteenth and seventeenth centuries, their precious metal repurposed for new religious and secular leaders both in Spain and the Americas. A most treasured bejeweled crown was made to adorn a sacred image of the Virgin Mary venerated in the cathedral of Popayán, Colombia. A symbol of the Virgin's divine status as a queen, the crown is encircled by golden vine work set with emerald clusters in the shape of flowers, a reference to her purity. The diadem is topped by imperial arches and a cross-bearing orb that symbolizes Christ's dominion over the world.

Although the practice was controversial, it was common to bestow lavish gifts, including jewels and sumptuous garments, on sculptures of the Virgin Mary. To gain salvation, the faithful sought her intercession and worked to honor her and increase the splendor of her worship. At the same time, the crown represents one of the most distinctive artistic achievements of a region whose wealth derived from the mining of gold and emeralds. Such a crown – worth a million dollars or more today – was crafted because several members of the indigenous communities had claimed to have seen the materialization of who they believed to be the Holy Lady.

UFOS, ARMAGEDDON AND BIBLICAL REVELATIONS

Lila Acheson Wallace Gift, Acquisitions Fund
and
Mary Trumbull Adams Fund, 2015

* * * * * * * *

THE LADY IN WHITE LIVES IN A CAVE ON "HOLY MOUNTAIN"

An Exclusive Report Filed By Bill Cox
Editor, "The Pyramid Guide"
Author, "The Pyramids Speak," "Unseen Kingdoms"

Of all the cases of Marian phenomena, the following perhaps best of all suggests a strong UFO tie-in: Over the years, Peru has seen its share of mystical happenings. Many citizens have reported seeing far distant lights in the sky that behave "improperly," and visionary experiences transpire here as frequently as anywhere else in South America or the rest of the world, for that matter. But there is an area in the state of Huanaco that deserves special attention, for among the strange phenomena reported occurring there are the following:

· Mysterious floating lights;

· Unknown flying machines;

· Odd creatures that materialize in the surrounding hills, emitting magical-sounding hums.

· And most amazing of all, the appearance of a female figure dressed in white that has become known as "The White Lady of the Andes."

Our first inkling of anything unusual taking place in this particular region occurred when three local inhabitants, or "Hill People," as we will call them, arrived in Lima after a long, exhausting journey from their territory, which is located between the central and eastern ranges of the Andes, not far from the edge of the jungle on the banks of the Haullaga, a tributary of the Amazon.

STRANGE FIGURE

The state of Huanaco is in itself somewhat of a mystery even to the rest of Peru. Tradition holds that the first inhabitants of the area came from the heavens, and some years back archaeologists uncovered the now famous "Temple of the Crossed Hands," believed to be the oldest archaeological artifact anywhere in the Americas. Made of mud, this figure dates back 4200 years, and studies have shown that the formation of its fingers, wrist and forearm is totally of a different nature from that of the people who now inhabit this region. It is generally believed that a different race must have arrived in Peru in the remote past from another continent. What cannot be explained is the fact that since the statue was made out of mud how it has been able to survive the passing of time and the forces of nature. This would indicate that an unknown ingredient was used in its composition.

Quickly, the Peruvian Society for Interplanetary Relations organized a fact-finding mission to the region. Many interesting stories had long been reaching researchers from this area and we decided it was time to investigate.

The first group was headed by Cesar Vasques Salasi, a scientist from Ecuador. He was accompanied on the journey by two capable researchers, Senor Alessandri and Alvarez. Together they traveled to the scene and interviewed several witnesses. They were even told about a case involving a man who was caught in quicksand and was saved when he was pulled out of the sink hole by two little men with greenish tinted skin. From all they were told, it was obvious that the majority of reports came from an area known as the Rondo Plain, just north of the city. At an altitude of 7400 feet the investigators set up camp. During the course of that first night strange things began to happen.

Cesar Vasques Salasi later reported back to us that at 9 P.M. all of their group saw two UFOs which were not explainable. A short while later Jorge Aluarez was by himself a short distance from camp when he almost suffered a heart attack. There, standing before him in the dark, were several beings who were very short in stature, had greenish colored skin and scales on their bodies and tails.

As soon as it could be done, a well-equipped expedition was organized. This time twelve investigators chose to make the long journey, which I personally directed. The first stop was at the home of Senor Fernando Fernandez, who proved to have a wealth of knowledge and was very well-versed on UFOs in the region. He said that his research had indicated that most of the strange activity seemed to be centered near the town of Cayran, which is located in a valley and inhabited only by country folk. In Cayran, Senor Fernandes explained, life is devoid of social problems, politics, and crime. The residents live in sort of a communal fashion and are closed to outsiders who interfere in their daily activities.

RESIDENTS DRAW BACK

Upon their arrival in town, the researchers were immediately surrounded by many curious people who, when they found out why they had come, drew back and refused to answer any of their questions. To them the subject of their trip was "taboo." From what could be gathered, they were upset thinking that the tranquility of the place would be altered. To them, any investigation of the "Lady in White" was a sin, in their eyes at least, and very diabolical.

Initially, it looked like they had traveled in vain, that their investigation would not be successful. Luckily, the course of events was changed when two of the team of investigators came across two young boys playing alongside the banks of a stream. The boys were playing with a peculiar looking doll –a wooden figure of the Virgin, perfectly shaped. This doll fit perfectly the description that has been given of the "Lady in White." Naturally the researchers were curious and asked the boys a lot of questions.

The boys said the name of the Virgin was "La Purisima" ("the purest of the Holiest") and said that she lived in a cave outside of their town. They were not very helpful in giving directions, and would say only that she lived on top of a mountain accompanied by small "angels," and that she called the faithful with the aid of a bell which could be heard throughout the valley.

Said the investigators, "Naturally, we felt as if we were on to something very important, and with the help of a few small gifts, we eventually got the two boys (age 8 and 10) to cooperate. After walking over a mile and a half we reached the side of a very steep mountain with two rocks on the summit, one atop the other, at whose base there was an opening that an adult could only enter on their hands and knees.

"For the next two hours we looked for a possible way up to the summit. Being somewhat of a more experienced climber than the rest of our group, I went on ahead, inching my way up the mountain. Slowly but surely, I forged a path by hanging on to outcroppings and clumps of bushes that winded their way to the top.

THE LADY APPEARS

"Suddenly, about half the way up the side of the mountain, I saw a beautiful woman less than two feet tall. She was dressed in a white tunic, just like all the drawings of the Virgin. The woman's skin was a strong pink. She had very large, blue eyes and her hair was golden blonde. In one hand she held a red belt, and to me it seemed as if she were capable of reading my mind.

"After a few seconds of indecision on my part, I decided to try and communicate with her. 'Lady, I know you are not a spirit but a representative of another world, whose mission is to do good and look for love between the inhabitants of this planet and yours. I only wish to speak with you, so as to receive your message and share it with those who want to grow spiritually.'

"Before I had finished speaking with the 'Lady,' she started to move away, up the mountainside. To me it did not look as if she were walking as I did not see her feet touch the ground (her tunic was covering her feet). Within minutes she reached the cave at the summit of the mountain and vanished inside.

"Not one to give up so easily in my quest, I tried to follow her. Eventually, I reached the cave at whose entrance there was a small platform about thirty square feet. The platform was covered with flowers and vegetables obviously placed there by the faithful in gratitude for miraculous cures received by the local inhabitants. As the others in our party reached the top, I suggested that we search for the bell the 'Lady' used in order to summon the Mountain Folk. I figured that it would have to be rather large in order to be heard throughout the entire valley. Because of its size it would be pretty hard to hide in the cave.

UFOS, ARMAGEDDON AND BIBLICAL REVELATIONS

"Taking matters into my own hands, I asked the younger of the two boys who had led us to the cave to go inside the small opening and see if the 'Lady' was there. A few minutes later he crawled back out on his hands and knees and told us, 'Yes, she is there, but she is not alone – she is accompanied by two angels.' 'Two angels?' we asked, wanting a better description. 'Yes, mister,' answered the boy. 'She is with two little men, dressed in gold.'

"Once again I asked the boy to enter the cave and request permission to make contact with the 'Lady in White' and the little men. I told the boy what to say, that we were learned men and wished to tighten bonds with our space brothers. Upon his return the youth stated that the 'Lady in White' was willing to come out at midnight. I said that was not practical, since at this altitude we would surely become sick or perhaps even freeze to death. All our Geiger counters, telescopes and other measuring devices would do us no good since we didn't have the proper garments to sleep at this high altitude.

"It was obvious that she did not wish a physical contact with members of our group, and so we went away disappointed. But perhaps we shall return someday soon to this region and discover even more about the 'Lady in White' and the 'angels' who accompany her in the cave."

* * * * * * * * * *

MIRACLE OF THE WEEPING MADONNAS

From California to Puerto Rico, statues of the Virgin Mary are crying real tears and moving about as if to warn of impending danger.

The mystery surrounding the statue of Our Lady of Fatima, which is said to move about and shed tears in Thornton, Calif., a rural community outside of Sacramento, has received its share of national publicity in recent months. Some months ago, an attendant in the church noticed that the statue – which weighs nearly sixty pounds and stands four feet high – had apparently moved down the aisle by itself over night.

Over a period of the next six months – always on the 13th – the statue would somehow find its way to the altar, although it had been in its usual resting place on the 13th of the month, and perhaps this was in some way tied in with the famous apparition. To add fuel to the belief that this occurrence was something in the realm of the supernatural, the statue also began to shed tears. This, many believe, is Mary's way of warning people that some terrible event is going to take place very soon. Of course, there are the skeptics who point out that church attendance has mushroomed since the story was published in local as well as national publications. Now it is not uncommon for a thousand of the faithful to flock to the church for services, especially around the time of the month when the statue is supposed to move.

By pure coincidence, an "Inner Light" reader, Joyce Davis of Knights Landing, California, also heard of the miracle at about the same time we started work on a new book on the Virgin Mary. This book details several dozen appearances of the Mother of Jesus in recent years and the dire prophecies She has repeatedly given in order to save as many people as possible should there be a global disaster. Apparently, Joyce Davis was really emotionally touched by her visit to the church and as PROOF that this statue is no ordinary statue, Joyce came away with a fantastic photograph showing a fiery object which was not present when she took the picture. What she captured with the camera's eye is reproduced in this book (unfortunately in black and white), but let us allow Joyce to tell her own story: "On the date of December 19, 1982, I walked through the doors of the little Catholic Mission Church of Mater Ecclesiae with heavy heart and troubled countenance.

"I came not seeking signs and proof of what I had heard, but with a prayer, and an urgent hope and desire that I might obtain Divine Intercession in matters that had become very difficult to cope with and burdens which had become almost too heavy to bear.

"Upon receiving back a roll of film I had turned in to process, I discovered a very brilliant globe of white light, surrounded by a fiery aura, in the upper left side of one of the pictures. Nobody seems to be able to explain to me exactly what this manifestation is."

Though Joyce Davis remains puzzled, there is a possible explanation in that other, similar, manifestations have taken place on a global basis. It has been revealed that Mary has repeatedly told of a forthcoming devastating wall of fire which will sweep down over the Earth, destroying the chaos that mankind has created out of God's beautiful creation. Known as the "Ball of Redemption," Mary has warned over and over again that God in Heaven is fed up with the conditions down here on Earth and will cleanse the planet in the very near future.

In fact, Joyce Davis says that she has now had a chance to meditate on what the manifestation in her picture indicates, "And the answer I have received is: 'For the judgment I AM come,' a statement which I feel is self-explanatory, and which helps me to remain firm in my conviction that judgment will indeed come upon those who take so lightly the warnings that are being sounded to the uttermost parts of the Earth and which are still falling upon deaf ears."

Concludes Joyce, "I pray that the reason for the Virgin's weeping will soon be over, for there are those upon this Earth who have taken heed of Her urgent warnings, regardless of the taunts and ridicule of those who are presently at risk of being taken by surprise when that inevitable 'Three Days of Darkness' arrives due to their own disregard for useful instruction and the breaking of laws which demand justifiable restitution."

Indeed, the Madonna almost always seems to have a harsh message, a stern cautionary warning to deliver

* * * * * * * * *

THE SORROWFUL VIRGIN OF AIBONITO

Nothing like this has ever happened in the 160 years since the town, which is at the highest point in Puerto Rico, was founded. According to witnesses, the image of the Virgin Mary has been seen to cry in the local parish, and even the priest who has been taught to be hardnosed and skeptical in such matters, admits that the entire episode has him puzzled.

The Virgin was seen for the first time to weep on May 31, 1983, during a mass at which another, similar, statue was being crowned. The first person to notice the tears was a child who ran and told her mother what she had seen, even though she was not old enough to understand the significance of the event.

Daisy Santiago de Rivera, mother of the child who first witnessed the miracle, tells how the miracle unfolded: "We went to the mass and stayed in the back. Jessica and her older sister and some other little girls went to place some flowers beside the image of the Virgin which was being crowned.

"Then little Jessica asked if she could take some flowers to a second statue of the Virgin Mary and place some flowers around Her. I said she should do this because the second statue looked so sad that she was being left out of the proceedings. My daughter took the flowers, which were white lilies, and placed them by the statue. My sister was there praying. Suddenly, she noticed that there seemed to be tears on the face of the statue. Without saying anything to me, she walked to the front of the altar and waited for the mass to be over. Then, on impulse, I went over to the Sorrowful Virgin and I also noticed the tears. I was not able to pray. I thought I must be going mad.

Daisy saw the tear fall down as far as the lips. Her sister, who is a school teacher, saw the tear fall even further. Daisy's husband, Pucho Rivera, a band director, says, "Everyone who was there saw it. It was a miracle meant for us all!"

By the end of the service, word had spread of the miracle and everyone clustered around the statue of the Madonna to catch a glimpse of the tears. Though there was a lot of emotion, tears and prayers, there was no hysteria. It seemed that most everyone was wondering what message the Sorrowful Virgin was trying to convey.

The residents of Aibonito don't know what this all means, but they are certain that the Virgin Mary does not cry for no reason at all. They are looking deeply within themselves for answers, as are others who have witnessed the appearance and been affected by the miracles of the Heavenly Mother.

It does appear that the visions hold a dire WARNING! – Such warnings are part and parcel of the phenomena. The visions almost always tie in with a dark prophecy, but with an upbeat message that this darkness upon the Earth does not have to occur should humankind change its dire ways.

* * * * * * * * * *

VISIONS AT GARABANDAL

Garabandal is a small village in the northern part of Spain. It lies near the Picos de Europa Mountains and is a rugged area, although quite beautiful. The town's full name is San Sebastian of Garabandal and is quite difficult to reach. You have to climb a steep road which begins in Cosio. The population of Garabandal is about 300. There is no doctor in town, and until 1965 there was not even a resident priest. The pastor from Cosio used to come to the quiet town to celebrate Mass every Sunday. The visions began on June 18, 1961, in the evening. Four girls were playing on the outskirts of the town when they occurred. The girls were Conchita Gonzalez, Maria Dolores Mazon, Jacinta Gonzalez (no relation to Conchita), and Maria Cruz Gonzalez (no relation to the other two). Maria Cruz was eleven. The other three were 12. All were from poor families. The girls heard what sounded like a thunder clap. When they looked around for the source, they saw a bright figure who announced himself as Michael the Archangel.

The girls were awestruck. They said nothing and did nothing. They merely stared at the magnificent figure until it faded from view. During subsequent days, however, the Archangel Michael appeared to the girls again and again. Finally, he told them that on July 2nd they would see the Holy Virgin.

The news spread quickly, so that on July 2nd Garabandal was crowded with people from all walks of life. At six in the evening the four girls walked to the place where Michael had appeared. In a short time, Our Lady appeared to the girls accompanied by two angels, one of them being Michael the Archangel.

The girls went into ecstasy, their faces radiating the light that they saw around the Holy Mother. The girls described what they saw in this manner: "She is dressed in a white robe with a blue mantle and a crown of golden stars. Her hands are slender. There is a brown scapular on her right arm, except when she carries the Child Jesus in her arms. Her hair, deep nut-brown, is parted in the center. Her face is long, with a fine nose. Her mouth is very pretty, with lips a bit thin. She looks like a girl of eighteen. She is rather tall. There is no voice like hers. No woman is just like her, either, in the voice or the face or anything else. Our Lady manifested herself as Our Lady of Carmel."

MORE VISIONARY APPEARANCES

During 1961 and 1962 Our Lady appeared several times each week. The four girls were not always together during the visions. Often, only one girl would be present. The visions did not always come at the same time of day. Sometimes they were in the afternoons, sometimes in the evening. Often, they were seen early in the morning. The people of the village noticed that although the girls worked as hard as usual, carrying bundles of grass or wood, working in the fields, they never showed signs of fatigue.

THE STRANGE ECSTASIES

During the apparitions the four girls went into ecstasies lasting from a few minutes to several hours. Their faces revealed an extraordinary sweetness, beautiful and beautified and transformed as by an interior light. Time did not seem to count; they never showed signs of being tired despite the length of time or their weary uncomfortable posture, kneeling on rocks, with their heads violently thrown backwards, or on cold days of winter with snow under their bare feet and no protection against the cold.

At the end of their ecstasy they would return to their normal state, with no signs of excitation or nervousness, but only a deep and profound peace and joy. During the time of ecstasy they seemed to lose sensibility – burns, hits, pricks failed to make them come out of their state of rapture. Powerful beams of light were flashed in their eyes without causing even a flicker. Under normal circumstances these lights would have burned the retina and caused blindness. Their eyes had an open and joyful look. When the vision appeared they fell instantly on their knees, striking the hard rock with a loud noise which was frightening, but they showed no signs of wounds or injuries. They were then unaware of the material things around them, being completely absorbed in ecstasy.

MIRACLE OF THE HOST

An area above the village of Garabandal is called the Pines. A small cluster of pine trees stand on the hill, and according to the four girls an angel with a golden chalice appeared on the Pines and asked the girls to recite the Confiteor. He then gave them Holy Communion. The incident occurred often, especially when the priest in Cosio could not make the trip to Garabandal to celebrate Mass.

Films were taken of the event, although it was necessary to use very bright light. The lips and the tongues of the four girls on the film indicate that they were actually receiving the host.

On May 2, 1962, an angel told Conchita that God would perform a miracle so that it would be easier for the people to believe what was happening. He would permit them to see the Sacred Host on her tongue.

By the date of the miracle, July 18, 1962, the town was jammed with people. They came from all over the country. Conchita remained in her home until midnight. She was in a state of ecstasy when she walked into the street. The crowd made room for her. Suddenly, she dropped to her knees and opened her mouth. She put out her tongue. There was nothing on it. Lanterns were drawn near. People stared. Then, slowly, a white host materialized. It was thicker than most and it remained on Conchita's tongue for a few minutes. Don Alejandro Damians stood three feet away and managed to get the miracle on film. In 79 frames of the moving picture the materialization of the host is quite clear.

Witnesses declare that Conchita's arms were at her sides the entire time. Don Benjamin Gomez said: "The girl's face was beautifully transformed into heavenly ecstasy. Her face was angelic. I can certify that she was there, motionless, moving neither hands nor tongue. In this motionless state she received the Sacred Host. We had enough time to contemplate this marvelous phenomenon without any undue haste, and we were many who saw it."

MARY'S WARNING AT GARABANDAL

On January 1, 1965, Conchita was told by the Virgin Mary that she would have a message for her on June 18th. Naturally, word spread quickly. When the day came, more than two thousand people were in Garabandal, many of them French, German, English, Italians, Americans and Poles. There were journalists from many countries and TV camera crews from Italy, Spain and France.

Conchita walked from her house at 11:30 P.M. to the Pines. She stopped at a place called Cuadro. Witnesses said she was in rapture for sixteen minutes. The entity who appeared was not the Holy Mother, but the Archangel Michael (Conchita learned later that Mary was so distressed by her message that she could not deliver it herself).

The message which Our Lady has given to the world through the intercession of St. Michael the Archangel is as follows. The angel said: "Since my message of October 18 has not been made known to the world and has not been fulfilled, I tell you that this is my last message. Previously, the cup was being filled. Now it is overflowing. Many priests are on the road to perdition and with them they are bringing many souls. The Holy Eucharist is being given less importance (honor). We must avoid God's wrathful angel by our efforts at amendment. If we beg pardon with sincerity of soul, He will forgive us. I, your Mother, through the intercession of St. Michael the Archangel, want to tell you to amend your lives. You are already receiving one of the last warnings. I love you very much and do not want your condemnation. Ask us sincerely and we will give to you. You should make more sacrifices. Think of the Passion of Jesus."

The last apparition appeared to Conchita on November 13th, 1965. Conchita revealed later that she was told that a miracle will take place on a Thursday at 8:30 p.m. Conchita knows what the miracle is, but is not permitted to reveal it until eight days before it takes place.

THE GARABANDAL MIRACLE

Conchita said: "The Blessed Virgin will not allow me to reveal the nature of the miracle although I already know it. Neither can I reveal the date of it, which I know, until eight days before it is to happen." No one knows when the miracle will occur. We can't assume anything. All we do know is that the hour of Our Lady is coming. Mary promised Conchita that before the miracle occurs, all mankind will receive a warning from heaven.

Conchita does not know the exact date of the warning, but she has been given an inkling of what it will be like. She said: "The warning will be directly from God and will be visible to the whole world and from any place where anyone happens to be. It will be like the revelation of our sins and will be seen and felt by everyone, believer and nonbeliever alike, irrespective of whatever religion he may belong to. It will be seen and felt in all parts of the world and by every person."

PHYSICAL PHENOMENA – MARCHES AND ECSTATIC FALLS

One of the extraordinary and unprecedented phenomena in the history of the apparitions was the ecstatic marches and ecstatic falls of the visionaries in Garabandal. In the moments before the visions and during the visions, the girls circled the streets of the villages, went up and down the mountain, entered the houses, and visited the cemetery, but always in a state of ecstasy. Sometimes they also fell to the ground in ecstasy, without ever being hurt.

The young women knew when the visions would happen, by a series of three calls (illuminations), each stronger than the other. After the third call, they ran to the reclusive place, where the first visions were given; there they prostrated themselves on their knees in the sharp rocks and entered into a supernatural ecstatic trance. Their heads melted back, the pupils of their eyes dilated, their faces beaded with perspiration with striking angelic expressions. They remained thus in this position for a few hours, without ever showing signs of muscular effort and fatigue. Thus they were insensitive to pin pricks, burns with matches and physical contacts. Even when, at night, during the visions, dazzling spotlights were centered on the faces of the young girls, their pupils remained motionless and dilated. During such trances the weight of the young girls became so excessive that two adult men had difficulty raising a 12-year-old girl. However, they rose with one another, with the greatest ease, to offer a kiss to the Virgin.

ECSTATIC FALLS

As the apparitions continued, a new phenomenon began to occur: the Ecstatic Fall. Only in ecstasy, whether on their knees or standing, did the young women fall behind, stretched out on the ground. They were never harmed by this, nor were their garments ever entangled. They were thus ecstatic, in a horizontal position and without using their hands to compose themselves, returning to the original position, on their knees or standing. When two or more of the young women, in ecstasy, fell together, their movements were perfectly synchronized. One witness, Canon Júlio Porro Cardenoso, said that it was identical to a jet of light inside a large conference hall where all the lights went out simultaneously. When the girls lay on the ground, after an ecstatic fall, the position of their bodies stood out somewhat as a supernatural sign, and many bystanders described them as magnificent "sculptures."

Another exceptional feature of the apparitions, coming almost at the same time of the ecstatic fall, is the Ecstatic March. From head to back, in a characteristic way and without seeing where they would go, the girls marched arm-in-hand back and forth, without the slightest difficulty, on rugged and dangerous terrain and sometimes with such swift steps that spectators could not accompany them. A witness, Ms. Ascencion de Luis, described in a report dated March 18, 1962, one of these seemed "to fly": "From the village, climbing the rocky ramp to the small pine forest that hung in the direction of the village ... The girl climbed the ramp and down again at incredible speed." Sometimes the girls resembled airplanes gliding in the air, when they apparently flew over the land, arms outstretched, touching only the ground with their toes.

WHAT REALLY HAPPENED IN THIS SPANISH TOWN?

I have never visited the town. Did not see the apparition. But I do believe I spoke to one of the witnesses. It must have been in the mid to late 1970s when I received a call from a lady living in Yonkers, NY. She told me that she had been in Garabandal and had witnessed the peculiar, unexplainable phenomena. I don't recall why she picked me to call, but apparently she had read something I had written on the apparition suggesting that it could just as easily be defined as part of the UFO mystery as it could be associated with Mary, mother of the Christ, which she had been led to believe it was because of her cultural upbringing.

Apparently, the individual I was speaking with was in agreement with my viewpoint. From what she told me, she had changed her opinion about the circumstances of the vision after coming to America and hearing about UFOs, which she did not know existed before. I acknowledge that I have no notes and don't remember any more of what she told me. But the telephone call did stick in my mind as I had been doing active research on Fatima and the prophecies associated with the multiple 1917 events. Perhaps one of our readers who has followed these events can cast additional light on these sightings of the Lady in White.

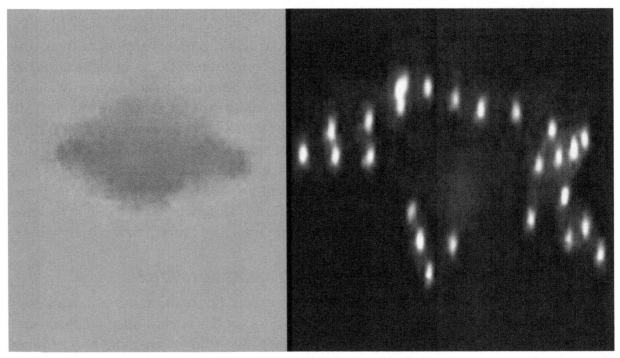

The Andes is known as a UFO hotspot.

The late Bill Cox used the pendulum to search for treasure throughout South America.

Valued at over a million U.S. dollars today, the Crown of the Andes was crafted because the local indigenous people had interacted with the Madonna.

The "Mother of us All" sheds tears for the state of the Earth.

Conchita holds the rosary aloft, as directed by the apparition.

Photographed during a period of ecstasy, the young lady falls to the ground feeling the presence of the Lady, who will have a message for all.

Three of the original witnesses to the manifestation at Garabandal receive a message from the Mother, invisible to all but them.

The Madonna was seen for the most part by the young witnesses, and they said she was majestic and beautiful.

One of the Garabandal children falls into a trance-like state as a communion wafer mysteriously appears on her tongue.

Sometimes the girls are said to have walked backward through the village.

The "Lady In White" was said to hold court in a cave in the mountains of Peru.

The "Crossed Hands" artifact is said to be the oldest archaeological relics found anywhere in America.

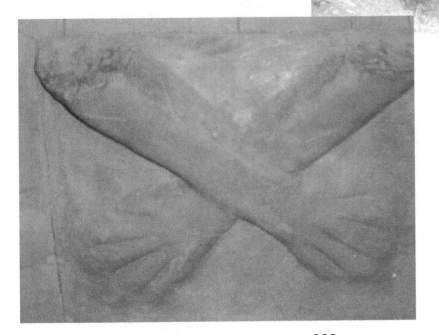

"Pyramid Guide" editor Bill Cox spoke with the witnesses who had visited with the Lady.

Art by Tom Goff.

Often associated with dire prophecies, statues of the Madonna are weeping tears around the world.

19

CUTTING ACROSS CULTURAL AND SOCIOLOGICAL LINES – THE MADONNA'S WIDE APPEAL
By Timothy Green Beckley

Additional Analytical Input From William – "Adman" – Kern
Astrophysical And Metaphysical Implications As Interpreted By Diane Tessman

* * * * * * * * * *

FACTS ABOUT MARY'S APPEARANCES

Our Lady is nearly always consistent when she makes an appearance. The fact is that Mary almost always appears to children or adults who are simple and innocent. She does not appear to the worldly-wise sophisticates. Many of the people privileged to see her are uneducated. It is as though she selects a clean slate on which to write her messages. The little people, the humble, the poor, the unlearned and illiterate are more likely to accept the apparition as true. The people with cluttered minds, and those who cling to pretentious philosophies, are poor receivers. Were they fortunate enough to receive messages from Mary, they would undoubtedly twist them, or question them, or even negate them and not pass them on.

Still another fact is that Mary always appears accompanied by a brilliant light. There is no exception to this. The light has an unearthly intensity, yet it does not hurt the eyes of those who witness the apparition. In the Fatima vision, when Francesco was questioned about the brightness of the light given off by the Virgin, he said: "The figure of the Virgin was brighter than the sun." Juan Diego at Guadalupe told of golden beams that rayed from Mary's body from head to foot.

Another characteristic common to all visions is that Our Lady always appears young and beautiful. Her youth in the apparitions represents a fresh new life of salvation for humankind. Our Lady also appears in white gowns. Witnesses have also seen blue and gold, but the dominating color is white.

UFOS, ARMAGEDDON AND BIBLICAL REVELATIONS

* * * * * * * * * *

WHAT'S IN A NAME?

By William – "Adman" – Kern

We are past the 100th anniversary of the apparitions of Our Lady of Fátima, and yet I know of no one, except for one of our intrepid researchers who has made what should be an obvious connection between the name of this famous Portuguese town and its more than subtle connection with Islam. The Blessed Virgin Mary appeared to the three shepherd children near the city of Fátima, that is an historical fact, but it's not generally known that the town is named after both a Muslim princess and the daughter of Mohammed.

During the 12th century, Christian armies sought to recapture cities in Spain and Portugal that were being occupied by Muslim forces. In this time period, a knight named Gonçalo Hermigues and his companions captured a Muslim princess named Fátima. Some stories say that after her capture, Fátima fell in love with Gonçalo and the two were soon after betrothed. Before their marriage, Fátima was baptized into the Catholic faith and took the name Oureana. Bet you didn't know the Portuguese cities of Fátima and Ourém are said to be named after this Muslim princess.

What's interesting is that the Muslim princess was named after one of the daughters of Mohammed, Fatimah bint Muhammad, a woman highly revered in Islam. She was given the title al-Zahra, "shining one," and Mohammed once said about her, "Thou shalt be the most blessed of all the women in Paradise, after Mary." (While Muslims do not hold the same beliefs about the Virgin Mary as Catholics, they still hold her with highest regard. Mary is mentioned more often in the Qu'ran than in the Christian Bible). According to Fr. Miguel Angel Ayuso, secretary of the Pontifical Council for Interreligious Dialogue, this connection can be a doorway to dialogue. He noted in a joint prayer meeting in 2014 how, "the Catholic Church recognizes that Muslims honor the Virgin Mother of Jesus, Mary, and invoke her with piety...Mary is mentioned various times in the Koran. Respect for her is so evident that when she is mentioned in Islam, it is usual to add 'Alayha l-salam' ('Peace be upon her'). Mary, a model for Muslims and Christians, is also a model of dialogue." Venerable Fulton Sheen draws an interesting connection between Muslims' reverence for Mary and the daughter of Mohammed and the appearance of Our Lady at Fátima.

This brings us to our second point, namely, why the Blessed Mother, in the twentieth century, should have revealed herself in the insignificant little village of Fátima, so that to all future generations she would be known as "Our Lady of Fátima." Since nothing ever happens out of heaven except with a finesse of all details, I believe that the Blessed Virgin chose to be known as "Our Lady of Fátima" as a pledge and a sign of hope to the Moslem people, and as an assurance that they, who show her so much respect, will one day accept her Divine Son, too. Surprisingly, besides attracting Christian pilgrims, the shrine at Fátima, Portugal, has also attracted Muslims in great numbers. They go to see the place where the Virgin Mary appeared in a city named after one of their most highly revered women. In the end, the Blessed Virgin Mary at Fátima called Christians to pray for peace in the world. In an age when violence is so often committed in the name of Islam, how much more should we have recourse to Our Lady of Fátima! Let us continue to work for peace in the world and look to Our Lady to be a bridge between Muslims and Christians, begging her to end the hatred that has caused so much violence around the world.

As with the Christian version of the sightings of the Madonna, there are miracles associated with the Muslim version of these accounts as well.

There is a miraculous incident related in Al-Bidayah by way of An-Nihayah. Once a lady sent Fatimah some bread and roasted meat. She put this on a plate and covered it with cloth. Then she sent a message to her father to come and eat. When he arrived, she removed the cloth and to her astonishment she found the plate full of bread and plenty of meat. She understood that this abundance and plenty had come from Allah. She praised Almighty Allah and asked Allah to mention and bless His servants. She started to serve the meal to him, beginning with Allah Almighty's Name. When he saw such a huge amount he smiled and asked who had sent it all. She promptly said Allah gave it to her and He provides sustenance to whom He is pleased without limits. Then the Prophet (peace and blessings be upon him) smiled and ate the meal with his daughter and her family. Yet there was so much food still left over that it was sent to the Mothers of the Believers. They also ate their fill, and then it was distributed among the neighbors.

The comparisons are there for one to see, cutting across cultural and social lines, while making it obvious that there is an external force behind the phenomena we are questioning.

* * * * * * * *

FATIMA DECODED

The reader, in fact, does not have to go about the task of cracking open dusty old books to realize fully the spectrum of such apparitions in our modern-day world. It has become common knowledge that visions of the Madonna come fairly widespread. A person has only to pick up one of the many supermarket tabloids to learn about sightings everywhere, from Omaha to Chicago, from Paris to Havana. On the other hand, if one wishes to skirt over such seemingly sensationalistic accounts as an apparition of Mary appearing on the side of a refrigerator, one merely has to step into any Catholic bookstore and find the section devoted to such sacred matters. Here the testimonials of the pious are quite plain, taking up volume after volume. Interestingly enough, it appears that visions of the

UFOS, ARMAGEDDON AND BIBLICAL REVELATIONS

Virgin Mary have increased many-fold since Fatima, and most assuredly so since the end of World War II and the beginning of the nuclear age.

The Marian or Madonna phenomenon has recently attracted its share of researchers, many of whom are not associated with any particular denomination, nor are they necessarily even religiously oriented.

ADDITIONAL PATTERNS

Previously, we have discussed numerous existing patterns that are repeatedly seen when researching the visions associated with the Marian phenomena. But it is justifiable that we reiterate several of them, so as to bring forth more strongly our views.

Instead, these investigators pore through tons of testimonials searching for possible clues and patterns that will lend additional credibility to the scores of case histories now recorded. Many of these patterns are noted throughout the pages of this book which, hopefully, will awaken scores to the fact that something of tremendous importance is taking place which needs to be re-evaluated.

One noteworthy pattern is that often, at the time of such materializations, the Lady will entrust to some worthy soul prophecies of forthcoming events. Sometimes the predictions are limited in scope and are of a personal nature of benefit or interest to just the immediate witness (such as that they will be turning to the priesthood or will be joining a convent). Other times they may be in the form of dire warnings that someone's life is in danger. Or the Lady can bring with her news pertaining to the nearest town or community, perhaps communicating the sad news of a forthcoming flood, or bridge disaster, or train wreck that is certain to cause many deaths and bring great sorrow in its wake.

On other occasions, she may appear before some tragic world event, such as a devastating earthquake or the outbreak of war. She may be seen by only one or two individuals, or by a small group, or perhaps by hundreds (or even thousands) gathered in a particular locality awaiting her arrival. Frequently, the Lady will appear over and over at one spot before vanishing, never to be seen again. Other times the apparition is a "one shot" deal, and comes totally unannounced and unexpected. As proof, some of the gathered flock may be healed. Some may develop strange powers such as levitation or a sixth sense. Others may go into a trance state and "speak" directly with her. Those with cameras at their side have caught some truly amazing phenomena on film. Some have photographed glowing bursts that look remarkably like a lady engulfed in white light. Others pick up enigmatic strobes, flashes, and maybe even a form dressed in a robe.

UNEARTHLY EXPLANATIONS

Noted author John A. Keel, who made a study of puzzling phenomena most of his life, has gone on record as stating that the most impressive UFO sighting of all time was, more than likely, the apparition of the falling sun at Fatima. "I have seen photographs of the phenomena," Keel said, "which were published at the time and the sun actually looks very much like a spinning disc."

Michael Grosso, a Ph.D. who teaches and lectures in New York, goes a step further when he proclaims, "To me, the events at Fatima look as if they were engineered by an intelligence of unknown origin." To back up his case that UFOs figure very deeply in this miracle, Grosso points out that many of the "witnesses at Fatima reported observing thunder-like sounds, sounds of 'rockets,' sudden winds, drops in temperature, dimming of the sun and atmosphere, light effects that tinted trees, faces and stones, and 'falling flowers,' an effect similar to the 'angel hair' described in association with some UFO sightings." He also notes that mysterious "flashes and balls of light were seen and the children involved reported being penetrated by a light ray, another common feature in UFO reports." Similarly, during the summer of 1917 (leading up to the sun's dancing) the children experienced, according to Grosso, "voice-like buzzing, smoke-like forms, and Lucia was heard saying the lady disappeared through a door in the sky."

I am fascinated by the fact that Michael Grosso first became fixated on the subject of UFOs upon witnessing the manifestation of a "squadron" of unidentified objects which appeared out of a clear sky and hovered over a cathedral in Greenwich Village. He witnessed the strange pattern from his Manhattan window. Grosso, we should point out, is not a person to be easily fooled. He is a scholar, teacher, author and painter whose interests span psychical research, mystical art, and the parapsychology of religion and philosophy. He tells us about a miraculous experience where UFOs seemed to play a cat and mouse game with him outside his window in Greenwich Village, which led to a leap in awareness. He has recently written "The Man Who Could Fly."

Those who wish to listen to him describe his tantalizing tale merely have to sashay over to our YouTube channel, "Mr. UFO's Secret Files," and give a listen to Dr. Grosso, who is a very compelling guest. The show was recorded in June, 2018, and is tagged, "The Ghost Box And The Flying Saint." – www.youtube.com/ watch?v=_lABbSJYWoU

During my own tenure as a reporter interviewing witnesses of various unexplained phenomena, often times I couldn't be absolutely certain if I was being told about a close encounter with an extraterrestrial or being offered another possible explanation for an apparition of the Virgin Mary.

Actually, the vision seems to be saying it doesn't matter what you believe but it is paramount that you believe. She seems to be warning of coming catastrophes. Many of them are outlined in the prophecies affiliated with the various visions we have outlined as well as hundreds more which would take several volumes to give all the details.

* * * * * * * * * *

UFOS, ARMAGEDDON AND BIBLICAL REVELATIONS

FUTURE HUMANS AND THE ARRIVAL OF THE MADONNA
By Diane Tessman

PUBLISHER'S NOTE: I've known Diane since the early 1980s. I respect her as a researcher, she having been a field investigator with the Aerial Phenomenon Research Organization (APRO) and Florida State Section Director for the Mutual UFO Network (MUFON). Her work on the UFO puzzle began when she was 4 years old, when she was abducted by UFO beings in 1952. Diane taught English as a second language for 11 years on St. Thomas, Virgin Islands. While living in Ireland she studied Celtic shamanism and folklore. She also lived near Giant Rock in the Mojave Desert of California, where George van Tassel met with the ultra-terrestrials who instructed him in the building of a "time machine," something which has not been lost to Tessman who, in recent times, has come to believe that while we may, indeed, be visited from time to time by extraterrestrials, the bulk of the craft and their occupants that we interact with are from our own future, probably residing in a parallel dimension which she identifies as "the dark plasma biosphere."

Diane eagerly expressed her well thought out opinions on the apparitions most often associated with the Marian phenomena.

* * * * * * * *

The reason I am thrilled by the potential truth that Earth's dark halo is home to another entire world of consciousness and therefore to life itself is that here is the full realization of Science and Spirit not contradicting each other but instead coming together to form a larger truth which offers a vastly greater perception of reality itself! Science and Spirit have been in a supposed war since humankind began on Planet Earth. In fact, this is an imaginary war propagated by both silly scientists and silly religionists. When humankind can truly perceive that Science and Spirit together form Truth and therefore, Reality itself – then humankind will have evolved a step forward!

For centuries, spiritual teachings have taught that angels are of a realm which is lighter in density; for millennia, metaphysics has proclaimed that ghosts are vaporous and plasma-like as they pass through walls and otherwise defy gravity.

Phantom plasma ghost-lights glow on the road ahead, and then dematerialize. Some UFOs seem not to be nuts-and-bolts craft but rather colorful, brightly illuminated plasma which can zap physical objects from one polar magnetic charge to the opposite polar charge.

UFOS, ARMAGEDDON AND BIBLICAL REVELATIONS

For centuries, the Quran has spoken of "jinn" who are said by Islamic scholars to be life-forms with transparent, shape-shifting bodies. Science agrees as we read about Trevor Constable's plasma-based "sky creatures," who are amazingly similar to Islam's jinn and might be the same phenomenon.

There is no reason for intelligent, enlightened humans to fear or hate jinn, which are sometimes painted as evil phantom humanoids by modern UFO writers in an effort to make them kindred to demons.

Jinn probably originate in the dark plasma biosphere of Other-Earth; in fact, it is believed Other-Earth has a huge diversity of life-forms just as Visible Earth (our Earth) does. All life-forms of Other-Earth can be considered "ultra-terrestrials."

I can't help but ask, are some ultra-terrestrials human-like, or at least can they shape-shift into a human form? The Greek and Roman gods would appear as human, then shape-shift to a huge size before the eyes of bewildered humans and then ride away in a glowing chariot through the atmosphere. Deities of other cultures, such as Hindu avatars, seemed unaffected by the physical laws we know. Our myths are full of entities which seem to be lighter than air, capable of shifting shape, and who sometimes glow and dematerialize. Angels, both Christian and generic, first appear as glowing balls of what is probably plasma, and then take form so that the human observer can recognize them as an angel or even Jesus or Mother Mary. It would seem that guardian angels and spirit guides and all apparitions could be of the "Other Earth," I have contemplated. Perhaps the invisible beings that offer spiritual friendship – like the Madonna – might actually exist in quantum terms that we are discovering as we study science's new viewpoints on physics.

And might this "Other Earth" have, since time immemorial, been "entertaining" us, frightening us, educating us and most likely even WARNING US? There are many examples we can find in folklore, religious texts and mythology which could be credited to these beings associated with paranormal phenomena. Consider Moses and the burning bush, described as a "fire without smoke" Bright glowing doves appearing during the baptism of Jesus and throughout the many appearances of the "Mother of Us All," as described in this work. Sure enough, such Marian events as the Fatima manifestations display plasma characteristics, beginning as glowing orbs and morphing into "Mother Mary," who is sometimes accompanied by angels.

LIGHT FIELDS IN UFO AND MARIAN SIGHTINGS

UFOs often display an enormous emission of light and colorful auras. I am sure you can recall the scenes from the movie, "Close Encounters of the Third Kind," where UFOs appear seemingly out of nowhere in a blaze of light. Light seems to radiate from the entire UFO. Common UFO descriptions include "surrounded with a red glow," or "wrapped in a blue haze." This indicates that the luminosity is not coming from the object but from the air around it. During the Dark Ionization Process, dark particles collide with atoms in the air; the air becomes "excited," first by xenon, the gas of lowest ionization, to gases with higher ionization energies. Colors are generated by these different gases ionizing.

The brightness and transparency of many UFOs are also explainable by looking at specifics of the Dark Ionization Process. Ghosts are also transparent and of a different luminosity than their surroundings. Ultra-terrestrials would likely never be as solid (dense) as we are; whatever process they use makes them visible to us, almost like a hologram. The fact that UFOs and ghosts stick out visually like sore thumbs in our bio-sphere indicates possibly that their world is built on entirely different aspects of light and gravity.

We should consider plasma magnetospheres: They are luminous orbs, globes, or ovoids of orange or blue or other colors. These are identical to many UFOs and UAPs spotted at night. Holograms within ordinary plasma have been created in our laboratories. There is no reason dark plasma could not function similarly, with dark plasma UFO occupants or their holograms inside the oval-shaped plasma ship.

OTHER FASCINATING TIDBITS

Booms and rumbling sounds are thermal shock waves and are often heard around Marian apparitions such as the Fatima visions. In UFO and ghost encounters, humans feel they have entered a strange zone where normal noises do not occur; all goes quiet. Sometimes humans get nauseated around UFOs and/or paranormal activity as if this strange zone was really poisonous or alien to human molecules. Some of the witnesses involved in the viewing of the observation appear to be under a spell, which they often call the Ecstasy.

Also, residues are sometimes left behind by plasma activity. These residues include "angel hair," ectoplasm, and similar weird materials sometimes found after UFO encounters. Usually these dissipate before reaching the ground but if the UFO lands or flies very low, angel hair is sometimes left behind and a smell like bitter almond oil is also sometimes present. Rose petals have been seen falling from the sky at the time of the Virgin's appearance. And cameras sometimes photograph UFOs or ghosts which our naked eye cannot see. We now have tons of photographs of the Madonna. They are as plentiful as UFO pictures, and just as impressive.

The Goddess of Us All, if that is how you wish to identify her, speaks to those who are enchanted by her presence telepathically since she does not have a physical body nor vocal chords. The UFO contactees throughout the last half century or longer claimed that they communicated with their "Space Brother" friends mind to mind, eliminating the need to speak.

UFOS, ARMAGEDDON AND BIBLICAL REVELATIONS
SOME IDENTIFY HER AS GAIA OR THE MOTHER GODDESS

If the dark plasma biosphere possibly accounts for Christian religious phenomena such as Mother Mary standing gracefully atop church spires, as well as dark plasma playing a role in creating Islamic jinn and Hindu avatars and gods, is there evidence that the pagan world interacts with dark plasma and its lifeforms? What about the pagan cultures of ancient times?

In Greek mythology, Gaea or Gaia, is the primordial Earth or Mother Goddess. She, in essence, was one of the deities who governed the universe. It was her task to make sure that the planet was not harmed by its often inconsiderate inhabitants.

Some maintain that the Madonna is our current "religious manifestation" or representative of Gaia.

Pagans past and present might not realize in physics terms that there is a world composed of dark (not visible) matter, but of all cultures, they may come closest to perceiving such phenomena accurately. Pagans say, "The ghost is a citizen of Mother Earth, too, just not of our dimension." Or, "A phantom spirit appeared to me; she was real and yet transparent. She had a sprig of holly in her hair. She smiled, then walked through a wall and disappeared."

Fairies, gremlins, sprites, angels, all these entities sound real and solid as experiencers report what they saw, smelled, heard, and sometimes touched and tasted. However, these exotic beings can never be tracked down and captured. We have tried! Might they be made of exotic matter which can present itself in any desired form, but then subsides back into invisibility?

One thing is certain: This unknown world belongs to Gaia, the living spirit of Mother Earth. Every experience with these entities happened here, on Earth. She created us, she created all life which dwells upon her through chemistry, evolution, and just a touch of magic.

What clay does she use for this invisible world? Might it be her dark plasma? We are bound together in spirit, whether Christian, Pagan, Hindu, Buddhist, Moslem, atheist or "I don't know," because all kinds of believers and nonbelievers have witnessed bizarre, manifested/then disappearing ghosts, jinn, banshees, aliens, gods, and more. This is not Mother Earth's baryonic (visible) world of matter, this is Gaia's exotic domain of invisible (dark) matter!

Is it intended to scare us? Maybe it is intended to inspire, please, or thrill us. Perhaps the fear dwells in us. Physics is working on the puzzle of dark matter, but it has been manifesting for us, visiting us, for tens of thousands of years.

OF NOTE: Diane is the Director of the Star Network Cat Sanctuary and Wildlife Refuge in Iowa, established 22 years ago to give a warm, good home to stray cats (and dogs), thus working on behalf of the Earth energies of Gaia. The sanctuary is supported by those who enjoy her writing and donations to the Network are welcomed. Diane is the also the author of "The Transformation," (her earliest work published by Tim Beckley, still in print), "The Earth Changes Bible" and most recently "Future Humans And The UFOs, Time For New Thinking."

Websites: www.EarthChangePredictions.com
www.TeamTimeTravel.com

Friend Her On Facebook — https://www.facebook.com/diane.tessman.54

Dozens Of Interviews On The Web — Check out "Mr. UFO's Secret Files" On YouTube. Search For: DIANE TESSMAN'S MAGICAL MYSTERY TOUR OF IRELAND, DIANE TESSMAN AT GIANT ROCK, AND THE SPACE BROTHERS PHILOSOPHY

In addition to being a UFO abductee, author, and newsletter publisher, the honey-haired Diane Tessman runs an animal care center out of her Iowa sanctuary.

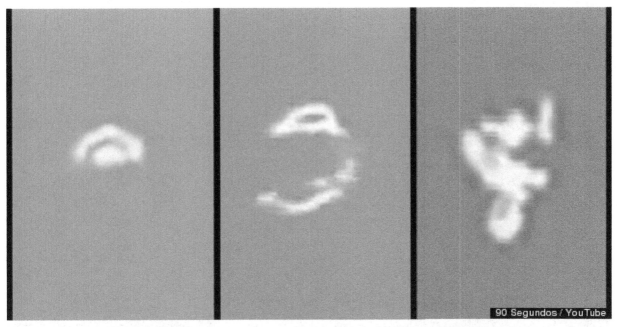

Shape-shifting light phenomena over Peru. UFO or religious icon?

Islamic woman burns candles on behalf of Mother Mary.

UFOS, ARMAGEDDON AND BIBLICAL REVELATIONS

Religious apparitions are often associated with a loud bang and a brilliant light.

Michael Grosso, Ph.D., had a remarkable experience looking out the window of his Greenwich Village apartment. Several unidentified objects cruised across the sky and hovered over a nearby landmark cathedral.

Gaia, the pagan Mother Goddess. Inspired art by Carol Ann Rodriguez.

Mother Mary's warnings to human-kind by American visionary Ingo Swann – one of the top sensitives of all time. Image: Madre Dolorosa by Ingo Swann, 1986. Oil on canvas. Gift of Artist Ingo Swann's beloved sister, Murleen S. Ryder, in tribute to their adored late sister, Marlys.

"The Revelations At Fatima" provides evidence that the visions of the Madonna are also of importance to the Islamic community.

From The Original Text by Timothy Green Beckley and Art Crockett
Revised and Updated by Téodoro Rampale

The Revelations At
FATIMA

20

SOME FINAL THOUGHTS FROM SEAN CASTEEL

The book you have just read is the product of many years of experiences with and research into the paranormal, most specifically UFOs, their alien occupants and the often religious-spiritual overtones to contact between the aliens and ourselves. As some of the contributors to this book believe, the nature of genuine religious experience and encounters with extraterrestrials may be inseparable, may in fact be one and the same though called by different names and seen in vastly different contexts.

None of which is new, of course. From its very beginnings in the mid-20th century, the UFOs (at times dubbed "flying saucers") of the modern era have been compared to angelic appearances in the Bible and seen as the driving force responsible for miracles attributed to all faiths throughout recorded history. What we have attempted to do here is to offer a survey of the religious implications of UFOs and the countless varied forms those phenomena take when they manifest in our all-too-limited physical dimension.

Along with some fresh approaches to the familiar ancient alien accounts, we have also provided an overview of Marian visions, which are much more frequent and well-documented than you may have realized. UFOs sightings in modern-day Israel are also included, as well as an analysis of why sightings in the Holy Land are so important to the entire world.

In an effort to be fair, the demonic take on the UFO phenomenon is the subject of a Q and A with prolific British author Nick Redfern, who believes there is a secret government group searching for ways to do battle with the demons bedeviling the U.S.

The religious and prophetic implications of UFOs and other forms of the paranormal are complicated, and we have provided no easy answers here. Is it even possible that there is only one single, perfect way of understanding? I think I can safely say, along with all the contributors to this book, that the answer to that question is a resounding, tantalizing, frustrating "No."

Sean Casteel

Sean Casteel has written about UFOs, alien abduction, and related phenomena since 1989 when he interviewed Whitley Strieber, around the time that the movie version of "Communion" was released. He was a contributor for several years to UFO UNIVERSE and was eventually given the title of Associate Editor. Later he began to write special reports and books for both of Tim Beckley's publishing companies, Inner Light Publications and Global Communications. The books he has written include "UFOs, Prophecy and the End of Time," "The Heretic's UFO Guidebook" and "Signs and Symbols of the Second Coming." His work has also been published in the U.K., Italy, Romania and Australia.

UFOS, ARMAGEDDON AND BIBLICAL REVELATIONS

William Kern E6, USN (ret)

Born in Washington, Indiana in 1936, William C. Kern served 20 years in U.S. Navy. As a Documentary Motion Picture Cameraman he participated in many NASA unmanned and manned space missions. Served 10 years in the intelligence community prior to, during and following the Vietnam conflict. He is currently the layout artist and ad designer for "Conspiracy Journal"," edited by Tim Beckley.

He served in USS Intrepid, (CVA-11), now a National Museum in New York. He was a photojournalist for the Great Lakes Bulletin, an award-winning military newspaper, and was the Official Photographer for the United States Navy Band.

In the early 1960s he was assigned to VAP-62, a heavy reconnaissance photo air group at NAS Jacksonville, Florida. Flying RA3B's, this squadron, with others, was charged with the responsibility of obtaining intelligence photos of Soviet missile emplacements in Cuba, evidence of which led directly to the "Cuban Missile Crisis."

Prior to the Vietnam conflict, he was assigned to the Naval Reconnaissance Technical Support Center in Suitland, Maryland and to Defense Intelligence Agency in Arlington, Virginia. DIA is the military counterpart of CIA. His duties while at these facilities is still classified.

During the height of the Vietnam conflict, he was assigned to the Fleet Intelligence Center, Pacific Facility, where over-flight intelligence information from SEATO was gathered and disseminated to friendly nations and to U. S. Intelligence Agencies. He received special training as a Courier and qualified with both the .38 Service Revolver and the .45 Model 1911 semi-automatic Service Pistol; and qualified with the .30 caliber M1A-1 Carbine. He was authorized to use deadly force to safeguard highly classified overflight materials which he transported for dissemination to Civilian and Military Intelligence Agencies of the United States, Australia, New Zealand, Canada and United Kingdom (Five Eyes).

He returned to CONUS in October, 1968 and was assigned to USS Constellation, CV64. One year later he arrived at NATTU Motion Picture School in Pensacola, Florida where he studied lighting, single and double system sound, casting, script writing, shooting techniques and camera operation and maintenance. He graduated 2nd in a class of 20 and was awarded a certificate of completion for his film on the hearing impaired.

From 1970 until he retired in 1975, he was assigned to the National Parachute Test Range (Naval Aerospace Recovery Facility), El Centro, California. His duties were as a Documentary Motion Picture Cameraman and he produced a number of excellent films, including RDT&E of the Bell Aerospace (Stratos Western) AeroCab egress system in Los Angeles, California, and the Desert Heat Evaluation of the C5-A Galaxy.

He was officially commended for these two films and others. He also filmed RDT&E features on the egress and retrograde systems of Apollo, Viking, Voyager and Pioneer manned and unmanned space projects.

For two years he was the "Voice of Mission Control" and military liaison between Navy, Air Force and civilian enineers during the development and testing of a number of sophisticated aircraft and missile designs, including the B-1 bomber and Tomahawk Cruise Missile.

He also did feature films on the Martin-Baker zero speed/ zero altitude jet aircraft egress systems; LAPES (Low Altitude Parachute Extraction System) used in Vietnam; Rogallo Wing; ParaWing; heli-borne man-tow insertion/retrieval system; mid-air "trapeze" recovery system for the Corona/Keyhole spy satellite; on-going RDT&E analysis of the egress systems for the space flight program, and other sophisticated classified aerospace systems and hardware, many of which are now in common use by military units and numerous civilian police forces.

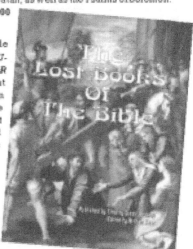

Made in the USA
Middletown, DE
29 June 2020